BUT I DIGRESS

On travels, pubs, walks, football
grounds and other obsessions.

Alan Forbes

A&A Travels

INTRODUCTION

Travel, for me, encompasses virtually any journey: whether that be a 30-minute train ride to London, a 600-mile walk, or a plane journey around the world.

Addiction takes numerous forms: many destructive, some, like ours, I like to think, productive.

This is my attempt to put into words our addiction: to collecting and some of the travels that this has taken us on. Most of us collect something, many of us become addicted, on some level, to adding to those collections.

My wife and I have 3 collections, well I have 4.....

PREFACE

This is a book about my collections/addictions, my travels and anything else in my life I digress upon. Hopefully someone will read it. Someone may even enjoy it. At last, I've started to write it. I may even finish it.

I've been made aware on numerous occasions, either directly or indirectly, that I talk an awful lot. In fact, some would say not just a lot, but too much. Well, they're entitled to their opinion and it would be difficult, particularly after a caffeine or alcoholic stimulus, not to deny this does happen, maybe on a very routine basis.

What I certainly would not deny is that I digress. Actually, I no longer attempt to deny I talk a lot. I have become increasingly aware of this. To the point that when I became a Samaritan some 7 years or so ago, probably a lot longer once this book is finished, if it ever is, it was difficult to contest the argument that I talk more than I listen. For those of you not aware The Samaritans is a listening service. Depending on how much the caller wishes to speak, and in some cases these callers could make me look a complete novice in the talking stakes - one caller actually talked at me for over 5 hours nonstop - I barely got a word in, literally.

When my talkative nature did come in useful was when a caller said very little other than that they were lonely and didn't know who else they could call at 3 o'clock in the morning. But I digress! I'm not sure if I'm going to point it out each time I digress, or if that insults your intelligence. Although I don't think I boast too often I think I became an ok Samaritan. I base that on the number of times a caller thanked me for listening to them. I may come back to The Samaritans in another chapter, not that it has much to do with the main subject - travel - but it does have a lot to do with why I travel so much: addiction.

I don't think I can avoid digressing. It's in my nature. What I must avoid is repetition. This, like the digression, is unintentional. When I digress, more and more frequently, I can't remember what I was talking about in the first place. Neither can the unfortunate or unfortunates on the receiving end. Sometimes they help me to remember. Other times they are just relieved that I've stopped for a moment.

The repetition is a result of me not remembering if I've said what I wanted to say or not, as opposed to talking for the sake of it. Those dearest to me - my adorable children (well 3 of them), my wonderful, amazing, beautiful fiancée - hopefully amended/updated to wife at some stage - and my best friend, Malcolm increasingly regularly inform me that I've already said what I'm saying. To the point that to the children my opening sentence regularly starts with "have I told you?".

Actually, Malcolm doesn't tell me whether I've already told him something: he never remembers. He is more guilty of this than me anyway, as he rarely knows if he's told his latest story or not.

Back to the point of the preface, before I digress again. Apparently, we all have a book in us. I've been told by a few, firstly as far back as sometime in the 80s. After I shared a diary, I had written on a 3-month trip in 1989 with a lucky few, the overriding sentiment was that I should write. 20 years later I started to collate my material for my book. 11 years later I'm writing this.

The reasons I haven't started writing earlier are numerous but the main excuse is that I didn't know where to start. I also have been too busy collating more material amongst other things. Another large reason, if I started, was how to proceed, what the main purpose of the book would be and whether it was really what I wanted to spend a lot of my time doing - writing rather than reading.

Listening and reading frequently teaches you something you didn't already know, whereas talking and writing you obviously already know the content. But - and I know you shouldn't start a sentence with that word, but I'm no longer likely to get told off for it - as much as I want to read, I want to release myself from this increasingly nagging and repetitive feeling that I want to, or should write.

Most books I read I enjoy but some have left me thinking that if I got my act together, I'd think my book would be better. This is my attempt to see if I could be right, although, of course, I know that's subjective.

So...... here we go. I hope this book may inform and even entertain. That is its main purpose. I think. Self-indulgently it is to see if it's true: if I have a book in me then everyone surely does. Let's see how much I can remember and I will apologize just this once, if an apology is needed, for digressing.

Warning: The first 6 chapters go into some detail on a 2-month India trip. This was not my intention, but helped me to get started. There's plenty of digressions, though.

ACKNOWLEDGEMENTS

First and foremost: Agnieszka/Aggers/Agi/Aga/ Agnes/Czekanska. Without you, there would be no 3rd and 4th collections. Without you the main collection wouldn't have flourished and been so much fun since you joined in. Thank you for being my perfect travelling lover, amongst many other attributes. You are a little bit quirky but then again.......

Thanks to: my parents, Mr. Davies and Mr. Newman, Stephen "92" Crawley, Pete Irwin, Jackie Forbes, Dobson, Malcolm, Jim the pilot, Sweaty Pete and all those who encouraged me to write and/or enabled my travels, Mike and Vanessa - they're not a couple, or at least they weren't even if they sound like it.

I think an acknowledgment is not only about thanks, although that is what it always seems to be. This is another thank you but not related to the writing of the book as such. Jordan, Callum and Molly - just Thank You!

CHAPTER ONE

I'm currently in India with Agnes for 7 weeks. We've been here for nearly 5 weeks and I started writing a few days ago. How much more I'll write here, who knows. There's so much to see and do, so much to plan and I have to feed some of my other addictions that it leaves little time to write. I have to read the Metro on line, both morning and evening additions (this is a fairly recent addiction, obviously, but reading a newspaper daily stretches back to my mother "saving the papers" for me whenever I was away for the best part of 30 years). I have to check BBC sport for cricket and football news and results every day. I have to read all the articles The Guardian send me by email - cricket only thankfully. I could go on but you get the picture. I imagine this counts as some form of OCD, at least the common perception of it. At least I enjoy all these tasks.

I better explain why we have travelled in India the way we have. I'll likely go into detail later but as this is meant to be the main focus of the book I'm going to confess now.

In the 1976/77 football season I started going to watch "dirty" Leeds on a regular basis. Travelling up from London I met a kid, amongst others, called Steve Crawley. Steve, as well as following Leeds, was intent on doing all 92 football league grounds. This appealed to me, more later, and became my first "collection". A few years later, a colleague at work, Pete Irwin, asked me if I had been to football that day to which I replied I had. He asked me if it involved a new ground, which it did (Blackburn 1 Leeds 1, I think). After asking how many grounds that was, little did he know the impact that his casual comment "I bet you've been to more airports" was going to have and still has on my life and not just travel.

I hadn't travelled too much at this stage so it wasn't too difficult to add up the airports I had flown to or from. Fortunately, when I met my first proper girlfriend, she was keeping a diary. As most diaries do, I imagine, or are supposed to, she wrote about her feelings much more than factual events. I decided I would keep a diary but my first one was, and they always have been since, purely factual. Not because I can't express my feelings. I just didn't want to put them in writing. Fortunately, this compulsion has lasted 40+ years so I had the early ones to start the airport list.

I wasn't aware of, then, and still have not met anyone who "collects" airports. I'm sure they're out there. Probably lots of them but I've never met one. Doing 92 football grounds is relatively popular, easy and straightforward. You go and watch a game of football at a league ground you haven't been to and add it to your list.

I decided there and then that I had to fly either into or out of the airport. Merely visiting the terminal would not suffice - that's caused a bit of heartache over the years. I also would not fly to an airport for the sole reason of adding to the list (with a few exceptions in the early days).

So, I was up and running. I had 2 collections, one most people understood and one that made most people think I was a weirdo. You can decide which is which or if both fit one description.

CHAPTER TWO

I'm not intending to write a travel book: there are so many already and far better than what my attempt would be. However, if I can inspire any reader along the way I'd be delighted.

India is just an awesome country to travel in. I wasn't necessarily thinking that on day 8 when I had the first, and hopefully only, stomach malfunction. Fortunately, I was pretty much done overnight and Agnes is so far unaffected. I enjoy toilet humour and travels inevitably provide much, but many people don't, so I'll give ample warning if I head down that route.

I've been here 4 times in total before but 2 very short trips indeed and the longer one was a while ago. Low-cost airlines have been a godsend to my addiction, particularly since I no longer have access to concessionary travel perks. In December we started to plan a trip to India. I couldn't resist it - over 100 commercial airports and prices from £15! Where to start and how to plan the route? How many could I squeeze in without being ridiculous and upsetting Agnes? I should point out that she decided to join me with this collection, as well as start her own. Quite fairly, she expresses concern when I roll off the number of airports we can visit. Have I factored any time to see anything of India? Of course, don't be silly, darling!

After several days of planning I had the route for the first 3 weeks. We'd make the rest up as we went along. Only issue is, as all you savvy travellers know, airfares normally rise the later you leave it. In India you have the added issue that trains fill up.

So, we left Heathrow for Hyderabad on 2nd of January. One of many cities we knew nothing about. What I'd either forgotten about or been a bit of a dick for not noticing previously is just how colourful India is. In particular the beautiful colours the girls and ladies adorn themselves in. Then there's the food of course - colourful and just dreamy. We may have another addiction to conquer after 7 weeks.

Let me digress (further) a moment. By accident, we have given up alcohol and coffee since we got off the plane in Hyderabad. Neither of us are alcoholics but, with a few exceptions we seemed to be having a couple of beers almost every day, and regularly share a bottle of red for the last 10 months. Time to have a break - certainly not difficult in our first few weeks. Coffee, now that's another matter. I think Agnes would admit she's been addicted to coffee for the last 20 years or so. No morning would pass without one.

I didn't drink coffee until I was 26, and then only

very occasionally. Aggers was well hooked while I was still in total control. Gradually, and for the last 10 years maybe, or maybe longer, I have succumbed. I find it much easier to pass a pub than a coffee shop. Coffee has been regularly available in India, alcohol initially wasn't. Do we feel any better for the abstentions? Physically, I'd say not (apart from me not needing to pee so often). Mentally I'd say we're bullish and proud.

If you've not been to India, or anywhere similar, the chaos hits you almost immediately, depending on how close your arrival airport is to the corresponding city. It used to hit you at the airport but on this trip all the airports so far seem positively serene. Many of them plush and modern - not how I remember it.

What we didn't expect was for it to start pissing down with rain on the way into Hyderabad! So, when our local bus had weaved its way through the millions of tuk tuks and mopeds and other buses and we reached our hotel, we went straight to bed.

If you do decide to travel in India do not be deterred by the hotels who mention that they only accept married couples. We've never had a problem and have been assured it only applies to locals. In fact, I saw recently a hotel stating that it would not accept anybody whose home address was within 100km. New one on us! You get the gist of what they are against.

We liked Hyderabad. Its diversity, its mental traffic, the Muslim quarter, the Golconfort and the tombs. I could continue but as I said I just want to give you an idea not the details.

What could be useful, although it may change one day, is being a little forewarned about the procedure of booking trains. I imagine most people do their homework before they travel. We're not great at that, prefer to wing it, but we had looked into the trains a little bit as we were to rely on them getting us to the next airport, if nothing else. And it looked so bloody complicated. And it's pretty tricky if you don't have an Indian sim card - and unless you're in a tourist area that's another challenge.

So, we headed off to the main station and joined the queue and filled out the form required to buy a ticket. Well, we would've done if we knew what train name and number we needed. By the time I had bought 2 tickets that queue had got a hell of a lot longer. But fear not, we had what we wanted. We broke ourselves in gently, not out of choice, it was all that was left, in AC3 class and headed off the next afternoon to Viyawada. Never heard of it? Me neither.

AC3 class is made up of 3 tiers of beds on one side, sideways and 2 tiers the other side, the direction of the carriage. It is, as the name suggests air conditioned. It is significantly more expensive than sleeper class 2, as you may expect, which we managed to book on our next jaunt. I won't go into all the detail of classes, but seat61.com gives a good resume. Indian Railways is a monster. Apparently one of the world's largest employers - about 1.5 million employees, I think. If you like travelling as much as arriving, it's great fun. 6 hours later, we arrived in Viyawada at around 11pm.

Bodies everywhere, literally. Live ones, I think, and hope. Even if you've seen it before I'm not sure if you ever get used to the oft repeated scene at an Indian railway station. It's difficult to determine how many are only there for one night and how many "live" like this. Very sad. We booked a bed out near the airport as our flight left in the morning. I say a bed rather than a hotel/hostel/homestay etc because although this was listed as an hotel it really wasn't. Just a dude with a few more rooms than he needed. He was a very friendly chap considering the hour and that our tuk tuk driver had to call him for directions. He was also quite hospitable and his English was pretty good. He proceeded to tell us that his main business was laundry and that in a few months he was heading to Scotland for a course to further his laundry skills. Once we saw the room we knew he needed this course pretty badly!

Neither of us are fussy travellers for sure, but, for the first time ever we had to ask to have the sheets changed. There was a black/grey stain across the length of the sheet. It didn't look like a stain that even the most ardent of detergent advertisers could show how they could remove. A simple wash would've done the trick. It just looked like the previous occupant hadn't washed their neck region for some considerable time and that the sheet had borne the brunt of the build-up of dust/dirt/sweat that had accumulated there.

The owner had retreated to bed before we made this discovery so it was left to the pensioner lying on the floor in "reception" to help out. Reception was an interesting affair. It consisted of a table and chairs in a car port just visible behind the owner's car. He did bring some cleaner sheets so all was well(ish). The health and safety was a work in progress and when we asked for a bedside lamp, as advertised, Mr Pensioner (he seriously looked the other side of 80) brought what looked suspiciously like a brand new IKEA version, still in its wrapping.

As in most situations in India though it's difficult and unreasonable to get upset. For a start the majority of people are so bloody friendly. Like anywhere it's not 100% the case but indifference is unusual in our experience. Curiosity is everywhere. "Where you from Sir?", "Where you go?", "how old?". What has to be a relatively recent phenomenon is the approach for "one selfie?". Our first experience was day 1 in a park in Hyderabad. The beauty for us is that while we posed for their pleasure, we were then able to take our snaps of locals without causing offence. In particular the females in their stunning saris.

The beaches with no other "whities" were a particular hurdle to overcome if trying to make any distance without being stopped. What did surprise us was a request in Goa, where whities outnumber locals 100-1. Why us 2? We were happy to oblige though as we had felt our celebrity status on the wane.

But I digress! Viyawada, was just a point to fly from to our next destination with no purpose other than just an addition to the airport total. I couldn't find anything in the guidebook about it anyway.

What seemed even more bizarre was, as the tuk tuk sped out of town, the central reserve of the dual carriageway, wide enough to be another road, was just lined with people sleeping. Even sadder, but not sure why, of all the places to sleep rough, you'd choose this. I'm sure there's a reason but our driver spoke no English.

Our flight the next day was nearly 3 hours late. Not a great start. Seeing as our train the previous night continued onto our destination, Visakhapatnam, the logic to get off at Viyawada would surely only appeal to airport collectors. Vizag, as it is shortened to locally, is a seaside city of around 1.5 million people. Yet, it is far removed from the normal chaos of most major Indian cities. Another worthwhile trip born out of the addiction. They have a submarine on the seafront as a museum. The first time we'd both been in a submarine. Some pretty good beaches, although inevitably with a fair amount of rubbish in places and a gondola, with great views from the top. I wasn't expecting a gondola in India, and it wasn't our last.

Was this to be the start of flying frustrations? Our departure from Vizag was by train to Raipur. A journey of some 10 hours. This time in 2nd class sleeper. 80 pence each for 10 hours!! Now that's a bargain for sure. The beauty of no air conditioning is that the train is open. Apart from the bars across the window you can enjoy the view and the breeze. As it had been mainly dark on our previous train ride this was our first chance to see some Indian countryside and rural life. It wasn't overly inspiring, but pleasant. It would've been much greener in and after the monsoon season no doubt, but we are in the middle of the long dry season. Predictably at the first sight of habitation litter was everywhere. We're even worse when you look at UK slip roads on motorways. Why on earth can't these bastards (in the UK) take their rubbish home with them, or leave it in their car? One of our few pet hates, rant over.

We only planned to have an overnight in Raipur as we would fly to Allahabad the next morning so we checked into the Le Roi hotel at the station. Booking.com description described it as very close to the station. Liars! There was a door directly from the platform into the lobby! After the normal confusion at check in - occasional language barrier mixed in with general confusion - we found ourselves in a really pleasant room. This coupled with our wonderful experience at the Treebo in Vizag was leaving us with a very high opinion of city hotels. Our first experience in Hyderabad had been somewhat underwhelming, very average to be honest. The rooms in Vizag and Raipur would not have been out of place in a 4- or 5-star hotel in Europe even if the rest of the establishments' facilities would.

After our best meal yet, sumptuous curries and simply delicious garlic naans all for under £3, selfie requests with waitresses completed we were happy with our brief Raipur experience. IndiGo, one of several low-cost Indian airlines efficiently informed us in the morning by text and email that we had an hour or so delay. Once we got to the airport this increased in increments to several hours, due to fog in our destination airport.

Finally, the flight was cancelled. We had planned to travel by train to Varanasi from Allahabad to witness some of India's most famous rituals. IndiGo did their best to reroute us but there was no guarantee we wouldn't get stuck somewhere else due to the fog over this part of the country. So we opted to rebook on the next day. We asked IndiGo to help us find a hotel near the airport.

This was not possible but they said we could have a special rate at the Hyatt in town. Hyatt? In Raipur? For £30? Too good to be true, surely. After a considerable delay we set off with our 3 fellow passengers to reach the Mayura hotel! IndiGo were paying for our companions to stay in the hotel as they were in transit. We would have to pay. The receptionist told us it would be the equivalent of £45. We called Sanjay, the helpful customer services supervisor who had arranged everything at the airport, to explain the discrepancy in price. With very little delay he said that IndiGo would pay for us as the price wasn't being honoured. Top man! And with dinner and breakfast. This was a treat, and in a suite to boot. After venturing out for another attempt to buy an Indian sim we luxuriated in our Hyatt! It was grey and cold outside.

We weren't too confident that our flight to Allahabad would operate the next day either as the weather seemed pretty set - foggy most of the day. The north of India is prone to foggy mornings and clearly, sometimes, the fog can last all day. Possibly many of their airports have auto-land facility these days but I've no idea which ones. I'm sure wiki can tell you. Mind you, I don't think that would have helped us as we were flying on an ATR, propeller job and I don't think they have auto-land capability. I'm not a spotter, by any stretch, honestly. My good friend Nigel positively despairs at my inability to identify aircraft types. I would say he is in the genius category, and he mows a mean lawn too. But I do know a few more things about aeroplanes than maybe the average passenger.

Whilst taking breakfast in the hotel we received a text from IndiGo that the flight was again delayed. Then not half an hour later another one that it was cancelled. We decided to leave straightaway for the airport in our courtesy taxi - well once the driver had decided which vehicle he would use and whether he should take his bottle of water or not. Seriously, he got in and out of 3 different cars at painstakingly slow pace. We told him we were in a hurry but this only seemed to make him more indecisive.

IndiGo very kindly agreed to reroute us via Delhi to Lucknow. Not an ideal solution to 2 airport collecting addicts as we had both already done Delhi a few times and Lucknow was planned further down the line. But at least it would get us to within 2 hours train journey of our next departure airport. Varanasi would have to wait for later in the trip.

It also saved us from that worse fate that can befall an airport collecting addict: sitting in the departure lounge but not being able to count the airport. This has happened to me a few times and the scars run very deep, believe me!

Allahabad, also confusingly known as Prayagraj, would also have to wait, or maybe disappear altogether. It's not so bad to fail to reach an arrival airport. There seem to be many cities in India that have more than one name and it doesn't always seem to be a name change from a previous British name, like Chennai to Madras for example. This can be quite confusing when planning airports and a real ball ache when trying to book trains.

Our journey to Lucknow via Delhi was uneventful apart from 2 things: even though we were flying with the same airline we had to change from terminal 2 to 1 at Delhi. This involved a bus journey of some half an hour. I had booked some flights with a 2 hour transfer in Delhi - probably a bit risky anyway, but if we have to change terminals, this time involving different airlines, it could be more than a bit tricky. The other thing was watching a pretty large monkey casually make his way past the terminal in the direction of one of the runways. Clearly Delhi isn't some little grass landing strip in the jungle. It's a major international airport with 3 terminals. Not a sight you would expect to see.

At this point it is maybe worth mentioning for those who haven't been to India just how many animals do populate city and town centres. Firstly cows. They are everywhere and, as you may know, sacred in this country. I don't think I will ever tire of seeing traffic going at breakneck speed but somehow managing to miss the sacred ones strolling along jam-packed city dual carriageways, country lanes and highways. Cows in train station booking offices, cows on platforms, cows on beaches, cows in temples. It's just hilarious. And they all move so slowly or not at all. They are oblivious to all the beep beep beep of the traffic.

Of course, there are numerous dogs, and pigs, goats, buffalos and chickens are certainly not endangered species, even though they also take their lives in their hands with the traffic.

On arrival at Lucknow we were somewhat shocked to find an almost brand new metro system waiting to transport us into the city. We're not great on planning and research - it can spoil the element of surprise. This was a pleasant surprise as we didn't have to bargain for a fare. 20 pence each seemed reasonable enough to us. We could have been in any city in the world as we sped towards the city centre, or at least the railway station. However, once we alighted there was no doubt we were in India. The noise, the traffic, the cows, the crowds. None of it a negative experience as such. It's just fun to stand and watch.

Which we couldn't as we had a train to catch to Kanpur. A chap who looked like he was more likely to be selling lottery tickets than train tickets was indeed able to furnish us with 2 tickets to Kanpur. 30 pence each for a 2-hour journey. I'm not bored of these prices so I make no apology, yet, for mentioning them. That was the easy bit. Finding the train which left in 3 minutes didn't go quite as well. As we jumped over bodies with the clock ticking we made it to a platform where we could at least watch our train crawling away from the station. 2 hours until the next one.

Not the biggest problem. In fact, we were both pretty peckish and I had spotted a Dominoes over the road - with a cow waiting at the door. Now, I can be a bit partial to a bit of junk food occasionally. Since Agnieszka my input has reduced dramatically, not that it was ever off the scale. I'm partial to a bit of pizza. Once I'd convinced Aga to at least view the menu, or say hello to the cow, while I did, she was sold. 2 curry pizzas - the toppings of which I can't remember - were so tasty we didn't feel guilty for going for a bit of western style junk.

We arrived in Kanpur around midnight. It was cold, dark and generally miserable. Our "hotel" was only about 800 metres or so away according to google but we opted to jump in a clapped-out old van, masquerading as a taxi, as it was too cold for a tuk tuk. The town looked an absolute dump. The hotel wasn't any better. And it was around £30. The next morning it was seriously foggy. I started to panic. I was almost more concerned that we may get stuck in this place if the flight was cancelled than I was that we may not add Kanpur to the list.

Breakfast, like the staff, the room and everything about the place was a miserable affair. The place was soul less. Actually, we appeared to be the only souls there. We decided to take a walk and then a tuk tuk to one of the ghats on the Ganges. This is why people go to Varanasi in the main - to perform or observe rituals. The Ganges, and Varanasi, in particular, are famous for it. Kanpur would have to be our substitute but when we got there, there wasn't a lot happening. We were offered a boat ride but it was cold and still very grey, plus we really didn't want to jeopardise missing our flight, if it happened.

Sorry to have such a downer on Kanpur but from our brief visit, and tuk tuk tour, it really seemed to be stuck in a time warp, and an India that would fit most people's vision, if they've not been lucky enough to visit. It's difficult to describe, particularly for a limited wordsmith such as myself. I know the grey and cold didn't help and only added to the general feeling, but it just looked a very poor, rundown and dirty city. Maybe we will return on a sunny day if England play cricket there again and see another side to the city which we missed this time, if it exists.

Even the airport was the first one we'd seen which had no modernisation at all. In fact, the terminal was the size of a large living room at best. We were very happy to see our Spicejet plane appear in front of the living room and even happier when it left 20 minutes early for our next destination, Ahmedabad. 2 more added to the list, but not without a slight drama.

We both feel that the more we fly the more nervous we become, particularly on approach. I am more aware of every little change in engine sounds etc than I ever was. I think I can only put this down to enjoying life so much I don't want it to end. Flying is safer than it ever was. Certain aircraft inspire a little more uneasiness. The ATR being one. Partly because of its previously poor safety record and secondly because of a somewhat strange man I met through work. He was a serious conspiracy theorist. I was to meet him in Zaragoza, to visit a ski resort he was bizarrely promoting. He had nothing else to do with the travel industry and how he became the rep for Ski Panticosa in Northern Spain remained a mystery. My business partner and I travelled on a short lived non-stop service from Gatwick to Zaragoza, some 2 1/2 hours on an ATR. He refused to join us on this flight and instead flew via Madrid, I think, and land transport of some description.

He explained when we met him why he hadn't flown directly and proceeded to detail every ATR crash and why. We still flew back the same way as we came. This has stuck in my mind, even though ATR safety record is much improved.

Actually we were flying on a Bombardier Q400, not an ATR72, but to the untrained eye they look very similar. As we flew on both on this trip I only realised one glaringly obvious difference: on a Q400 you board at the front and the bags are loaded at the back and vice versa on an ATR. It may be the other way round. As I say, I'm no spotter.

Our approach to Ahmedabad was going to plan on a clear, if hazy afternoon. At maybe 1-2000 or so feet we began to ascend. Overshoots, missed approaches or go around, are not that uncommon and a few reasons could be another aircraft on the runway, poor visibility, technical fault (eg landing gear indication fault, or real!) or pilot cock up. Naturally, the pilots are busy if this happens so it could be some time, if at all, before they tell the passengers the reason. I doubt very much that the pilot would come on and say "sorry folks, misjudged the approach a bit there, let me have another go".

In this instance our pilot let us know the problem fairly swiftly, if a bit muffled. "Monkeys on the runway". At least that's what I thought he said. Safely on the ground after a rather lumpy approach he apologised, and again said it was due to "clearing monkeys from the runway". I checked with the ground staff that I had heard correctly. They said I had. However, in India confirmation/ agreement can just be down to not understanding and not wanting to lose face. Just thought I'd mention it as a little anecdote as it was a new one on me.

Ahmedabad was also notable for us letting our guard down and getting ripped off for the first time. Of course, we have to negotiate each time we take a tuk tuk (known as an auto in India) and do our homework on the distance we need so we know what we should pay. This enthusiastic young lad collared us and insisted on taking us to the city. Every time I asked the price on the walk to the tuk tuk he said "meter, meter". To date we hadn't used a meter, but LP says in some cities they do, which we later found out to be true. Only thing was the readings on this meter made no sense. Well, we were in and off so what to do. We actually had a driver and a co-driver. We started to get a bit suspicious when they headed across the river instead of by it. Junior driver said it was because autos were not allowed on the route google showed. At this point, unlike everybody else we'd met so far in India, we were pretty sure these chaps were not being kind, by giving us a complimentary sightseeing tour.

Once we were reunited with the wrong side of the river and about 2 miles from our hostel/hotel they broke down. After much protestation from them they accepted that we would walk the remaining distance. I figured maximum 350 rupees (£4). The cheeky shit pointed to the defunct meter and said we must pay 3000 rupees (£33). As if! I gave him 300, he got a little bit too animated for my comfort, so I gave him 350 and we bade them farewell. Lesson relearned.

It was a pretty pleasant walk towards the bridge we needed to cross. We had to pay to walk by the river which I only mention as they had a seniors' discount. Life was now going full circle from pretending to be younger than I was to try and get a child fare on the bus or train, to lying to be older to get the lower price. We're talking of a saving here of around 5p so I was really hoping that the vendor would question my age, but no, he handed me my senior ticket without hesitation! (I was 59 1/2 at this time).

Ahmedabad was a pleasant enough city. Our stay at Hotel Good Night was unfortunately anything but. Immediately after check in I started my version of Delhi belly and didn't finish until the morning. Fortunately quite short lived and completely gone within 48 hours. We did manage a tuk tuk tour of the main sights, the wells being of particular interest, both for their architecture and novelty - never come across them before.

In the afternoon we set off by train to Surat. We couldn't get a direct train so we changed in Vadodara about half way through a 6 hour ride. The first ride was completely uneventful. The second made your worst London rush hour seem like a sparse Sunday morning stroll. These guys certainly know how to pack into a train. All 20+ carriages. We grabbed a space on the floor on our rucksacks by the open door. The pandemonium each time we approached a station as bodies clambered over us must've looked comical.

Nothing to say about Surat unless you want to buy some gems, which we didn't. If I'm honest, which I hope to be, this was an airport collection. We headed 6 hours south to then fly north to Udaipur.

Should you ever go to India, make sure you go to Rajasthan. We only had a short time there because we didn't want to escape the UK winter to feel cold in India, and we had some airports to collect.

We saw our first whities, en masse, in Udaipur. It's a fantastically located city on several lakes and the Palace is a gem. Don't bother with the car museum, hugely overpriced by Indian standards and only about 15 cars. We really enjoyed our 2 days there: it's a great town/city to wander around and one benefit of reaching a tourist destination was that we were finally able to obtain an Indian sim! Our main purpose for this was so that we had an Indian number to enable us to book train tickets on line. We are not so mobile dependant that we couldn't last without the internet on the move but we thought this would at least help us avoid the queues at the station.

What had previously been met with a flat no or minimum 3 days to connect was now done in an hour! Mind you, in the long run, it only helped us book 2 trains on line before Indian Railways inexplicably blocked our account. We couldn't create a new one because you can't use the same mobile number for more than one account! We subsequently bought another sim a few days later, only to lose it within a few days!

Back to Udaipur. I'm a dinosaur when it comes to social media but Agnieszka is relatively active. So my "36 friends" can see what I'm up to should they be so inclined. One of these friends happened to see that we were in India and, low and behold, she just so happened to be in Udaipur on the same days as we were. There's something quite pleasant about meeting friends abroad unplanned and we enjoyed a few hours together strolling around the Palace.

Our homestay in Udaipur is worth a mention for the amazingly comfortable bed. So comfortable in fact that we could not resist spending a few hours in it in the afternoon. Any feelings of guilt didn't last long. Also the 2 sisters who ran it were so friendly and helpful. The terrace was great too to watch life below. It really wasn't very warm in Udaipur but that was nothing to compare with what awaited us in Jaisalmer.

Our journey to Jaisalmer was by taxi. The result of my first planning faux pas. I thought there was a direct train when booking the next flight from Jaisalmer to Jaipur. Not sure why I thought that. Our other options were 15 hours by train via Jodphur, a night bus or an expensive flight with airport repetition. We really didn't have enough time for the train option. The reviews of the night bus made it sound like it was more suitable for transporting your pet gerbil or similar. Keen as I would've been to add Jodphur to the collection there is some kind of limit to the madness: flying back to Ahmedabad from Udaipur to Jodphur, taking all day and paying jointly £160, no.

So our kind homestay hosts arranged a taxi for the 500km/300 mile journey for £75. Including a 2 hour stop at the hugely impressive Kumbahlgarh Fort our trip took just short of 12 hours. During this time I think our driver spoke about 3 sentences. Whereas many Indians are very, very chatty this chap wasn't. I don't think it was a lack of English. That doesn't stop most of them. He just wasn't very talkative. Still his driving was fine and the traffic pretty sparse most of the time.

We had booked another homestay in Jaisalmer, within the walls of the Fort, for £2 per night. Normally, as the saying goes, if something sounds too good to be true then it generally is. But all the reviews were good and so it turned out to be. Only problem was it was freezing, almost literally. We learnt that, apparently, this was Jaisalmer's coldest ever winter. They are just not set up for it. Meals were nearly all on open rooftops, ours no exception. Great if it's not 3 degrees. We piled the extra blankets on and actually slept through the chill of night. Only thing was, on day 1 it didn't warm up until around midday and day 2 about

3pm!

We couldn't fully enjoy the facilities of our £4 expenditure for the 2 nights we spent in the Fort but bargain of the century it certainly was for us, if you don't count all the freebies. We even had an en-suite, although it took Agnes to notice that it didn't have a sink, which was a bit odd.

We were as unprepared as they were. Fortunately Agnes had thermal leggings and top, I only had a top, but these were still inadequate. It did rather take the edge off our time there but not so much that we didn't appreciate what a special place it is.

After the weirdest tuk tuk journey to the airport (I'm sure there must be a main road but our driver chose dirt tracks seemingly going the long way round, to the point that we wondered if he had an ulterior motive) we found our first airport with some character. Well, Kanpur airport had character, just not a very nice one. Whoever designed this new looking terminal had the sense to make it blend into its desert surroundings.

As I will no doubt mention again later, the airport collecting is foremost about the location (mountainous, beaches, jungle etc) and secondly if the terminal has some character. So far, our Indian collection had provided neither. Big airports are to be avoided where possible these days. At least Jaisalmer broke the mould slightly. It had a middle of nowhere feel to it. Jaipur was another jolt to the senses.

I don't know why but I had imagined Jaipur to be a smallish, even quaint city. Far from it. Maybe a bit of forward research wouldn't go amiss occasionally. It's very busy with the usual traffic and general street chaos. It does sort of live up to its name as the "Pink City". Although I would opine that the buildings giving it that name are all orange! There is plenty to see and a trip out to Amber Fort is a must. There are many forts in the area but this one was on Agnes's list.

For now, we, or at least I, are/am calling this a list and not a collection. We met a couple last year who, when we shared our collecting addictions with them, told us about Lonely Planet's 100 must see places on earth. For now, we have started to tick these off, if it fits in with our (airport) travel plans. There are quite a few in India but it is certainly not an addiction - yet. If for only one reason: LP can be very useful for sure but they don't always get it right. At the end of the day, this is subjective.

For example, our next destination Agra and, of course, The Taj Mahal. It is undoubtedly iconic and very beautiful but I feel we have seen 2 places since, in India, that surpass it.

We had, hopefully, treated ourselves to a nice upgrade in Agra. Generally, Agnes is the accommodation researcher and I do flights, of course. We had splashed out on £46 a night here. The room was very plush and the bed comfortable. Weird situation as it was a 30 odd room hotel but one where the manager had 2 rooms on Airbnb. This guy could not have been more helpful: booked trains and buses for our onward travel, sourced the sim within 20 minutes, that we subsequently lost and spent the best part of 2 hours trying to "fix" Agnes's phone.

When we arrived in Agra that evening it was cold and foggy. The next day was grim as anything so we decided we would head out to Fatephur Sikri and save Taj for the next day, in the hope that the sun would break through. I had been before, albeit 30+ years ago, but it was well worth another visit, and, yes, you've guessed it, a tick on Agnes's new list.

It stayed grey and cold all day but this Fort is still hugely impressive. We skipped Agra Fort as a) we didn't have enough time really and b) we don't want to get forted or templed out.

Luckily for us by around 1030 the next day the sun was making a much better fist of burning off the fog and mist. Our hotel was only around 500 metres from the East entrance to Taj Mahal and the crowds we feared were nowhere to be seen. Within the grounds it was busy, but I would say around 95% Indians which somehow doesn't have the same negative impact as a bunch of Europeans, Americans and, dare I say, Chinese.

We even don't mind paying up to 15 times more as foreigners than Indians pay. I did tell one ticket vendor at another site a few weeks later that I was Indian. I thought she would likely smile but she just asked me for my Indian ID. Teach me to be a twat, eh?! I know there's 1.3+ billion people living here so it stands to reason that at any one time there's going to be a bunch of them visiting their historical attractions. Who would we be to moan about that?

Normality and logic would dictate that we would fly onwards from Agra but obviously not when I'd done Agra not once but twice before. I admit to being a little selfish in my pursuit of airport collecting. Duplication is unavoidable and Agnes is increasing her total much quicker than me at times, but if it's a choice of a new airport for both of us or just her, well, I'm in charge of this collection!

6 hours by bus later we found ourselves back in Lucknow. Our unplanned reroute had already added Lucknow to the total but I'd already booked a nice little £25er to Calcutta with a bonus stop in Patna. The bus journey was uneventful and we hopped on the metro out to our overnight by the airport. Once we found it, after a back and forth on the train, with the owner calling us from the street, this was basic, very basic but for £6 with a late arrival and early departure it sufficed. It was still cold and the mattress was made out

of concrete but the critter running the joint.....
ex merchant navy so he spoke some reasonable
English. He insisted on giving us some cake at
6am and then proceeded to accompany us in the
electric tuk tuk to the airport. A true gentleman.
His establishment was located on a busy dual
carriageway with the metro above it. It was noisy,
cold, smelly and dirty but he was charming.

CHAPTER THREE

13 new airports. Not too bad for 17 days. My target for this trip? 25-30. Out of well over 100 possibilities. A year or so ago I came up with a target. Unlike football grounds, and our other collections there is not an attainable, finite number. Airports, well it's not feasible to do them all. Not if you want another life as well, and these days, have a conscience and a lot more money than I have.

Let me clarify. My airport collection consists of commercial airports, landing strips, private airfields, even the odd seaplane commercial "airport" and a couple of commercial helipads. I make up the rules, my rules, nobody else's. I don't count landing in the pub car park by helicopter, or by hot air balloon in a field but otherwise it's pretty varied. Some of these odder additions will be mentioned later. India presented an opportunity to get significantly closer to the target and at a reasonable price.

Now let's get that, currently, very large elephant out of the room, shall we? When I started collecting airports nobody had heard of global warming, climate change, carbon footprint etc.

Even now it's one of the hot topics, and should be the hottest, more and more flights are being operated. India alone is planning to build 100 new airports in the next 5 years alone. Personally, I think we are past the tipping point or whatever you want to call it. Aviation is apparently the single biggest contributor at 20%. What about the other 80%!

As much as I admire those who have chosen not to fly, the change my not flying will have is so utterly insignificant I'm not stopping yet. It is down to governments to curtail flying. The well-meaning and principled few will have no effect whatsoever.

My conscience is fairly clear on this as I don't go out of my way to pollute the planet in other ways. The flights I take will operate for the foreseeable future whether I travel on them or not. Luckily Agnes feels the same. So that's that out of the way. No need to bang on and if you don't agree I guess you didn't pick the book up in the first place. Who knows where we will be should I finish it!

Calcutta!! Forget the airport (not completely, obviously), I've wanted to come to this city for a while. Why? Because when I told people how shocking I found the poverty in Bombay, back in 1986, those supposedly in the know, at that time, said wait until you see Calcutta. For many years I was definitely not going anywhere near Calcutta. Whilst I can confess to a certain interest in morbid travel - Auschwitz, Killing Fields for example - I, rightly and obviously, do not enjoy observing the suffering of others. I like to see how other people live, of course. It's one of the beauties of collecting obscure airports. Normal travellers would say it's one of the beauties of travel. That's what I meant.

When the cricket World Cup was played in India in 2011 my mate Jim the pilot offered me to travel with him to watch England play India..... in Calcutta. He was flying to Bangalore on duty and I could "hitch" a ride if I sorted out the onward flights to Calcutta. Game on! A few weeks before we were due to travel India announced that the refurbishment of the "Lords of Asia", Eden Gardens would not be completed in time for the England match. Obviously, I was gutted.

In a way we were lucky that they announced a few days later that the game would now be played in Bangalore. They had talked about Delhi and Bombay so it seemed unlikely there would be a chance to get another new airport in as well as Bangalore. 2 wasted tickets to Calcutta and a chance to visit the most iconic cricket ground in Asia. Still, it was a great match. No need to mention the score. If you don't like cricket, you won't be interested. If you're an avid fan you'll know.

Almost 9 years later Calcutta sorted. The airport and the cricket ground. And what a pleasant city. Our favourite so far. What were all those folk talking about? Maybe I was influenced by the "the black hole of Calcutta" saying. I'd never bothered until now to find out what it meant or referred to. And the icing on the cake? The Ambassadors. I'd been telling Aggers about these lovely old cars that I remembered so well from my first trip to Delhi. It wasn't surprising that we hadn't seen any as they were surely considered gas guzzling relics of a previous era. But here they were, at the airport. We thought that they might just be a tourist attraction so jumped in one to the city. The roads were awash with them. Mainly yellow ones, some white, the odd blue one. This was what I'd wanted to see in the rubbish car museum in Udaipur. Perhaps that was why they didn't have one: they're all in Calcutta. I had to look into the history.

They had 2 factories, one near Calcutta and one near Madras. This seemed the only explanation why Calcutta had kept them all to herself. Production finished in 2004 or 14, can't remember, and if I look up everything I can't remember I'll never be finished. I'm not a big car buff by any means but I like cars from the 60s and 70s. If I'm still around in another decade I'll likely like cars from the 80s as well. Some I do already actually, thinking about it.

Our beautiful Ambassador delivered us to Hotel Cecil. Bang in a busy central district full of life. We relieved ourselves of our bags and headed off in search of Eden Gardens. What we liked about Calcutta was the street life, the old colonial buildings, the big parks, open spaces and the riverside walks and the food. It seems almost everything happens on the streets: people taking showers in the open pipes, men with typewriters set up against walls, hairdressers and the more common shoeshine. And street food everywhere. It was difficult to know where to look, as well as avoid the traffic.

There were 2 notable additions to the streets in Calcutta: trams, not many of them and very old. According to sweaty Pete, much more of him later, and probably much later, they are more than a century old and the only surviving ones. When it comes to buses, trams, trains, train track, UK especially, no need for google if you know Pete! And manual rickshaws. If you're not familiar with these, or there's another term I should be using, think of a man (we didn't see a woman doing it) where you would normally expect to see a bicycle (there were plenty of those as well) or a horse (some of those as well). These are not a tourist attraction - we barely saw a tourist - but used by locals. Invariably the men are barefoot to boot. Not the easiest way to earn a living, and not any faster than walking.

Sadly, by the time we got to Eden Gardens the match had finished. It was only an under 19s game so of no interest but the ground was certainly impressive. I could only imagine it at full capacity for the World Cup match that wasn't to be. We weren't alone in the stadium as a reasonable number of Indians were popping in to take a selfie or two, such is the ground's reputation.

On our long walk back, we were really struggling to find a suitable eating venue. Maybe we were in the wrong area. Finally, we popped into the Oberoi (think Savoy if you're not familiar with the brand) for some help. I was concerned they'd think we wanted somewhere posh but after explaining our needs we were directed to Bhoj restaurant. Best food yet. We learnt that Bengal cuisine is differentiated from Indian. Also, that Chinese, as we'd seen on virtually every menu was not as we know it but Indian Chinese. The proprietor was extremely helpful with his suggestions and so keen was he for us to try different things that he threw in a few extra dishes for free.

He asked Agi for a like on Facebook and when she later checked him out, we found out that he was indeed the expert he made out he was, with many qualifications on food, more than 15,000 followers and regular blogs on food. We even treated ourselves to desserts and then so did he. A beautiful feast with change from a tenner!

Next stop was Bhubaneswar, 8 hours south by train from the hugely impressive Howarth Junction station just over the river from the main city. We planned to chill for a few days here so had booked an apartment with a nice terrace. The next day we hired a driver for the day to take us to the coastal city of Puri and the largest lagoon in Asia, Chilka. It was a most pleasant day. The city part of the beach was packed with locals who were mostly fascinated to see us. The Indians have a different approach to a day on the beach. Some do sit down but most just stand and look at the sea. Some venture in but still fully clothed. It's a funny sight. Considering most females are either dressed in saris or hijabs and very few males wear shorts they seem to not care a jot how wet their clothes get.

Just 100 metres on and the beach was virtually deserted. We think this was because access from the road was a lot further away. We had to leave the beach after some time as a really very smelly river blocked our way. We headed inland and found the hotel that our host had recommended we broke our fast at. Cheese on toast with garlic! Why had I never thought of that. I'll certainly be giving it a go when we get back, either with or without the normal mandatory marmite. So good we had to order a second batch, as well as the chilli and cheese version.

After some haggling on the boat price, we headed out on Chilka Lagoon and were lucky enough to see Irrawaddy dolphins for the second time in a couple of months. The next day we did as we promised we would and chilled most of the day although we did take in a few of the temples for which Bhubaneswar is, apparently, famous.

Now followed 3 days of which most people would consider slightly odd behaviour. We flew the next morning from Bhubaneswar to Jharsuguda, then took a train onwards to Ranchi (5 1/2 hours). The highlights of this day were a very pleasant little airport at Jharsuguda, a lovely train ride to Ranchi, another bizarre hotel experience and more glorious food. By now we were used to asking for our food to be spicy. Strange as it may seem, we found some of the food a little bland at first. We're not hardcore but like a medium spice at least.

The Fabhotel Palash Residency Hotel had one of the weirdest entrances I've encountered. It was basically the entrance to a warehouse stocking washing machines etc, a night club and a hotel with a different name. Once inside the rooms were huge and comfortable but locating the restaurant was another equally bizarre challenge.

Day 2 of this stint started with a flight from Ranchi to Delhi with a connecting flight to Indore. This took 6 hours in total, followed by a 4-hour bus ride to Bhopal. We had booked a homestay by the lake on the outskirts of the city and not so far from the airport. It turned out to be a memorable experience. Our host was a retired Brigadier from the tank division of the army. His maid served us soup and cheese on toast (no garlic) at 10.30pm. So kind. His house was full of so much character, and so was he. He told us that he kept a very tidy garden as we would see in the morning. He certainly wasn't exaggerating. It barely had a leaf out of place. Mind you I'm not sure how much of it was down to him as there were 2 gardeners there already before we left.

He and his wife had been invited to the city's celebrations of India's Republic Day so they had left before we had breakfast. It was pretty brisk first thing but once the sun was up, we enjoyed the warmth in the garden admiring the lakeside setting. We both wished we had been able to spend one more night there but the flight schedules meant it was one or three, sadly. The sacrifices an airport collecting addict has to make.

As we reached Bhopal airport on the morning of day 3 we had our own little treat for Republic Day. We were presented with an Indian badge and some cookies and the security staff were all wanting to pose for photographs with us. Not your normal airport experience. Our flight to Pune left 20 minutes early, as had our flight from Ranchi to Delhi. The other two were on time so it seems that what could have been a difficult schedule to maintain had passed without a hitch. In fact, it did, with two minor issues on the last leg - the bus to Aurangabad. Firstly, we went to the wrong bus station. At least this allowed us to see a little more of Pune as we weren't stopping. Secondly, barely out of town our bus stopped for what seemed a random check and we learned that the suspension was faulty. We waited an hour for the next bus and then continued on our way.

It's worth mentioning that, if you haven't travelled on Indian buses, long distance or local, they truly rule the road. Well, after the cows of course. It's akin to a national express or mega bus competing in formula 1. They weave in and out of lanes passing within millimetres of tuk tuks, cars and lorries alike. They really leave no margin for error whatsoever. Yet we survived, so far, as it seems do the majority.

So, as well as increasing the airport count by 6, we had many interesting experiences along the way. We took buses rather than trains as there were either no direct trains or the timings didn't fit in. We certainly prefer the train wherever possible. Now in Aurangabad we had a couple of days of serious sightseeing. Our host and hostess arranged a tuk tuk to take us to Ellora Caves. These temples carved out of the rocks are, in my opinion, far superior to Taj. They are a UNESCO site but I would imagine, unlike Taj, pretty unknown outside India. Not wishing to overload on superlatives let's just say they are simply amazing. Our very friendly tuk tuk driver said most people take 2-3 hours to visit them. We are slightly heathen compared to some as we would normally take less time to visit places than guides/guidebooks would suggest. Such was our awe with this place we spent between 5-6 hours there. Admittedly we visited all 34 caves/temples and this involves a lot of walking.

Our time at the other sites such as Dalatabad Fort, Bibi Ka Maqbara (dubbed mini Taj) amongst others was consequently restricted to brief outdoor viewings but we didn't mind. We'd seen one of the 2 sites we had come for and were blown away. We had had our 3rd thali meal the previous evening, and to date by far the largest. If, like us, you didn't/don't know what thali consists of it is basically a large metal tray with breads, rice and an indeterminate number of small bowls of various curries. Our first experience was a small affair of about 4 different dishes in Hyderabad. Maybe we could have had more but we were thali virgins. In Bhubaneswar we upgraded to about 6 or 8, or even 7. Here there must've been double figures and we turned down more. It was a veritable feast. All for around £2 each. Ridiculous.

As we knew, Indian food in India is about as similar to Indian food in UK as McDonald's is to Dominos (alright, they're both junk food but you get my drift). Still, I don't think we realised quite how different. Agnes actually thinks we may have become addicted. Apart from that pizza in Lucknow and 2 risottos in Visakhapatnam, that I didn't mention - they were bloody gorgeous by the way, hence 2 - we have had curry for breakfast and dinner for 6 weeks now. Our only real diversion being the odd bar of chocolate or pack of biscuits for the train or bus journeys. And plenty of fruit.

Then there is the masala tea. As we are off hot drinks as such, we have only given in occasionally but our hosts here made a delicious one. Very sweet, which is good for me. I don't drink tea as a rule but for this I am happy to make an exception. I have also progressed onto fresh lemon, honey and ginger tea, a fantastic alternative to coffee but not available as a free refill in Wetherspoon so I'm sure it'll be back to the cappuccinos when we're "home".

Suitably inspired by Ellora we set off the next day, sharing a taxi with a Malaysian/Indian couple who were our neighbours, to Ajanta. I wondered if this would be a let-down after the high of the previous day. Well, we were certainly let down by the journey. We should have expected it as the 90km route showed 3 hours on google and was the same as our host predicted. Virtually the whole road was destroyed. The technical term would be that it was under repair but when you dig up the surface and make it far worse than your average dirt road and just leave it like that, I think destroyed is more apt. Our driver spoke little English but seemed unperturbed as we bumped along at walking speed. Why some dick or dicks had decided to dig up the whole road rather than just sections is stupidity at best. This isn't just India as we had a similar experience in Thailand but it does make our motorway repairs in UK seem logical by comparison. I kid you not, I reckon we saw about 20 people "working" the entire length.

A wildly optimistic local said he thought the road would be completed by the end of this year. At the current rate it's unlikely to be finished by the end of the decade.

The reason I'm harping on about this is because it is the only route to another UNESCO listed site. As it transpired, we did all feel it was worth enduring but it was so unnecessary. Why not resurface one side of the road whilst keeping the other side open? No, let's close one side completely and dig up the other side at the same time. I can't imagine what it'll be like in the monsoon season. I don't think our Malaysian friends were too impressed and they've been coming to India every year for the last 15, exploring different regions after their annual Hindu pilgrimage.

Moving back to more positive experiences, Ajanta is totally different to Ellora. The caves aren't as impressive but the setting is far superior. Our driver dropped us at the viewpoint so we could then walk down to the caves. They are set in a horseshoe-shaped canyon. It is a spectacular setting in the dry season but after monsoon with the waterfall and river in full flow, and hopefully the sun out, it must look sensational. Including the walk down and out to the car park we spent around 4 hours there. You could get a bus to the car park but we all enjoyed the peace and tranquillity the walk provided. The journey back took even longer but we felt more tolerant as we knew it had been worth it.

The next morning, after a rather heated dispute in a bank, we headed out to the airport to add to the collection. The dispute arose because the previous evening having been declined a withdrawal at the ATM, I was a tad alarmed to see that 12 hours later I had been deducted 10,000 rupees from my account. Whilst the staff openly admitted that this had happened before they steadfastly refused to put anything in writing. Bureaucracy rules. They would only repeat that we would get an email confirmation that the money would be refunded within 48 hours. 2 weeks later still no email!

Our journey today was from Aurangabad via Bangalore to Mangalore. Or Bengaluru and Mangaluru if you prefer. It's odd that the old names still seem to be in use more than the new "official" non-British versions. Bangalore was the first new airport for only Agnes. I'd done well to avoid repetition although, to be fair, I'd only been to around 10 Indian airports previously. Bangalore airport is extremely modern and, therefore, not much different to any other major international airport in its facilities. What did strike me was that the beers were nearly £10 a pop. I thought it was a mistake but it wasn't, and, as financial controller, it filled me with dread if Agnes were to carry out her threat to break her abstention in Goa! Surely the prices couldn't be that inflated.

Mangalore airport is in a pretty hilltop

setting and much smaller and more attractive than its rhyming counterpart. We had become increasingly indecisive, a common trait of ours at times, as to whether to head into the city or head north by a similar distance to a nondescript town. The advantage of the latter being that we could take the same train an hour later in the morning. As the tuk tuk fare was the same we chose to head north.

Let me digress for a moment. Well, actually this whole chapter is one massive digression, filled with lots of little ones, but let's not overdo the whole digression theme. Tuk tuk drivers in India are an interesting contradiction. They are actually referred to as autos. A few cities have electric versions. They're normally black and yellow, but we've seen green and yellow. They come in different sizes too. Some are clearly built for two passengers but some for six. In the latter case I'd say we've seen as many as ten people squeezed in. They do the school runs, sometimes carry cargo only. In some places every driver touts incessantly for a fare. In others they pass by even when you try to flag them down or, if they are sat playing on their mobiles, do not try to disguise their lack of interest in your offer of business. On a few occasions they have simply refused to take us to our destination. It's too far, or too close? Who knows? Then there's the haggling over the fare. We've worked out roughly what we should pay, sometimes by checking on Uber (yes, they do tuk tuks too), or just by the mileage involved. Normally they start too high but on a couple of occasions they started lower than we were prepared to pay! In Kerala they do use meters which started out as an advantage but then a couple of cheeky chappies wanted 50% more for their return "empty leg". Not how it works for us matey.

In some cases, we may need to haggle down a couple of quid as they start off with a ridiculously inflated rate as we are clearly foreigners. In most cases we're talking about 50p or even just 20p. I get a bit caught up in the haggling at the time and it's normally after we're on our way, or rarely if they've driven off without us, that I realise I'm debating with a guy (we've never seen a girl tuk tuk driver or indeed hardly any female drivers whatsoever. I think we've heard more female pilots on our travels so far) who probably lives on around £8 a day. At this point I feel unkind, but then offload my guilt onto Agnes and come to the conclusion that we are no doubt already paying way over the odds. And that it's all part of the game. I did tip the walking rickshaw driver over 100% when Aggers took a short ride. He gave a big smile in return.

What has been another pleasant surprise is that the fumes on the streets have been significantly less apparent than in our recent travels to South America and South East Asia. We have avoided

Delhi and Mumbai so the issue may be more noticeable there. Considering the amount of tuk tuks, mopeds, buses and lorries there have not been too many belchers of the nasty black stuff. Also, traffic jams have been surprisingly few and far between. We are very keen walkers but India's streets do not lend themselves to pleasant stomps. The traffic in all directions, the cows and their poohs, uneven if any pavement are just some of the hazards. In most cases we have resorted to tuk tuks for most journeys of a kilometre or more, Calcutta being the pleasant exception.

Concluding on the digression on transportation for now, the buses and trains can both range from overcrowded in the extreme to almost deserted. In our experience it's simply not true that all trains are packed to the rafters. We have avoided overnight trips because we want to and have the time to see where we are passing through, an essential part of our travels. We have seen some sleeper trains looking pretty chaotic but in the main have either been able to book a seat on the day or day before or find a seat if we have to book an unreserved ticket. We have also only been asked for a ticket on between a third or half of our train rides which surprised us.

Sorry, one more thing. On many train routes we have been on single track. This necessitates several instances of waiting at a suitable spot for opposing direction trains to pass. This can vary from 5 to 50 minutes in our experience so far. Just like in UK an on-time departure doesn't automatically bring an on-time arrival. The train doors are left open which is lovely in the warm weather and a great way to observe the scenery if the barred open windows become too restrictive viewing.

A bit out of sequence but as I write this we are on what must be a busy route as it's been double or quadruple track the whole way so far. Maybe we will arrive on time. We left at 6am and it was a joy to watch the sunrise as we cruised through the countryside. This particular train is of the sparsely populated variety so we are nicely spread out. One previous ride, more later, left on time, at one point was running 2 hours 15 minutes late and ended up arriving 45 minutes late. Our journey was only 5 hours of a 38-hour trip this particular train performed once a week!

OK, while I'm on a digression frenzy, back to the Indians. There's only one real habit to dislike: the noisy clearing of the throat, invariably followed by, admittedly, a pretty impressive gob, if you are impressed by gobbing. I'm not. I don't remember too much from my school days, you may be pleased to know, but I do remember Mr Saunders, our kiwi biology teacher, telling us how much disease is spread by spitting. And that his enjoyment at going to watch Crystal Palace was marred by the yobs next to him spitting throughout the match. My enjoyment of going to watch Crystal Palace is spoiled by them just being Crystal Palace. I also remember Louise Thompson falling a not inconsiderable distance from her stool, having fainted during the childbirth video. I wonder if she went on to have any kids herself after the trauma?

The spitting can be incessant. Coronavirus is currently a month in. Assuming it's ancient history by the time you read this if it reached India, I'm sure it would be an epidemic. Apart from the guttural haemorrhaging and spitting and a bit of uncleanliness here and there, there's not much to dislike and plenty to admire. Missing from previous visits appears to be human pooh infested beaches and the red spit caused by khat chewing seems much less prevalent. We saw a propaganda leaflet on one flight that explained the current government's 5-year plan, started in 2015, to increase the toilet availability from 15% of the population to 100%. The leaflet explained they had reached 95%. This would explain the lack of pooh. And good on them for it. The boys still like to pee in full view, wherever takes their fancy. Not bad news for me and my bladder issues!

And they don't like to queue. For example, you can be in the middle of a transaction for a train or bus ticket, purchasing something in a shop or buying a ticket for a monument for 15 times more than they're paying and they'll interrupt, thrust their money or bit of paper at the vendor who will invariably stop tending to you to get rid of them.

Sorry but being British it doesn't sit too well.

Litter, particularly plastic, is not as big a problem as we expected and the government appears to be trying to bring in one-time plastic bans. But the countryside and beaches are frequently blighted by all sorts of garbage as soon as there's any kind of human habitation. Railway lines and their immediate surroundings are particularly badly affected. And all city and town rivers we've seen are filthy and absolutely stink. Other than that, it's all good!

One other habit of note is the wobbly Indian head movements, made quite famous in certain comedy sketches. This can be quite confusing in day-to-day life. Shake means yes, nod means no? Or an all-round wobble indicates agreement, or disagreement? We just smile and move on, none the wiser.

Right, where was I? One of the big drawbacks of being a digresser. Yes, our overnight north of Mangalore. Another pretty weird check in experience. On a number of occasions, we have done our homework on booking.com and then headed to the establishment to check it out, found so far, in all cases it to be acceptable so proceeded to ask for a room. Sometimes we've been offered a rate far higher than online, or simply told to book on line with no explanation. On this occasion the rate was higher so we booked on line. Then we were told twice to cancel the booking, twice we refused as we would be charged a cancellation fee. Whether this would materialise or not we stuck to our guns and headed off to our room. Again, the quality of the food belied the surroundings. Again, we woke up to find our bellies agreed with us. This establishment actually had a separate bar. An exclusively all male affair and very smoky. We weren't tempted.

We managed to walk the 2 kms to the station, the next morning, as on this occasion there was a side road next to the busy dual carriageway which didn't possess the aforementioned hazards. A shop called Leeds Wines amused me. Rather than the city station in Mangalore we boarded in the countryside for our 4 hours jaunt up to Goa, our pockets some 150 rupees lighter. Now fully used to the warmth infusing our previously chilled bones we felt in holiday as well as travelling mode. The journey wasn't as scenic as Lonely Planet led us to believe. The track didn't hug the coast line. In fact, we rarely glimpsed it. It was also the first and only, to date, track that ran lower than the general landscape, obscuring the view for much of the way. Having noticed that we hadn't encountered one tunnel so far in India we passed through about a dozen on our way to our destination station, Canacona.

I had been to Goa on my first trip to India, back in 1986. I don't remember too much of it, but we got an "airline staff rate" at the Fort Aguada Hotel, where the staff proudly told us Mrs Thatcher had been a guest. We being Steve, an airline colleague and friend. He reminded me recently that we ended up in the police station at Goa after an altercation with the taxi driver who tried to fleece us on the journey from the airport. We won, I think. Goa, of course being the state, Old Goa and Panaji being the main towns.

Where to stay in Goa? Our research told us a lot of the north beaches are blighted by over tourism, both foreign and domestic, with a few exceptions. Our choice was made for us as one of Agnes's friends was staying in Patnem and we wanted to spend time with her. Patnem is an hour or so south of Old Goa and proved to be a great choice. After we got over the cultural shock of arriving at a station with 99% whities waiting on the platform, albeit small numbers, narrow lanes with more whities wandering around and locals only to be seen in shops and beaches almost exclusively frequented by Europeans, 90% brits, we settled into 5 blissful days of winter in Goa.

It's a fine line between somewhere being commercial enough to have a good time and being spoiled by tourism. And, of course, it's a matter of opinion. In our opinion Patnem was still in the former category. It's a beautiful beach without doubt. It is lined with small huts for accommodation and restaurants but all below the tree line. There's no nightlife and the clientele, although varying greatly in age range, all seemed pretty relaxed. By all accounts lots of returners and long stayers.

With the commercialism comes an excellent choice of restaurants with treats such as milkshakes, lassis and fresh fruit juices of all varieties, pancakes and beer! We had done 4 weeks and resisted the first 3 nights. Well, I did. So that made it a month for me. Aggers felt it was time for a red wine. After all we were socialising so she made her return after 4 weeks exactly. Late afternoon on day 4 it was time for a Kingfisher Strong as the sun went down. And it was strong, 7.6%. And very refreshing too. But that was it for Goa and the beach. Not bad, eh? 1 beer. And they were extremely cheap, not like Bangalore airport.

It was after a conversation over dinner the first night with a friend of one of Agnes's friends that I finally got my shit together the next day and started this book. Mike is/was a film producer/director, is producing a video game involving snakes and writing a book about snails, both taking over the world. His reason to be in Goa, again, was to try and finish his book, which is 2 1/2 years old. He has a producer and an editor, lucky chap. If I ever finish this, I'll probably just email it to a few friends and family members!

He is a thoroughly nice chap, if slightly mad (see his book and video game themes) and once I confessed to my addictions and added a few anecdotes, seemed completely convinced that I had enough material and liked the title, if it doesn't change. Agnes's friend, and ex work colleague, also admitted to having started her own book. I felt I was out of excuses, which had always been lame to say the least.

So that's how and why I finally started to write. Back to the beauty of Patnem and the adjacent beaches. To the south there are 3 beautiful beaches, the second of which you need to take a 50-metre boat ride to reach, all virtually deserted. At last we could do a proper stomp in India. Well, a mini one of around 8 miles. To the north is Palolim. This is bigger than Patnem and certainly busier but in our opinion still a cool place to hang out. There's still no chain or resort type hotels. It's a similar set up to Patnem, just on a larger scale.

We loved it on the beach. We had a great little hut for around £15 a night. I'm sure we could've done a deal if we were staying longer. The food was great and I'm sure we could easily live there for a winter on less than £25 a day. We both felt sad to leave but as I'd already booked the next flight and we had more places we wanted to see before we ran out of time it was time to hit the road again.

As soon as we were back on the train for a short ride to Madgaon Junction we felt a buzz from being on the move again. The green of the palm trees against the blue sky as we rattled along filled me with the pleasure that travel so often brings. We had taken a walk to Canacona station a couple of days previously to buy our tickets for the journey to Madgaon and then onwards to Belgaum. I'm glad it was a nice walk as it was utterly pointless otherwise. No, we couldn't buy a ticket from Madgaon to Belgaum. Not possible, computer broken. No, we couldn't even buy a ticket to Madgaon, only on the day. This information was imparted to us by the dude shouting across his ticket office as he couldn't even be arsed to get off his to speak to us. His colleague at the next window was eating his lunch, and his other colleague playing on his phone. When I asked him if he could move to the window to talk to me, he said they had an emergency as the track was buckled. If they'd been any more relaxed during this emergency, they'd have slept through it! We tried 3 travel agencies back in Patnem who advertised the sale of rail tickets - false advertising. Finally, in Palolem we got the tickets we wanted. The seller apologised profusely that his admin fee was almost as much as the cost of the ticket, 100 rupees versus 136 for the ticket. We cared not.

The journey to Belgaum, apart from the aforementioned late running due to waiting several times for trains to appear from the opposite direction, twice for nearly an hour, was by far the most scenic so far. We climbed up through the mountains with fantastic views in a fashion akin to Swiss rail journeys.

CHAPTER FOUR

Belgaum was a nondescript town. As we expected. Our visit was purely airport related but had already been justified by the lovely train ride. It was further justified by the comedy show we got for free at the Navratna Palace Hotel. Don't be misled by the use of the word Palace in an Indian hotel name. They can be as shitty as Crystal Palace. The rooms here were ok but the sheets were not clean and, as we had experienced in several establishments, they provide a blanket rather than another sheet. These blankets always look like they haven't seen any water, let alone detergent, for a very long time. In addition it's now too warm to use a blanket, thankfully. So we requested clean sheets for the bed and an additional sheet in place of the blanket.

You had to be there. As you weren't, think Alan Partridge operating the Tesco check out and the little old lady just not getting it. If you haven't seen that, YouTube it. If you haven't seen any of Alan Partridge I would very strongly recommend you watch the 2 series from around 2001/2. In summary the hotel staff simply could not understand what these 2 foreigner weirdos were banging on about.

Agnieszka is my perfect travelling companion and girlfriend/fiancée. At least I think it would be harder to find a better version of either. On top of obviously being extremely gorgeous in almost every way she is very, very easy going, rarely complains, always wants to try new experiences and takes any hiccups in her stride. I could go on and maybe will later. For the purpose of this digression she has slightly different views to me on hygiene. I think that's the best way to describe it. Her requirements are quite simple and not unreasonable. I've come to agree with most of them but am still work in progress in some areas.

Taking ones shoes off when entering your own or someone else's home has always come naturally to me, well, at least for as long as I can remember. Some people clearly aren't bothered but it does make perfect sense if you think about it. What has never occurred to me pre-Agnes was to do the same when entering a hotel room. Makes sense again. What never occurred to me was not to sit on the bed in the same shorts that I had been wearing on a 10-hour Indian train ride, for example. I get the logic, but it just never entered my head. I think this has actually been an addition to Agnes's fight against unwanted bacteria on this trip.

This wasn't the first time we had asked for cleaner bedsheets, you may recall, and wouldn't be the last. I don't ever remember having to do this anywhere before, so can only assume I'd never come across unclean bed linen or that I'd been too pissed and then too hungover to notice. Or, that sober, I wasn't very observant. Back to the Navratna Palace. Initially our request was being dealt with by 2 staff. One just shrugged and disappeared. The other chap persevered. I don't think it was purely a language barrier that was holding us back. The look on this guy's face was one of utter bemusement.

To summarise, we wanted a clean sheet on the bed and additional sheet to cover ourselves, no blanket. Firstly he returned with another sheet, no cleaner. Then he returned with a new sheet, still in its wrapping. Another issue for Agnes. Well, you obviously wash new bedding, towels, clothes in general before you use them as you don't know how clean the factory or its employees who packed it are. Really? Never occurred to me. Ignorance is bliss, or was. I suggested to Agnes she might have to make an exception here as how was I to explain to the dude that the sheet was too clean!

As I said, far from an unreasonable girl/woman so he unpacks the sheet, complete with pillowcases and proceeds to chuck it all on the floor so he can remove the original sheet. Where else would you put it!!? I volunteer to sleep on the side where the brand new sheet has come into most contact with the floor. He then climbs all over the new sheet in his shoes as he attaches it to the filthy mattress. I tried to divert Agnes's attention at this point by saying I'd seen an elephant wandering down the street. Didn't work.

Clean from the factory bed sheet attached and pillowcases replaced (which hadn't been necessary before he chucked the pillows on the floor to change the bed sheet) he feels his work is complete. I motion for one more sheet. He returns with another blanket! Finally the penny drops and we get our second, brand new, sheet. Job done. In my world we're sorted. What could be cleaner than brand new bedding? Smiles all around. Well at least me and him. As I said you had to be there. Agnes was and even she had to laugh at her own personal bed from hell materialising before her very eyes.

A little later we opened the door to go out for some food and there was all the packaging from the new sheets, the unwanted blankets and the old sheets strewn across the floor outside. I can only guess whether he had a silent scream moment when he left us or whether he just left them there to use on the next unsuspecting guest.

We couldn't find any suitable looking restaurant in the vicinity, so returned to try the Navratna Palace's. Perhaps this was where the Palace element fitted in. The surroundings couldn't be considered palatial but the food wouldn't have been out of place. Once again the flavours that make you omit noises normally reserved for pleasures encountered in the bedroom, and I'm not referring to clean sheets.

Back to the purpose of us being in Belgaum in the first place. I have never been in the habit of reading reviews. How can you make a judgement on a hotel when one person gives it a ten and the other a one, staying on the same day? Why am I going to trust a stranger over my gut instinct? That's how I've viewed reviews until recently. Influenced by Aggers, who spends a considerable amount of time reading reviews on Airbnb or booking.com before committing, I have now started looking at reviews before booking hotels. It's easy to get carried away and before you know it you've wasted another 30 minutes of your life translating what Vladimir from Russia thought about Fawlty Towers in June 2014.

When booking internal flights in India I was familiar with Spicejet and IndiGo and we had flown GoAir and Air Asia recently. Two I hadn't heard of were Vistara and Trujet. I came across an interesting route operated by Trujet so decided to look for some information and reviews. Without exception the reviews were awful and they had a 1 (out of 5) star rating. Tales of being stranded by cancellations, waiting months for refunds, constant delays were all too common. In the past if I hadn't heard of an airline I would just book it out of curiosity. Having reviewed Trujet I decided we best avoid them. That's what reviews do to you. I reviewed Vistara, nothing but positive so we booked them. And they were pretty decent. Having only booked as far as Jharsuguda before we left UK our plans remained relatively flexible after that. I'd found a good route to Goa (avoiding repetition of Goa, which Agnes accepted without complaint) and in my search to find the closest airport to leave from, up popped Trujet with the only direct route from Belgaum to a new airport. To Mysore, which we wanted to visit and it fitted in with our attempts to see big cats. The flight was about £15 each. Surely they couldn't be that bad if they were still flying? I couldn't resist, but chose not to book anything else onwards in case they did live up to their reputation.

I managed to check in on line 48 hours before so felt quietly confident. Then the night before departure I decided to check flight arrivals and departures for Belgaum and Trujet didn't feature. The internet could provide no details of this flight apart from on Trujet's website. Strange and a little disconcerting. We headed out to the airport in hope more than expectation. The Trujet flight was on the departure board and they also had a lot of check in staff. The plane arrived in plenty of time and left 20 minutes early. Bloody reviews!

After a very nice Trujet flight we arrived in Mysore, also now known as Mysuru, and took a bus to the city. We got off at the Palace, another, previously unknown to us, UNESCO site. It looked stunning but we were starving and had a safari to organise. After a delightful breakfast we spent a good couple of hours trying to work out which safari park we could get to, which gate we needed to be by and how we could avoid paying £150 a night for the privilege. We failed in the last bit but at least had a plan.

Off to Mysore Palace. Another site I would rate above or at least equal to India's most famous. Mysore also has many other wonderful old buildings but we decided to head up Chamundi Hill for an overall view of the city. We found ourselves a very nice tuk tuk driver who offered us a very reasonable price for a tour, spoke excellent English and even a few words of Polish, much to Agnieszka's surprise. We'd heard a few Poles in Rajasthan, Agra and Goa but Mysore was certainly off the well-trodden tourist route. Our tuk tuk driver said they had enough pass through to make it worth him learning some basics. It was a very pleasant hour or so and his price very reasonable so we accepted his invitation to extend our stay to visit St Philomena's church. He suggested to stop very nearby to sample some local oils being made, such as water lily - good for keeping pesky mozzies at bay apparently.

It was interesting but prices were stupid, we didn't want to buy so, left. It wasn't a hard sell but clearly Mr tuk tuk would earn some commission if we bought. We came outside and he was nowhere to be seen. We asked his mate where he was and he said he'd call him and that he'd be 5 minutes. He said to wait inside but we declined and said we'd wait at the junction by the church. After around 15 minutes he still hadn't turned up so we decided to walk back to our room. We hadn't paid him but how long were we supposed to wait? He did us a favour in a way as our walk back, around 45 minutes took us through a different part of the city.

What we had seen so far gave the impression of a fairly wealthy looking city by Indian standards. Lots of nice old buildings, wide, relatively peaceful roads and plenty of open space. Now we were back in the normal chaos of an average Indian city. We felt guilty but not culpable for not having paid him. When we got back to our establishment (I wouldn't want to mislead you by calling it a hotel, even though it was fine and kind of was) we explained our predicament to one of the boys and said if the driver turned up that we would be back in an hour or so and would pay him. We had told him where we were staying.

We headed out for some dinner and decided to walk about 30 minutes to a rooftop restaurant. Just before we reached it a tuk tuk idled up beside us as they do. I thought it wanted some business but it was our man! Mysore is a city of 1,000,000+ people. We were relieved to see him, explained how long we waited, and gave him his money. He smiled, said thank you, and told us that he had gone to get some petrol. No harm done. We had our second beer of the trip, not so much in celebration but out of frustration at our pathetic indecision over which of the 2 adjacent rooftop restaurants to eat in. We sat down in both before returning to the first one. Pathetic, but I doubt the food could have been any better in Roope where we didn't eat than Park Lane where we did, at the second attempt. If Roope had had just one Indian beer available from their menu we may've stayed there despite the fact of having to go down two floors to an under renovation hotel room to wash your hands - weird. When we got back to our hotel there was our tuk tuk driver having a casual chat with one of the staff, seemingly not a care in the world. It was the same guy at the hotel who had told us not to concern ourselves as it wasn't uncommon for tuk tuk drivers to disappear without collecting their fare! Really?

We took a government bus the next morning to Bandipur Safari Lodge, about 80 kms south. Anybody we spoke to, including the lodge said take a taxi (£25) but why would we when a bus would take us close, or so we thought, for 70p each? 2 hours later the bus pulled up directly outside the lodge. Cash back! We had paid £150 for lunch, dinner, breakfast and 2 game drives. Good by African safari prices but seemingly pretty expensive for India. First impressions weren't great. Described as a tranquil setting it was directly on the main road. The rooms were neither better nor worse than anything we had stayed in so far. Bang average. Buffet lunch was ok. There were only 2 English couples and one single Indian gentleman, Djoshi, occupying 3 of the other 22 rooms so the place was quiet. The latter has since become Agnes's new friend, or one of them. The brits were not very sociable and it sounded like they had pretty much blanked Djoshi the previous day. He had travelled down from way up north in the foothills of the Himalayas. He latched onto us but Agnes in particular. We learnt that he was an only child, his mother had died when he was 5 days old. His grandma had raised him. Now in his 60s he had done well for himself. Having come from a simple background he formed his own travel agency, sold it and now still runs his own hotel. He was lonely though and didn't mind admitting it. A week later and he is still messaging Agnes each day.

The 6 of us headed out on safari. The brits, seasoned safari goers, had failed to spot a cat in 4 attempts. Many deer and a couple of elephants later our first attempt was coming to a close when the driver spotted a leopard (get it? Spotted a leopard). He was lounging around on a branch about 50 metres away. Well spotted indeed. Our experience was not like previous ones in Africa. The landscape was thick forest, no open plains so the only real chance of spotting wildlife was on the tracks or very close by.

One leopard seen, now all we needed was a tiger to avoid the hassle of reaching Nagarhole national park from Bandipur national park. Tigers weren't having any of it and Aggers wasn't ready to give in. Previous evening's research had left us none the wiser how to get to Nagarhole and which of the 4 gates we could access. The staff at Bandipur lodge seemed to know less than we did. Remarkable, considering they all said they had grown up in the area.

Agnes's new friend to the rescue. Djoshi had a driver who had brought him from Mysore and he wasn't ready to lose our companionship - Djoshi, not the driver - so he offered to divert by 80+ kms to take us to the nearest gate if we gave his driver 1000 rupees. Not a bad deal as public transport didn't seem to exist on that route (the reality was that it did but nobody, even at the local bus station, seemed to know about it. We saw a lot of buses). After hugs and an offer to stay at his hotel we parted company with Djoshi. We had 2 hours to wait for our safari. Several tigers had been seen that morning. Rather than a nice jeep, like we had at the lodge, we set off in a government bus, open at least, but one of three in a convoy. We split up once in the park itself though. Rumours and phone calls between drivers hinted that the tigers were close but sadly never close enough for us. We saw a couple of elephants and a ton of deer but not what we had come for.

In the afternoon Agnes was hinting that she wanted another go in the morning if we were unsuccessful again. The attempt was fairly underwhelming, the nearest town where we had found accommodation was 30 minutes away and we didn't know how we were going to get there and back so, to my relief she was happy that we would head straight to the coast the next morning. We will try again another time.

The lodgings we had found in the nearest town, Heggadadevankote, thankfully shortened to H D Kote by the locals were simple but clean. The difference was how super friendly the owner was. We ended up reaching them by hitching a ride in one of the beautifully colourful trucks we had seen so many times. Driven by a young chap who spoke no English whatsoever he just beamed at us the whole way. I was close to a tick on my pretty much non-existent bucket list but not quite: I want to ride in an articulated lorry. I can only think it's because I wanted to be a lorry driver until I was about 8, or a coach driver, but I've only had this wish in the last couple of years. In a way this was better. His cabin was so high up, it had a bed, well a bench with a cushion on it and his equipment was so antiquated.

We learnt from our host that it was a bit of a scam by the government run lodges to keep information hidden so that they could fleece would be customers. We paid £5 to stay with Azlar and £17 each for the safari. If we'd taken a second safari it would've still worked out about half price for the lodge plus a bit of food. Azlar took us over to the restaurant in the bus station and joined us for a chai while we had a very tasty dosa each, think a crepe on steroids with savoury filling. Very nice. He insisted on paying. It was only about 90p in total but the gesture was what felt so nice.

The next morning required 2 buses of around 3 hours each to bring us to Kozhikode (pronounced like the Corrie in Coronation Street, we later learnt, explaining why nobody understood us when we pronounced it like cozzie as in swimming costume). The second of these, after literally a 30 second connection, was scenically spectacular. Neither of us had realised how far above sea level we were. No idea how high but high enough to necessitate a series of hairpin bends with beautiful palm trees and rice fields far below. These local bus drivers earn their money. They look like something from the 50s, the buses that is. Manual and very noisy gear boxes. They chuck them around the bends. Maybe they have power steering maybe they don't but nothing seems automated. The beauty for us is that they have no windows so there's no aircon and we can enjoy the natural breeze. Must get pretty hot, and wet, in the summer though.

We arrived in Kozhikode with no plan as usual. Our next flight was booked in 5 days' time from Kannur 80 kms up the road. Our purpose in Kerala was to visit the backwaters and a nice beach. The vast majority of tourists and travellers do this in the south in Alleppey, near Cochin (Kochi). I had briefly done this before so, selfish as ever, tried to convince Aggers that the non-touristy north would be a better option. At first she was set on the south but after she had done her own homework and I had teased her with the opportunity to tick off 2 more on her LP list she was happy to indulge me.

Another reason for me wanting to stay in the north, you'd be forgiven for thinking this the only reason, was because I'd found a cheeky little flight from Kozhikode to Kannur for £16. As I said that journey is 80kms/50 miles by road or train. It was a mysterious little flight as one day it appeared on Skyscanner (my bible for booking flights) the next day it was gone. A bit of research and it came up on Air India's website (not the most reliable) as a Delhi-Kozhikode-Kannur-Delhi route. This would explain why the price remained the same as it was a double drop so unlikely ever to be full on the short sector we wanted.

Both airports were, unusually for India around 30-35 kms from the city. To a normal traveller why would you trudge out both those distances for a 25-minute flight. To an airport collector it was a no brainer. Rome2rio, another bible for train and bus information, although not always accurate, told us there were no buses to or from either airport and a taxi would be required. As I had now booked our 3 remaining flights for the trip, one of which was from Kannur, the appeal of the Kozhikode-Kannur flight had diminished by 50%. I suggested to Aggers that maybe we should leave Kozhikode as an entry point for our next visit to India. She was having none of it. I was impressed. This girl clearly had her own target in mind!

What should have been a simple task to get from the bus station to the nearest beach by tuk tuk was anything but. These tuk tuk drivers really are an interesting bunch. We had found a restaurant on google that looked like it would fit the bill for us to have brunch and plan how to split our time between Kozhikode and Kannur and book the last remaining flight. You would've seriously thought we were asking them to drive us back to UK or some other outlandish request. Beach Road? The main beach in Kozhikode? Beach hotel (where the restaurant was located)? All requests greeted with the same incredulous head wobbling that only Indians can do. I kid you not, we must've asked half a dozen bemused drivers before finally finding one who, with the help of a passing pedestrian, was able to understand our destination - 2kms away! All these dudes have smart phones but they clearly don't use maps. It seemed a bit like asking a black cab in London to take you to Buckingham Palace and them not having a clue where it was. I'm glad we persevered because the thatched outdoor restaurant was a lovely place and the food divine. We were also treated to more Fawlty Towers type service - not the angry Basil behaviour but the confused Manuel variety. If you have a fresh pineapple juice on the menu surely your head waiter should know whether it is made with fresh juice or any other added ingredients. He moved the glass from one side of the table to the other and back again but it wouldn't make the milk in it disappear.

It's a bit strange but, without exception, every single place we have eaten in, the menu has been in English and often only in English. We have always got what we ordered, at least I think we did as sometimes we didn't really know what we were ordering. We now have a better understanding, as we damn well should, of the contents of an Indian menu but we still see something new even after 7 weeks.

Both Kozhikode and Kannur have backwaters and beaches but, a little bit like the national parks, information of exactly how to reach the backwaters was scarce and lacked detail. We decided we would take the flight the next day to Kannur as that would leave us 4 clear days before heading north again. We spent the majority of the rest of the afternoon trying to find somewhere to stay. Our first attempt was thwarted by an overwhelming smell of either cigarette smoke or chemicals in the rooms we were shown, the second was full, the third was really very nice. We set off to the beach to pose for more selfies, accustomed to and comfortable with our new found celebrity status.

We found a bus that would take us within 2kms of Kozikhode airport for 20p rather than a taxi for £15 and walked the remaining distance. 20 minutes after take-off we landed in Kannur. This airport looked new, very new. In fact it is. It only opened 14 months before we arrived. Previously Kozhikode was the nearest airport to Kannur. It's been built on a man-made plateau on the top of the hills at what must be a huge expense. Only very recently have I become a little anoraky about checking the history of certain airports. This one was interesting, to me. Kerala state supplies a very large number of workers to the gulf. I can only surmise that this would be the main purpose of the airport, to facilitate workers from Kannur region to travel back and forth from there rather than Kozhikode. It has a huge, very nice but deserted terminal and the ramps up to departures must be a mile long in total. It took 30 years from conception in 1988 to opening in 2018.

Unless Kannur has a plan to increase its almost 0% of tourism arrivals by 1000% or its workforce to the Arab nations by 500% this airport will remain refreshingly peaceful but surely the vast expense would have been better allocated elsewhere in the Indian economy. Still, they do have a very helpful if under utilised tourist office. We know it's not busy as they asked us to sign the visitors' book. Unless all other tourists had been too grumpy to comply there had been about 10 of them this year! They gave us some very useful hints on how to reach the backwaters and, immediately of more importance how to reach Kannur without paying £18 in a taxi. It's not that we are tight but we are on a budget and, as I've said before, taxis really are a last option mode of transport for us. Why would we be happy to pay more for the taxi than we did for the flight!? As well as the Indian menu we also have a pretty good handle on what we should pay for a tuk tuk. We accept that we will likely always pay more than the locals but within reason. Actually we had been told that even the locals have to haggle with the drivers. We knew that 3kms should be no more than 50 rupees maximum so, being stubborn, we started to walk out of the very long airport entrance road when faced with a 200-rupee quote. It's interesting that sometimes they'll let you walk away or drive off themselves rather than strike a deal. Within 30 seconds of refusing the tuk tuk 2 very kind chaps stopped and gave us a lift to Mattannur from where we could catch a bus to Kannur.

We were in the city at the same time we would

have been if we had taken a taxi I reckon as buses do all the overtaking in India, not cars. We decided to stay on the nearest beach to the city for the first night and then head north the next morning. Payyambalam beach is only a couple of miles from town, 4 kms long, very quiet, unspoilt and, in the main, very clean. Sunfun Beach house is located by the middle of the beach, across the dirt road as all guest houses are. There's not many of them. We actually made 3 separate bookings at Sunfun. We still hadn't found a reasonably priced place to stay on the backwaters so we would head off in the morning and see what we could find. We allowed ourselves one night and then booked the next 2 separately in case we wanted to cancel and stay longer on the backwaters if we found anything suitable.

After our first night we weren't even sure if we would return at all to Sunfun. We had booked a suite as the other rooms were full. It had a great balcony overlooking the ocean but the room itself was far from what we wanted. Smelly bathroom with no light working, unclean overall and a concrete mattress. No restaurants nearby, although the takeaway (curry) we ordered was very nice. You know you pick up the vibe on a place pretty quickly? Well I think we do. Although the owner was very amenable he wasn't on site much and left 2 young boys in charge who were clueless really. We had another sheet incident (we wanted one instead of the blanket as usual). This one was added to as the boys were clearly pissed, which was funny in itself, and the first sheet they brought literally looked like it had been dragged through mud. They brought us 6 more dirty sheets and, in the end, offered us curtains to cover ourselves. It was amusing but I would say this room was worth half of what we paid for it.

On our return we were due to stay on the newly added top floor so we thought it could only be better, we wanted to leave our bags there and it was almost 50% cheaper. The beach was lovely and we both fancied another day or 2 doing very little before our last week of being on the move before heading home. We chose not to take our free breakfast at Sunfun having witnessed the state of the kitchen when getting water. It was filthy. Maybe so were some of the other kitchens where we had eaten but ignorance is bliss, isn't it!? We headed off, as instructed by the tourist office at the airport, to catch a 30-minute train ride to Payyannur. From there we should head to Kotti jetty, 5 minutes walk away, where a government ferry would take us on a 2-hour trip on the Valiyaparamba backwaters to Iritty jetty for all of 10 rupees.

Google directed us through a small building site but down a narrow path after this, sure enough, at the end of the path, was, indeed, a ferry. Only thing was this ferry looked like it hadn't moved in many a year. There was, though, a chap, flat out on a bench nearby. When he stirred I asked him if the boat was the government ferry. Yes it was. When does it leave? 1030. In ten minutes. Result! Neither this ferry nor this chap looked like they were going anywhere in 10 minutes. However, from nowhere 3 other seamen materialised and sure enough off we set. Not before one other passenger joined us at the last minute. Looking a little out of breath and as if he had just left the office, he looked very much the Indian highflyer. What was he doing on this ramshackle ferry? He sat right behind us but it wasn't until an hour into the journey that he made any contact. Very unusual for an Indian. Usually "which country, where you going, what's your good name?" is the very least you get within 10 seconds of someone setting eyes on you. One chap was even after Agnes's father's name and then mother's - the kind of interrogation normally reserved for official immigration procedures. Agnes had also been called granny, auntie, sister and even sir by cheery locals by this stage of our Indian travels which I found quite amusing.

Back to our ferry companion, who by this stage had been joined by a few locals as we made several stops at jetties along the backwaters, which were delightful, by the way. After an hour of me glancing over my shoulder very surreptitiously in his general direction in the hope that he may be enticed into imparting any local knowledge he had, he finally produced the goods, and by heck, did he produce! Of course, I had been too British to start the conversation, actually not normally a fault I suffer from, but for some reason.......

So, Sudhir owns a property on Valiyaparamba island. We could stay there if we wanted but he didn't have a licence for foreigners. I could almost see his brain ticking over to see if he could circumnavigate this problem and boost his business. We get into the usual where are you from etc. He tells us he has a sister in UK. I dig a bit deeper resulting in the answers South London, Croydon, Shirley, West Way, opposite Benson school. Of course we are going to meet people who know people who live in London. In fact on day 1 in Hyderabad we met an Indian couple who lived in Bromley. But this was spooky. I was born in Shirley, my first ex-wife went to Benson school and one of our friends' parents lived opposite Benson school. It couldn't be the same house could it? The friend's parents were surely long dead. Buoyed by this discovery of coincidence Sudhir ventures that if we wanted to stay with him we could say that we were friends of his sister if the police asked. Why would the police come to his home and where would they come from in this almost deserted spot of paradise? Well, apparently there were plans to demolish any property that had been built in recent years without planning permission so the police were quite active. Sudhir suggested we get off at his spot and see if we liked his home and wanted to stay. If we didn't we could hop on the next ferry and continue our journey, no harm done.

We were already in heaven. This place was beautiful. To steal one of Lonely Planet's phrases in their Romania book when describing a certain village "so beautiful it should be arrested". And we hadn't even seen the beach yet, but the backwaters provided me with glowing praise from Aggers for persisting with my gut feeling to head north even though she knew that it had really been driven by the airports having already been done by me in the south. 30 minutes later we were doing a site inspection of Sudhir's home. Did we want to stay? Too bloody right we did. How much? "Whatever you're comfortable with" came the reply. We were more than sorted for tonight, hastily cancelled our Sunfun booking for the following night, contemplated cancelling the last night booked there and settled in for 48 memorable hours. The beach? I think we have both travelled enough to have a reasonable opinion on this. More so than an ex-friend who once described Kos as the most beautiful island in the world. No offence to Kos but, even though it's subjective, that's stretching it a bit. Maybe, "Kos is the most beautiful island I have visited" would have been more apt. I hadn't been to Kos at this point (apart from the airport in the middle of the night, more later) but when

I did a couple of years after receiving this pearl of wisdom I'm afraid I didn't share the opinion.

Sorry, I digress. I actually think I've done amazingly well so far. I'll let you into a little secret. I want to finish writing about India on the plane when we leave in 2 days time. Not after numerous distractions and God knows when later. So, I've resisted countless opportunities to digress but I promise I won't let you down once I've finished India.

Where was I? Yes, the beach. Without digressing again at this stage, I've seen a few in my time, all shapes and sizes. This was a beauty. Sudhir's place is equidistant from the beach and the backwater, around 20 metres from each. As we stepped out onto the beach and looked left and right all we could see to the horizon was sand, sea and palm trees. An infinite amount of all 3 of them. It was stunning. I've avoided proper swear words so far and intend to do so. I do find that they slip out as much in awe or happiness, or even more, than they do in anger and frustration. But this was.... Nope, I'm not going to say it. It's so much easier not to write a swear word than say it. I've only just realised. Even if I do write it I can erase it. I'm actually going to write it and then erase it. It was absolutely   gorgeous. Just to prove I wrote it I've left the gap.

The room Sudhir provided us with was lovely too. Simple but clean and nicely furnished. This was someone's home, not a business. He had created 3 bedrooms as well as his home for friends and family to stay in. On the second floor was a lovely spacious balcony and terrace. He had a really pretty garden at the front, facing the backwater and open land at the back. He was his own nearest neighbour as he owned the land next to him on one side. This had a small derelict building on it which was his escape plan should he have to demolish his two-storey home.

Over the next 2 hours, before we took to the beach, and the next 2 days we learned an awful lot about and from Sudhir. This guy could talk way more than me, let alone Agnes. But he was interesting and also listened. The basics: he was 55, didn't look a day over 40, married for 26 years with 2 grown up daughters, retired from the army 5 years ago, currently was living in Bangalore. His wife brought him to this spot 4 years ago for a birthday or some other treat. He fell in love with it immediately, bought some land, built his castle and now visits twice a month, interestingly for a few days each time during full moon and half-moon. He normally comes alone. His wife and daughters prefer the city. He catches a night train from Bangalore in each direction and stays 3 or 4 nights each time. He comes all year round, even during the monsoon. He shared many memories of his army career, his time in Dubai before proper retirement, his life stories, Indian life, politics, religion. You name it. He was also very open about his family life, in particular his love life. He had this way about him that he could boast about his success with the ladies without boasting. Agnes reminded him of the girl he should have married but she dumped him before he asked, so he talked of her a lot.

He liked a drink so it would've been rude and extremely unsociable of us to carry on our self-imposed exile. We did decline coffee though. He had ordered in beers, which he didn't drink, just for us, and had a seemingly unlimited supply of rum. He shared the food he had brought with him for himself for 4 days. It was immediately such a natural and relaxed atmosphere with someone we had only met an hour or two ago. We set out to walk the beach to our right. Sudhir had told us it was about 10kms in each direction. We weren't about to walk 20kms as it would be dark for half of it probably, although we had the full moon, and we wanted those beers he had ordered in. So we would be faced with that almost impossible decision, for me at least, although Agnes always wants to see round the next corner too, of when to turn back. There were no corners. A sand spit did appear on the horizon quite soon though so we endeavoured to reach it, in the hope that it may decide for us. Around an hour and a half later we had reached our turning point. This was where the backwaters met the sea. A large man-made breaker either side had caused the build-up of sand to contain erosion, I assume. The beach was now perfect for us to the north as we had no option but to turn around. It was a simply beautiful walk. An occasional fisherman here and there, an odd (not by nature) villager contemplating life where the palm trees gave way to sand and 2 boys cycling home from school along the hard sand (very nice bikes by the way) were our only company. Plus plenty of birds and crabs. Agnes's phone told us it was a 10km round trip at best. Clearly Sudhir wasn't much of a walker. Too tame a pastime for him!

Please don't put your fingers down your throat. I know that sounds a bit cheesy but I make no apologies. It was up there with the best of the beaches we've been lucky enough to set foot on. We once again gave thanks for the fact that the vast majority of tourists go for 5-star luxury all-inclusive holidays, or Benidorm, if they can't afford that and that still leaves some areas unspoilt for the likes of us. They become increasingly harder to find. I will relate stories of former paradises blighted by overdevelopment, or turned from desolate graveyards into shopping and dining paradises depending on your take on such matters, in due course.

We enjoyed a perfect sunset over a couple of large Kingfishers, tucked into a few rum and colas, before setting out to a local establishment for some dinner (obviously delicious) all accompanied with more musings from our host. The next morning we awoke for a near perfect sunrise over the backwaters, broke our fast and after more Sudhir story time headed southwards on the beach. As if things couldn't get more perfect, we were treated to the sight, between 50-100 metres offshore of dolphins doing their stuff. Several of them. To be honest they didn't perform too many full jumps out of the water (this wasn't SeaWorld thankfully) but enough to enchant us. Sudhir later told us he had never seen dolphins there in 4 years. Again there was initially no natural turnaround point for us. I cared not but our heels were still a bit sore from yesterday's barefoot stomp and the sand was a bit softer in this direction. Which was a catch 22, not so hard on the heels and joints but a slower walk.

Agnes identified a distant palm tree sticking out from the orderly row as a potential spot. Once we reached that we could see the hill which signified the southern end of the island. It was likely deceptively further than it seemed but, after an idyllic rest under aforementioned sticking out palm tree, we decided to press on and catch the ferry back at some stage. A couple of miles later our turnaround decision was made for us by a navy checkpoint. Initially not what we expected but, seeing as a naval base had been constructed at the southern end of the backwater, not a complete shock as we knew the beach may become military property at some stage. The sentry's rifle seemed as out of place as those we've encountered at some very underpopulated temples we'd visited. We didn't think we were about to meet our deaths on the beach but we weren't inclined to press on past him, claiming we didn't understand his intentions.

Not that the naval base was a blot on the otherwise perfect landscape really. There was no evidence of it from the beach at all apart from the tiny sentry post and you could only really see the main building as you approached the far end of the backwater. I was happy the decision was made for us as I knew Agnes was ready to make it otherwise. With precision timing the military would have found hard to equal, we arrived, after about a mile and a half backtracking through sporadic but quaint little settlements, at the nearest jetty just as a ferry was pulling in. We had been unable to make head nor tail of the timetable advertised on the boat the previous day and found it even harder to get the crew to understand where we wanted to get off. Finally the penny dropped with the words "yesterday same".

Sudhir was once again impressed with our efforts and the rest of the day followed a similar pattern to the previous with only a different sunset and restaurant for dinner. Yet again we were reminded that "assumption is the mother of all fuck ups". I quote, not my swear word so it doesn't count

- my book, my rules. The same happened in Goa and would happen when we returned to Sunfun: one perfect sunset followed by a relatively disappointing one where the sun disappears before it sets. Everything seems the same but then it isn't.

The next morning, after the same sunrise as previously and some breakfast, we said our farewells to Sudhir and headed off to watch a Theyamm dance that was performed November to March and not for tourists. We couldn't thank Sudhir enough for making our stay so memorable and I'm sure we will stay in touch: he's been pretty active on WhatsApp since we left and although he's most definitely a lady's man he seems to be my friend rather than Agnes's. I think that is because he wouldn't like his wife to be backwards and forwards on WhatsApp to another man so thinks I would feel the same. Not so, Agnes also has another friend, as you will learn shortly. Our experience reminded us yet again how much more you can get out of travels if you don't forward plan everything. We were prepared to just have a day trip to the backwaters if we didn't find anywhere to stay. There was a very small place close to Sudhir but they wanted £55 a night on line, more than we were prepared to pay. We gave Sudhir what we were happy with and he seemed happy too. He didn't need the money for sure and he seemed very happy with our company.

Agnes enjoyed the dance. It was ok but rather

repetitive so, after an hour, we set off for the bus back to Kannur and a new, to us, tuk tuk scam. After several not interested in our destination one finally took us to Sunfun on the meter. He then proceeded to ask for double as he had to go back! No thank you. Bye. Sunfun, whose location had seemed idyllic to us a few days ago, now didn't fare so well when compared with Sudhir's but the top floor rooms were a vast improvement on the previous room. The place was empty as well. We set off along the beach to find somewhere to eat, succeeded and enjoyed another evening with just a few locals on the beach for company.

CHAPTER FIVE

Our flight the next day wasn't until 1810 so we just chilled on the beach and balcony until it was time to leave. What I forgot to mention was Agnes's other new friend, Azlar, the generous chap from HD Kote. He had told us that he was from Kannur and that he would be visiting his family there shortly. As we were leaving the very nice outdoor restaurant the previous evening, I remarked that a passing 7-seater car looked like it had about 20 people in it. No sooner had I said that than a beaming Azlar ran up to us. Fortunately, I recognised him instantly, while the charming Agnieszka beamed back at him as she would any stranger who approached her with such joy. He introduced us to his mum, wife, sister, sister-in-law, brother, brother-in-law, children and several other relatives in the aforementioned vehicle. It was really very nice to see him. He seems a charming chap. He messaged Agnes later to say how happy he was to see us and that his family were delighted to meet us. Next time we must stay with him in Kannur he offered.

Other musings on Kerala. There were absolutely no cows on the streets anywhere. How come? Sudhir to the rescue. Kerala is predominantly

Muslim so they eat them. Drrr! We knew that, but just hadn't clicked where we saw beef and steak on menus everywhere. Kerala is also a communist state, not that you'd notice as a tourist. Interestingly, it is not a dry state, yet other less Muslim dominated states are. In fact there are many more Muslims in India than I remembered or realised. Possibly as many as 30% of the population. That would make around 400 million, not including all the illegals from neighbouring countries. It seems a credit to the people that they live in harmony side by side. Maybe not in Kashmir but, then again, maybe that's just the governments and military, we don't know.

We repeated our journey to Kannur International and marvelled once again at the no expense spared project. Once more, our flight left early allowing us to arrive in Hubli just before dusk. Another recent habit is to avoid arriving or departing on flights in darkness. The interest is normally the landscape around the airport more than the airport itself. Even though most in India had failed to deliver, on both accounts, this was our only flight planned to arrive after dusk.

Hubli was just a stopping point on our way to Hampi. LP said no need to stop any longer than necessary and, in our limited experience, they weren't wrong. Apart from not being cold it was on a par with Kanpur. We had found a place to stay online near the station for our 6am train to Hospete the next morning so took a tuk tuk straight there from the airport after the standard haggling. Confusing H's for us, Hubli, Hospete, Hampi. The first 2 with at least 2 different spellings, as usual. Hubli was busy busy. 2 things stood out: barely a female in sight and monks everywhere. Most of them in face masks. Were they from China? Did they have coronavirus? We cared not and found out from a young chap who was checking into the same hotel as ours that there was a big monastery nearby and they were in town for some R&R.

Only, like us, this chap didn't stay in the hotel. God it was rough. The reception staff were indifferent to the point of hostile, the room we were shown was filthy and crawling with wildlife, even on the bed. We were out of there sharp. They cared not. They had enough monks to keep them busy. We moved on. The next attempt we got as far as checking in, paid for the room and then the wildlife appeared. Cheeky buggers were hiding when we inspected the room. Both these places cost around £6-7 so we weren't expecting much but even where we had paid similar or less we were not faced with such grimness. Now we realised we were following this young chap. We went back downstairs and got our money back.

Before we did Aggers had a very rare breakdown. She's the only girl I've known who can't really cry. She can do the movements but nothing comes out. She was apologising for being fussy about the rooms. She had no need really. I didn't fancy either of them. Our next stop was ok, nothing special, but pricey. It was 8.30 and we had to be up at 5.00 so saw no point in overspending unless we had to. Next stop, full. Next stop, the young chap we were following around nabbed the last room. Finally, our last attempt provided an acceptable price and suitable cleanliness. They were actually pretty friendly too, which couldn't be said about the rest of Hubli folk. Fortunately, all this took place within about 100 yards of the station so we still had what we wanted. It just took a little longer.

Having seen the state of the hotels in the area, I wasn't too keen to try any of the eating establishments. Since our first night, which I had kind of forgotten about and then felt too ashamed to admit to, you may have noticed we've been loving the food. Most mornings we wake up thinking "well that's ok then", having had no adverse reaction. It has kind of annoyed us that we have felt like that. It hasn't held us back from sampling such beautiful food and we haven't sought out touristy joints where they existed. I've used hand sanitizer outside a hospital for the first time in my life and taken normal precautions. With 2 days to go, Aggers has avoided any upsets and I've had one brief episode. Let's not drop our guard though. We bought a packet of biscuits and our usual 55% cocoa chocolate and headed back to our room.

That first day/night we were kind of overwhelmed with the food choice, didn't understand the menus and guess what, we had a pack of mature Cheddar and Danish Blue in our luggage that we didn't want to leave to rot at home. So, on our way back from sightseeing in the evening in Hyderabad we had stopped at an apparently famous biscuit shop, part of a chain, ironically called Karachi biscuits, if my memory serves me correctly. We tucked in when we got back to the room. It was our secret and we would deal with the menus the next day, which we did.

The following morning the train pulled out on time as they invariably did, but this one arrived 20 minutes early. If you hadn't arrived early at the stations we stopped at I guess you missed it. It was a pleasure to watch the sunrise over the open countryside and the train was blissfully empty. Hospete Junction is about 15kms from Hampi so we were in Hampi in time for brunch. Another UNESCO site, we had never heard of. This one is clearly more well known as there were plenty of travellers, tourists and hippies around, numerous places to eat, shop and book travel and tours. Think inland Goa and you may get the drift. However, it is not much more than a village, and another must see in India.

The variety, quantity and beauty of the temples

in and around the surrounding area, once again, hugely impressed us. I think it is fair to say that the area is certainly on a par with Angkor (barring the huge main temple of Angkor Wat) and Bagan. Although almost all of the temples have suffered varying degrees of destruction it was a wonderful place. We spent the afternoon walking around the temples in the vicinity and then climbed up Matanga Hill for fabulous views and a sunset which was spectacular until it did that frustrating thing and disappeared before it set. Actually we didn't quite reach the temple at the top as it was quite slippery on the stone, we were barefoot and Agnes is not good with heights. We had a magnificent view anyway and both wanted to have many more. It was only the next day that we realised the size of the temple at the summit. Even if we had known it would've made no difference. Without being over dramatic it really was a case of one slip and out.

We hired a scooter for our full day in Hampi to reach some of the outlying temples. It was a lovely day. It did get pretty warm for temple touring but we weren't about to moan about that. On the opposite side of the river on which Hampi lies is another township, called Virupapur Gaddi. I mention this because of quite an odd situation. Lonely Planet from 2017, our companion for southern India, mentioned that many of the hostels and restaurants by the main temple had been bulldozed a few years ago and that Virupapur Gaddi could suffer the same fate. There were still plenty of places to stay and eat in Hampi, whether these were the survivors or had made a comeback we knew not. As we bumped our way down into VG (I don't want to keep writing the whole thing as Google doesn't recognise it on predictive), primarily to catch the tiny ferry back over to Hampi, we noticed that every hostel we passed had a closed sign displayed.

After finding out we couldn't take a moped on the same size ferry we had been able to further up the river, we enquired why the closed signs. It seemed that the proprietors had finally lost their battle with the government over their right to reside and demolition was due to start in 10 days. Only people who had booked before the demolition was announced had been allowed to stay. The guy we spoke to rated their chances as 1 in 10 to have the ruling overturned.

When we got back to our pad I spoke to the owner about what we had seen. He said, as per Sudhir's place, all the properties had been built without permission. This had been ongoing for 20 years. I had ventured that this would be good for business for him. Not so! Apparently the clientele in Hampi and VG have different agendas. Hampi visitors, like us, go to see the temples. VG folk go for booze, drugs and ladies of the night and are not bothered about temples. Why not stay in North Goa then?

Even though in the same state and no more than 100 metres apart the local laws governing such matters varied significantly. We were so not into booze we hadn't even noticed it was missing. The latter service, unsurprisingly, was of no interest to us, and the middle one of occasional to Aggers and long since not on my menu (more later on that episode of my life, maybe). On reflection it did seem that the visitors on the VG side, where there were only 2 temples of note a few miles away, looked a bit more hippy/backpacker in general than our fellow visitors, but never judge a book by its cover, eh?

We capped off our stay in Hampi with 2 more significant temples within walking distance as the sun set. Make sure you go there should you go to India. Our next airport visit was a unique one. Around 40 kms from Hampi there is a seriously monstrous steel factory. The founder built a runway next to it to transport employees in and out. A few years back Trujet started commercial flights there. Two a day, one to Bangalore, one to Hyderabad. It was our first cute little terminal. There was nothing cute about Kanpur's, even though they were a similar size. We had fought a battle with the Hampi tuk tuks to get a reasonably priced ride to the airport the previous evening, to no avail. There were definitely no buses, only prebooked taxis at 1600 rupees (remember we could hire one for the whole day and travel over

200kms for 2500, so not a good deal). Rome2rio reckoned on 5-700 for a taxi but that was certainly not going to happen. We decided we would sleep on it and take a chance in the morning.

We had noticed that, even in the big cities, life doesn't get going very early in the morning, and Hampi at 6.30am on a Sunday was like a ghost town. I'd imagine it's like a ghost town on any day of the week at that time. Luck, or skill and judgement, was once again with us as a lone tuk tuk dropped a couple of girls off just before our hostel. The driver was clearly keen to get a return fare out of Hampi and said he would take us to the airport for 2000. We said 1000, walked away and after a tame request for 1500 he agreed on 1000. Just as well, as our options looked very limited.

As we approached the steel works a nasty smog lay above. Unsurprisingly really. The airport, named after the owner, was right next to an entrance to this massive complex. There were a couple of different names, as usual, but let's settle for Vidyanagar, as per the Trujet boarding pass, even though their route map calls it Bellari! Another Trujet on time departure took us to Bangalore. But not before we had broken our self-imposed coffee fasting. We were hungry. The tiny but cute little airport offered very little in the way of sustenance but did have a coffee machine. Easily led by Aga, as usual, I joined her Americano order with a cappuccino. With a packet of digestives, warm sunshine, despite the factory haze, and our favourite airport so far to stare at we reflected on how happy we were that we had broken our coffee dependency. Agnes would freely admit to it being far more her weakness than mine, so brownie points to her on this one.

By the way, or may I digress, every flight we had taken it made us smile at the sheer volume of staff, both airline and security, who were present. Boarding cards, or flight booking confirmations are checked at the terminal entrance, fair enough. Then they are checked again about 5 metres in. Clearly not much trust in their colleagues. Then again before security, during security, at the boarding gate, as you either get on the bus to the aircraft or at the top of the jetty, as you get off the bus or halfway down the jetty and then as you approach the steps/ramp or end of jetty and finally by the cabin crew. Seriously that is 9 times, every time, without fail.

Vidyanagar really emphasised this. Staff probably outnumbered passengers 2-1 as, again without fail, there was approximately 15 ground staff surrounding the aircraft on the ramp. We travelled mainly on 70-seater aircraft. When I was a lad, quite an old one, and did my stint loading and unloading bags on the ramp at Gatwick we would sometimes only have 2 of us to deal with a 189-seater and never more than 4. Similar numbers of staff in train stations (apart from the booking offices which, without fail, had long queues and few staff to serve), bus stations, restaurants, banks and shops could be observed trying to busy themselves. We were astounded to be told by a very pleasant young lady we got chatting to in a pub in Bangalore, yes that's right, we went to a pub, that unemployment was a problem. Suitably rewarded employment maybe, but unemployment? That shocked us.

We had decided not to take a chance with a 2-hour connection so booked an early morning flight the next day to our next destination. We deliberated about trying to change our flight as we had arrived on time and Bangalore held little interest for us, to no avail. Then we deliberated again about staying near the airport, as the city centre was around 35km away. Finally we reverted to our original plan and took the bus to the city centre. This was our first experience of UK style airport rip offs. We paid 240 rupees each for this journey. We could make a journey 4 times longer and pay half the price. Obviously it is still very cheap and don't get the wrong impression. We're not bothered about paying it, just interested in the discrepancies. We checked into the Treebo nearest the bus station as we would have to catch a bus back to the airport at 4am. Unlike our previous Treebo experience this was nothing to get excited about but it did the job, apart from the reception staff telling us that iPhones and iPads couldn't connect to their internet, only android. What the hell!? And they wanted 300 rupees for an extra key card. Actually at first they said "not possible" but as we insisted came up with the charge. The reason we wanted an extra one was so that we could leave iPads on charge, as it was one of those rooms where you use a key card for electricity, and the technology being cleverer than to replace it with a driver's licence. In some places we left our power thirsty equipment with reception to charge but the lad here and his manager did not inspire us to do that.

We both felt ourselves getting slightly ratty with the little obstacles you come across, not just in India, when travelling. At the beginning of this trip we just laughed or smiled. Now when the power didn't work, or security moved us on but let Indians remain, as happened in Hampi, we became a little irritated. Was this because we were coming to the end of our trip? Or would it continue, if we didn't resolve to stop it, if we had another 7 weeks to travel, and were only at the halfway mark? I'd like to think it was the former. I made a conscious effort to return to smiling when a tuk tuk driver asked for 4 times what I knew was a fair fare. A polite "thank you for your offer, kind sir/madame but at this present moment I already have access to a rooftop view of this magnificent temple, but thank you again for thinking of me". However, if another airport security told me not to speak while he conducted his search, I may again question why he felt that to be necessary, as nearly all his colleagues I had met wanted the usual "which country" etc chat while they went about their business.

We took a rather circuitous route towards our intended dining venue in Bangalore. This was because we couldn't find the first choice and ended up passing the Treebo again on the way to our second choice. Bangalore was, as I remembered from a previous brief trip in hope of sampling England (cricket, clearly) World Cup glory, a far more cosmopolitan city than most in India although it did have the normal Indian chaos in places. We had reverted to LP for some restaurant suggestions and had decided we may have a break from curry, if this meant we could dine al fresco. We walked through Cubbon Park, one of the highlights of Bangalore as suggested by Sudhir, and LP. It was a lovely park and, on a sunny Sunday afternoon we could have been in Central Park or any other main park in many a city in the world. The only difference here was that the occupants of this park, as in almost every non foreign tourist area, were exclusively Indian. There is not the same cultural diversity in India as we have in UK, particularly London. Yes there are Muslims, Hindus, a few Sikhs (very few we had seen), dark skinned Indians, lighter than us (except for bottoms and front of bottoms I imagine) skinned Indians. There were undoubtedly Bangladeshis amongst them, maybe even some Pakistanis and the odd Sri Lankan, but the population was entirely made up of Asians. The cultural differences lie in the caste system (although we had been told that this was less prevalent in India these days) and religions, I guess. We had not seen one African or Afro-Caribbean in nearly 7 weeks, not even a British originating one. That seemed weird.

We arrived at restaurant choice number 2 in a swanky district full of Audis, Mercs etc, Aggers even saw a Ferrari pass by, on a trailer admittedly. The restaurant had the required courtyard setting so we sat down to order a beer. This was no easy matter as the waiter could not tell us what size beers we were ordering and, when we said we would have a pitcher, said he had nothing to keep it cool in. We were a little non plussed. Did this joint which offered bottles of white wine for near on £100 not then keep them chilled for you. OK so we were only ordering a £10 pitcher of beer but still. A guy looking suitably like a maitre d' came over and resolved that issue. 10 minutes later, still no beer, original waiter comes over and asks if we were ready to order food. "No not yet, we would like a drink before we eat". "Kitchen close in 5 minutes". Our newfound resolve to smile and not sneer was already put to the test. Coupled with the fact that the locals in this joint all had dogs with them that they were failing to control and were smoking while their fellow table companions were eating - both of which, dogs on leads and smoking, you rarely see in India - told us it was time to leave. Posh was clearly not meant to be on our agenda.

We had seen "The Bier Club" on the opposite corner and had been tempted in the first place. We headed straight there, positively leapt upstairs, proceeded to order two wonderful tasting craft ales and whiled away a couple of hours watching the world pass by from our first floor, outdoor, seats. Watching the traffic merge in the 5-way crossroads below us and thinking of the road rage this would inspire in UK made us marvel again at how the Indians just get on with it. Someone pulls out in front of you, causing you to brake sharply or swerve? Why would you get excited about that? Just get on with it.

God, I do enjoy a good ale, particularly after nigh on 7 weeks without one (Kingfisher is ok but it's no craft beer). We ordered another and then tucked into some nachos and risotto. We didn't feel guilty. That's what some locals do in Bangalore. We were just experiencing a bit of middle-class India. I doubt upper class Indians would consider beer and nachos upmarket. We also had a most interesting conversation with a girl/lady who was celebrating her 38th birthday. Her husband was not so interesting as he could barely stand up. What was so interesting to us about this young lady was that she was from Kanpur. When we said we had been there she looked very shocked. "Why did you go there?" As there was no other explanation I dared to tell the truth. She looked a bit dazed, it was her birthday after all, but seemed to understand what I meant, even if she was thinking why on earth would anybody collect airports.

When she asked what we thought of Kanpur I asked if she would be awfully offended if we said it was our least favourite city in India so far. Not only was she not offended she agreed! It's title we saw it proudly proclaim on one large noticeboard "The Manchester of the East" was true. It really was a dump (obviously Manchester UK is not a dump, but as a diehard Leeds fan that made me chuckle. You would need to understand the rivalry between a certain shit team from Manchester, who play their home games in red, to appreciate the irony. What really pisses me off about Manchester United fans is invariably when you meet one for the first time and the footy conversation comes up they call themselves a United fan and seem bemused when I ask which one - West Ham, Newcastle, Colchester, Cambridge? Or sometimes I just say, "oh yes so am I, do you get to Elland Road often?").

But I digress. This lady explained why she agreed with us and it was comforting to know that our opinion formed within a fleeting visit to Kanpur was shared by someone who had spent most of her life there. Suitably refreshed by beer, food and conversation we headed back to Treebo via the park again and, in addition, passed 2 wonderful pieces of architecture - one housing the city court and the other the local government. Our quick trip into Bangalore had turned out to be most enjoyable and rewarding. Agnes ordered a peanut masala from room service, my idea of hell, while I was satiated.

After a rather early start for our 0650 flight to Tiruchirapalli (Trichy) it was a pleasure to arrive at this small municipal airport (number 28 on this trip) after the congestion of Bangalore. We walked out onto the main road and took a tuk tuk into the city. Even though Trichy has temples and other sites on offer our intention was not to stay there. It was the closest alternative airport to our intended focal point, Madurai and the world famous Meenakshi Amman temple. We just had 2 decisions to make, where to break our fast and bus or train. Our first breakfast choice, courtesy of LP, confused us. How could it offer views of the Rock Fort several miles away, from ground level in the city centre? Turns out they have 2 branches, not immediately clear in LP unless you read to the end of the description. Second choice looked fine with outdoor seating. We would return after we had made our transport choice. Aggers was keen on the deluxe A/C train at 1010, described as India's first semi-high speed fully air-conditioned train with modern on-board facilities including automatic doors. Unlike her to favour A/C. I swayed towards the open buses which left every 15 minutes and took the same time. Agreeing that we would need to rush our breakfast to make the train and pointing out that she was as averse to A/C as me, we, as thankfully is the norm, were in agreement. I was mildly interested to see India's most modern train, but only mildly.

The cuisine in Southern India is so different from the north. Not sure where the dividing line is or if there's also a central cuisine but there are very different characteristics and we have found many menus in the south offering North and South India options. Discovering new options all placed on our banana leaf "plates" towards the end of our trip just reaffirmed how much we want to come back. Yet again our lack of planning came up trumps as, had we booked the train in advance, we would not have met the friendliest bus driver I think we've ever encountered. He spoke not one word of English, literally, so we never found out what he found so amusing, likely about us. He regularly burst out in hysterical laughter so that when he offered us his boiled sweets I took one to see whether this was what made him so bloody happy. Rather selfishly I told Agi that she best not take one in case he was a smiling assassin and was poisoning us. Unlikely in the extreme. As soon as we left the city centre he turned on his music, selected his favourite track with his remote control, and proceeded, almost literally, to dance in his seat. Surely he couldn't keep this up for 2 1/2 hours. He didn't but he regularly turned round to beam at us, mutter something unintelligible, roar with laughter and continue on his merry way.

What capped it all was his appearance. He could have been a doctor, judge, headmaster, bank manager if you formed an opinion when passing him in the street, yet, here he was, happy as Larry (whoever Larry is. I just googled it and realised how much the internet can be blamed for my digression. Not only does it tell you who happy Larry is, but also Bob (your uncle), Pete's (sake), (bloody) Nora, Fanny (your aunt), I could go on), seemingly not a care in the world driving a clapped-out old bus. The freedom of the road, eh? We wondered if he was always this happy or if the presence of two whities on his Trichy - Madurai run had something to do with it. Maybe it was just that his bus was less than half full, allowing us to stretch out in his immediate vicinity, rather than being crammed with bodies all around him. One final chuckle as he dropped us at his final stop finished off our last long distance bus ride in very fine fashion.

Aga had booked us a hotel with a rooftop view of the temple, which had initiated our visit - alright the airport picked it out for us firstly - and less than 100 metres away. The initial view of this unique temple, or symmetrical set of temples already made the journey worthwhile. Another stunner. It was closed until 4pm so we headed off on a walk around the outside and also visited the Palace. Lonely Planet described the iced coffees served at the rooftop restaurant of The Supreme Hotel as "brewed by God when you sip it on a hot, dusty day". How could we resist? We had already broken the seal in Vidyanagar, so what the hell. And it was very hot, and extremely dusty. In fact, we both agreed that if you took away the heat, the sunshine and the temple, Madurai bore a lot of similarities to Kanpur. Again, it shows you the power of the sun to transform. The streets were in complete disrepair, dust, sand, cement, holes everywhere. And transform not just the place but the people as well. Welcoming smiles contrasted with stern glares in Kanpur. And so many people bare feet. Out of choice, it seemed, unless they chose a mobile over flip flops if they couldn't afford both. There were a few other whities in Madurai. Clearly this temple was well known to some as there isn't really any other apparent reason to visit Madurai.

Back to the coffee. LP was not wrong or exaggerating, it was divine. I'm surprised we only had one. The views were great and the evening sunshine so pleasant, particularly as we knew we had 3 weeks of winter in Europe coming up. The food was good too, although the date pancake was different, to say the least. Having seen literally

1000s of bananas for sale on the streets I could not comprehend how banana pancake was off the menu. As astounding as no coconut water for sale in the beach huts in Palolim, Goa even though they had netting above to stop you getting killed by falling coconuts!

Our rooftop was a bit different. For sure it had an unbeatable, and much closer, view of the temple but you could have fitted a tennis court on it and yet there wasn't a chair or table to be had. Clearly someone was missing an opportunity, or so it seemed. There was an interesting sign by our 3rd floor reception "please use the stairs to go down to save electricity". Fair enough but as we got to the ground floor by the lift who exited it? Sure enough. The 2 guys from reception. Clearly it only applies to guests not employees. The temple was fascinating and so impressive. The attention to detail mind blowing. Certain areas were Hindu only, or no foreigners. Get away with that in London! Coupled with the fact that neither of us have mastered any religion, let alone the many gods of Hinduism, our visit didn't take too long.

Agnes had told me early on that she needed one day to shop at the end of our trip. One day? She wanted to buy some Indian clothes for herself, mum, gran and friends. Not too many as we managed the whole trip with 7kgs hand luggage, but she wanted time. We both hate shopping so the thought of spending our last day traipsing round countless shops was not an appealing one. I couldn't fathom why a shop hater wanted to devote a whole day to such misery. "It's the colours, the choice, I don't want to rush and I need you to help me make decisions". I clearly wasn't getting out of it. It would be unfair to protest to one who almost always wants to do the same thing as me and, if not, will agree to split. What I did manage was to move the day slot from Chennai to a morning slot in Madurai. I was happy with 50% reduction and after much haggling Agnes was happy with her purchases. Part of me thinks we paid way over the odds but if you're allowed to walk away from the deal, not once but twice. Whatever. We were happy and as this particular journey came to an end we were becoming more benevolent, particularly with the tuk tuk boys.

We flew off that afternoon for Chennai, thereby completing airports 29 and 30. Not a bad effort some would say. Why, would be the more likely response from most. I was impressed with myself. Aggers was impressed with me and herself. We had seen so much along the way, yet left so much to see, and more importantly another 70 odd airports, at least, to fit into another itinerary.

Madurai airport was a smallish affair and like nearly all airports of this size had lovely gardens at its entrance. It was a shame that most of the terminals were clearly new builds so lacked the character that history brings. Chennai airport appeared to be undergoing a major transformation from old to new with part of both still in use. We hopped on the metro towards our Airbnb Agnes had booked for our last 2 nights and then jumped in a tuk tuk. She had chosen this particular venue for its beachside and airport proximity as much as the host's description. We've had experiences in the past, mainly but not limited to UK, where the host says how much they love meeting people and then proceed to show you to your room never to be seen again. Lion, yes that was his Airbnb name, went seriously over the top in his description of how much love he could offer. Let's see what the reality was.....

As we entered the apartment block we wondered what we were letting ourselves in for. Run-down, would be kind. Never judge a book by its cover (one of my favourite proverbs). An airy, spacious, clean if simple apartment, well 2 in fact awaited us along with a warm and friendly greeting from our host. A small balcony with a sea view completed what was another excellent choice by Aggers. We had to curtail our first chat with Lion as we were so hungry. Dinner was again sumptuous. Curries will be even more of a let-down in UK now than they had become for me. I reckon we will stick to Wetherspoon's fish and chips. At least you know what to expect.

Sunrise over the ocean the next morning promised a fitting start to our last day in India.....

CHAPTER SIX

In reality the sunrise was one of the best things about our last day. We intended to have a relaxing day and that is how it transpired. We ventured out to Marina Beach around 10am. I didn't have high hopes for this beach. Just as well. Strewn with litter at first it then moved onto rubbish of the human pooh variety. Time to step back. On a previous trip to Kerala I had had that decision of when to turn back on a never ending beach made for me by the scene of loads of people taking a dump at the water's edge. It was not pleasant. Fortunately, until today there had been no repetition. It was also very hot. Strangely, much hotter on the beach than in the streets, so we headed back to our apartment.

We enjoyed one last beautiful curry but not before another chat with our host, Lion. This one was a little curious. He started by giving us his business card and then proceeded to tell us that immortality will be achieved within 10 years. Great news. Only problem, the Artificial Intelligence required to bring each person this mortality will cost between $1-3m! I think we were getting a sales pitch. Not to part with the millions of dollars we don't have. The AI isn't ready yet. But to either give him some funding for some project or other or to be guinea pigs to have the AI tested on us. Clearly neither would be happening but we agreed to give him our email addresses as we were curious as to what he had to say but didn't want to waste any more time listening now. We had a curry to devour.

Lion was such an optimistic, animated chap it was difficult to be annoyed by his approach. When he said he wanted to have a chat we figured it was more of the same of our encounter the previous day: swapping stories, learning more about India, hearing about his bucket list. We were suitably shocked when he said number one on his bucket list was Ibiza!! To sample the music. A 48-year-old dude from Chennai who'd not yet been out of India and his biggest ambition was to go and listen to trance music in the Balearics? Superb! We didn't touch on whether he wanted to sample the class A's whilst there. When we managed to divert him from his lecture to us we also learnt that he had renounced his religion, Islam, 10 years ago, thought it ludicrous that he should remain faithful to his wife of 26 years, sold his car to reduce his footprint and refused to go to the cinema with his daughters. An interesting character indeed.

We are currently halfway through our 10 hour flight back to London. We both felt a touch of sadness to be leaving India but obviously excited to be catching up with our loved ones before our next jaunt. India had been so much fun. The negatives we expected rarely materialised. As a proportion I'm sure we witnessed less homeless and beggars than we do in London. Yes it was very dirty in places but the positives almost always outweighed any negatives. The frustrations were always minimised by the humour that accompanied them. Talking of humour, I've yet to mention one particular amusing habit of some men of a certain age and above: they dye their hair, and sometimes their beards, orange. We're not talking a dark orange, or a brownish orange, or a kind of ginger but a very bright orange. Apparently it's henna so in time fades, leaving a very fine mix of grey and orange. Some are also partial to the finest Bobby Charlton/Ralph Coates style comb overs I've seen since, well Bobby Charlton or Ralph Coates. Another characteristic of amusement is how hairy some men's ears become. We all get them to a certain degree, if we live long enough, men that is, but some of these were truly prolific. Best way I can describe it is to think of an ear moustache.

We were surprised, once more, about the lack of backpackers in India. Yes we saw some in Goa and Rajasthan. Not many at all though. We experienced the same in the Far East and Turkey last year apart from the very obvious tourist spots. We barely saw another non-Indian looking person on a plane, train or bus that we travelled on. Most cities we visited we were alone with the colour of our skin. Where were all the backpackers? Are they becoming less adventurous, sticking to the well-trodden paths? Not just backpackers, but it seems so many people are missing out on so much. We carry small backpacks so do not fit the stereotype of a backpacker. We're too old for a start. We just saw so few foreign travellers, it was bizarre, almost eerie.

I'm sure there's many other traits I may have forgotten to mention but it's time to move on to the real purpose of the book. Writing a diary on India, as it has become, has got me started but it's just a massive digression really, full of minor digressions. So this is maybe how my book would have been if I'd started 30 or more years ago. As it is I don't remember much in detail and if I had I guess I would've written 20 books by now, or given up after one. So, where was I?

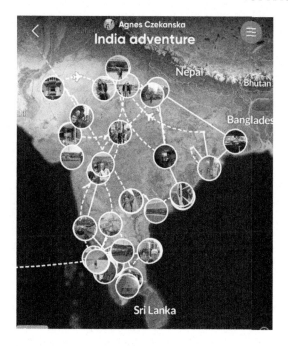

CHAPTER SEVEN

Now back from India and in the gloom of European midwinter it's back to the book proper. Diary writing is easy I reckon, particularly if everything is fresh in the mind. Back to the story, which I'm finding a little harder to formulate. As many people have expressed that we all have a book in us, I have often opined that we all have addictions or collections of some sort. The former is probably true, the latter maybe not so much. There are obviously many well-known and documented addictions. Some less well known than others. I've just had a quick google to find some weird ones: a woman who drinks her own pee. She also washes her eyes, sinuses, and teeth with her urine. She claims it tastes like water, and she has no intention of stopping.

So that's pretty weird. I feel pretty normal collecting airports. Being addicted to getting dumped (romantic rejection) also makes me feel ok. I guess I can kind of understand being addicted to coffee enemas. I suffer from the opposite of oniomania - I would say I am allergic to shopping! At least shopping malls. So is Agnes, fortunately. So there's some very serious addictions, some amusing ones, and some weird ones. I could class my addiction as collecting but then again I only have 5 collections.

I'm not sure, but let me not labour the point. Collections are the same: there's the bog-standard stamp collecting, well, back in the day, and the less usual collecting milk float numbers or visiting every Tesco in the country. Lots of people like to make lists too. Normally shopping lists, or to do lists. Collections of the inanimate nature require lists, or spreadsheets as they've now become, I imagine.

Not for me. I am still adding to the original list started with football grounds in the mid-70s and it's a bloody mess. Maybe one day it will become several spreadsheets.

Like many a young boy, I used to collect football cards and stickers. George Best was so elusive. I still remember when I finally "got him" to complete that year's album. Like many of the little pictures he didn't look particularly real. David Herd, also of Manchester United, looked particularly weird!

I'm sure if you stop and think you all know someone's addictions and collections, if not your own. I don't think there's a particular point in time when I felt that my collections were becoming addictive. Maybe it is wrong for me to think of them in this way and an insult to those with life threatening addictions, but when I let out an audible whoop when it was announced that our flight back from Windhoek, Namibia would need to fuel stop in Luanda, Angola on the way to London I think most people would think I had issues.

My friend, Peter, sweaty Pete to his kids (because he sweats apparently, not because they think he's a weirdo) has some interesting collections. And he assures us he is not alone in most of these. He is trying, and quite successfully, to obtain a photograph of every single bus that has ever operated the number 64 London bus route. He has travelled on every single section of passenger railway track in UK and will think nothing of travelling hundreds of miles to do a new piece of track, previously unavailable, that may be less than 200 metres in length. He has a photographic memory when it comes to buses, train track, Leeds matches. He can tell you the history of every Routemaster bus ever produced, should you be interested. I think I could write a few chapters on Pete but as this book is meant to be about me.....

Well where I was, was in UK and Poland for a total of 3 weeks before we set off on our travels again. No new airports, no new football grounds during this time but we did make a sizeable addition to one of our other collections. When I finally got my shit together and managed to persuade Aggers that I wasn't a total dick and that her and I could possibly have a nice time together she eventually gave in. At this stage she was already aware of my airport collection and had indulged me on a couple of occasions during our first relationship and then a few more in our "just friends" phase (obviously I wanted more than that, she's too gorgeous to just be friends with but she at least seemed keen to visit new airports with me even if it did mean booking single beds!).

When she realised the extent I would go to just to add one more airport to the total, she decided to join me. She was able to recollect, we think, all of her airports, with maybe one or two discrepancies - she was no diary writer although ironically she is now. We celebrated her 100th and my 700th at the same time which was a nice coincidence, Culiacan in Mexico. Another place we had never heard of prior to flying there. Memorable since, not only for the landmark totals but for Agnes's conversation with the taxi driver on the way into town. Agnes speaks pretty reasonable Spanish so was having a chat with the driver and asked him what the main industry was in Culiacan. He replied agriculture. "Oh, what do you grow?" she enquired. All sorts - cucumbers, tomatoes, oranges, bananas etc, you know, the usual, he informed her. A few days later when we were in a 5-star resort in Los Cabos, compliments of Aggers' job at the time, enjoying a drink with the hotel manager, he asked how we had arrived in Cabos (I'll get back to that in a moment) and when we said we had been to

Culiacan he was quite incredulous, what the hell were we doing there? This is one of the cocaine capitals of Mexico, consequently one of the most dangerous cities in Mexico! He did find it rather amusing when Agnes told him that we had asked the taxi driver what the main industry was. A year or so later we heard that her colleague had been shot and nearly died not far from the resort. Maybe Los Cabos wasn't any safer than Culiacan (where Diego Maradona was manager for 2 seasons, somewhat ironic considering how much of the local agriculture he had been partial to!). At least he survived.

We had planned to fly to Mexico City on this trip using a friend's concessions on BA. As this was standby we hadn't booked any internal flights. Just as well as a week or so before we were due to leave, Lufthansa crew went on strike so our half empty flight was suddenly overbooked. No problem. We would fly instead to San Diego in California and make our way down from there. No new airport for me in either case but a new one for Agi. We then took a tram to the border, walked across the border, taxi to Tijuana airport (now there's a city whose reputation precedes it) and, no word of a lie, within 20 minutes of arriving at the airport we were taxiing out to Culiacan. Very speedy work by the Volaris ground staff - we didn't even know where we were going let alone have a ticket. We did manage 8 new airports on that short trip to Mexico, which unexpectedly allowed us to go whale watching in La Paz amongst other bonuses.

Now, I'm not sure whether to digress further here or get back to the original topic. Actually it fits in nicely so....... whilst we were in Puerto Vallarta on the same trip we were walking along the beach one afternoon when we heard someone shout Alan! Can't be me they're shouting at. Unlikely to be Alan Partridge in the vicinity either, otherwise I would definitely have turned round. The second Alan! wasn't followed by a chorus of Dan's!! (Partridge fans only) but a slightly louder Mr Forbes! Well maybe it was me they were after but I didn't know anyone at all who would be in Mexico at the same time as us, let alone Puerto Vallarta. I've only ever met one other Alan Forbes (I'll get back to that one or this is going to get silly) and it was unlikely to be him they were hollering at, so we turned around. As you can probably imagine I am rarely lost for words but there was one of my cousins from Canada and his wife! Beat that for a coincidence. I'd not seen him for about 18 months and we don't keep in touch, after he stopped emailing me porn, unless we are arranging a visit, so neither of us had any idea the other would be there.

It was very funny to say the least. He had seen us walking along the beach as they were having their lunch. He said they were pretty sure it was me (they'd not met Agnes) but finished their lunch before following us. I took slight offence at that.

If the roles had been reversed I would have left my lobster instantly and chased him straightaway. Clearly he was a little cooler about the one in a million. He wasn't so cool at dinner that night when he asked how my mum was and I had to remind him she had been dead 7 years! Luckily I had the last laugh (again Partridge fans only).

As an inspiration for travel Mexico is a must. Forget Cancun, or maybe go there at the end of your trip for some beach. Los Cabos was overrated. Just because Jennifer Anniston or similar loves it doesn't mean it's nice, but there are some great places to visit. Although Puerto Vallarta is also blighted by mass tourism the old city is nice and Saulita beach nearby is fabulous and San Sebastián in the hills for some reason is not mentioned in Lonely Planet. It's so nice I was even moved to write to them to suggest they include it. They never replied, but if it features in later additions I'm claiming it. Other highlights include Copper Canyon (I'll come back to that if I don't forget), Palenque, Canyon de Sumidero, Oaxaca and Puerto Escondido to name a few. Even much maligned Mexico City is well worth a visit.

So, yesterday we flew out to Budapest and as we were getting on the bus from the aircraft to arrivals I got a tap on the shoulder and as I turned around a "thought it was you on the plane" comment. Only one of my son's best friends from school who he is still in regular contact with. Small world, eh? He was with his girlfriend, who has Hungarian grandparents and consequently a Hungarian passport, as well as British and Australian ones, but had never been to Hungary before and didn't speak a word of the language. She was right when she said she thought the additional staff set up for coronavirus checks would be a bit shocked when she handed them her passport but didn't understand a word they said.

I've gone back to our current travels as this is no ordinary time. We've had the gulf war, 9/11, SARS, ash cloud and other scenarios that have disrupted travel but this is certainly unprecedented in my time (I'm neither old enough for the world wars or unfortunate enough to live in a country ravished by war). We booked a cruise a few months back for 3 reasons - we wanted to travel through the Suez Canal, it was very cheap and it lasted 3 weeks. I'll find a time to come back to cruises as we are neither addicted to them or collecting cruise ships, cruise lines or ports. As coronavirus shuts down more of the countries we are currently descending into Dubai, not the Dubai most people know but the airport for cargo flights and low-cost carriers. We paid £59 each for Gatwick to Dubai, via Budapest (not new to the collection). What a bargain and taking us to a new airport to boot. Even if it is 50 kms further away. But will the cruise operate? And if it does where will we end up? Well, we'll know the first answer tomorrow afternoon but it seems unlikely we will end up in our final destination of Rome in 3 week's time. In the last 2 days 4 large cruise lines have cancelled all their cruises. First things first we need to get into Dubai and onto the ship if it indeed leaves tomorrow. We both have colds! But no coughs or fever.

Well, how the world has changed since I finished that paragraph over a month ago! Maybe by the time I finish this book we will know just how much coronavirus changed all our lives. Or maybe lockdown (who had ever heard of that 3 months ago?) will have lasted so long or become so recurring that, even with all my digressions, I have no more to write. Within half an hour of finishing that paragraph we learnt that between leaving Budapest and arriving in Dubai our cruise had finally been cancelled. We were neither particularly shocked nor majorly upset. Worse things were happening. We had a plan B should the cruise have been cancelled before we left UK: we would return to India. Spring would be on the horizon so we could head further north to some of those areas that were not practical for us to visit in January and February and have a little more time on the beaches in the south.

Our cruise line, Costa (not going to name drop them if the refund doesn't come through), were very efficient in handling the cancellation. As we had no onward travel booked once we arrived in

Rome, just a plan to be in Poland 3 weeks later for Agnes and her mum's birthdays, they said they would fly us wherever we wanted to go. I'm sure this would have come with a caveat if we had said Australia or Cuba - both under consideration. We initially said we would like to fly to Gatwick as it seemed the logical option. However, when collecting airports logic goes out of the window. Not that this was the time to be thinking of adding to that collection. Literally by the hour we were learning of countries imposing quarantines or banning foreign arrivals completely. India and then Sri Lanka being amongst the growing list. So plan B and C were not an option. We applied for Australian e-visas. Agnes's came through by return. For some reason mine took 48 hours, by which time we were home and before that Australia had also imposed a 14-day quarantine. So logic, realistically, seemed the only course to follow.

After a night of luxury in JW Marriott, compliments of Costa, we were back home 72 hours after we had left and around 48 days sooner than we planned. We had given up our jobs to travel. Well, Agnes gave up a well-paid director position. My career in dog walking was coming to a more natural conclusion. The idea to "retire" and travel full time had been hatched 4 years earlier. As soon as my youngest daughter was 18, and presumably off to university we were off. A 6-

month delay did transpire but March 14 2019 we were off. A loose plan of spending all year in warm climes was all we really had. We knew that our health and that of our loved ones could impact that idea at any time and that finances could also play a part. What we never could have imagined was that the health of the whole planet would be in jeopardy and that our plans would eventually come to a complete standstill.

At this stage UK was in single figure deaths and Italy, Spain and France had only partial lockdowns. It, therefore, didn't seem too selfish at that point to be considering how we could at least feed 2 of our home-grown addictions whilst overseas travel options continued to disappear rapidly. This conveniently takes me back to our other, Agnes inspired, collections, which, of course, I had to join her on. Quite rightly, not content with embracing my collections, she wanted "her own", which I could accompany her. Well, let's say accepting one and embracing the other of mine. Agnes is in no hurry to add to her 3 football grounds but accepts my obligation (to myself) to remain current on football grounds. Her first idea for her collection could only add to the belief, my belief, that I am an extremely lucky man. "Let's (try and) visit every Wetherspoon in UK and Ireland".

How long do you reckon I needed to think about that one? What were the chances of me saying, "sorry darling but you're on your own with this one"? How long do you think it took me to realise how many times we would be able to merge Spoons visits with football and, to a lesser extent, cricket? I already loved Agnes as much as I thought possible. Now here was a girl who not only hated shopping but was now suggesting that we had a very sound reason to go to the pub as often as possible. Granted, none of us need any more reason to go to the pub other than we want a drink. I actually think it is fair to say that Aggers likes a drink more than me. Or should I say, she likes to drink more regularly than me. I've always been a bit crap at having just one drink. Once I have one I get the taste for it. Invariably I could get the taste for too much at one time. Having always had a poor constitution when it came to drink this led to some fairly horrendous hangovers. I'm not talking headaches. Or generally just feeling dire. We're talking full on 8-hour vomiting sessions which would normally not begin until around 10 am the next morning, therefore writing off the next day until anything as late as 6pm.

Why, some of you may ask did I not learn? Let's put some figures out there. This probably only happened around half a dozen times a year. The rest of the time I either surprised myself with how much I had managed to consume, and the variety, without feeling hungover or I had actually realised when to stop. Unlike the real drinkers (normally men) who can consume anything between 10-15 pints plus, my limit has been 4-6, depending on time and strength. I just don't have the capacity for more. When a lunch merges into a dinner I can drink a reasonable quantity of wine, maybe a bottle or 2 but not 4 or 5 (dare I say normally hardcore lady drinkers). Spirits? Very hit and miss. On a 10–12-hour flight I could get away with a gin and tonic to start, a couple of beers, a few glasses of wine and several Drambuies and feel nothing other than jet lag. My most pathetic effort was vomiting the next morning after 3 1/2 pints. I had to pull myself together as I had a 4pm flight to Havana and 3 kids to look after!

In my defence, cigarettes played a major part in my more pathetic hangovers. I was never a proper smoker. In fact, I was well over 30 when I had my first straight cigarette. Whilst never proclaiming to be prolific on the class A front I had dabbled and was even partial to weed for a few years. On most occasions the joint I would have partaken in would've consisted of some normal tobacco so finally I thought why the hell not? Initially I would maybe have one or two (of someone else's) cigarettes when particularly drunk. Over time this progressed to having a cigarette with a drink - if someone else was. This then meant that, instead of having a couple of cigarettes at the end of the evening, I may smoke 6 or 7 through the course of an evening. Or more, if this was one of those lunchtime into evening sessions, which were always loosely in the name of, and paid for, by work.

To summarise, my drinking was erratic. I never drank alone, well not until the later years of flying solo. I never drank at home without outside company until I met Agnes. Many of my heavy boozing sessions between 1990 and 2010 were work inspired. I would stop short of calling them benders. Consequently I could easily go a week or more without drinking, and therefore smoking (I never once smoked a cigarette without an accompanying glass of something alcoholic, not once, promise). My hangovers were even more erratic and very unpredictable. Hence, I could never really "learn my lesson". I could drink and smoke heavily, for me, and feel as fit as the proverbial fiddle or I could drink and smoke lightly, by my standards and barely worth a mention by others' and be struck with what felt like a bout of food poisoning.

In contrast, Agnes tells me that she has only ever had one hangover! She is prone to being exceptionally truthful so I have no reason to disbelieve her. But one hangover? I've not seen Agnes drunk in the 9 years we have known each other. I wouldn't say she is a little and often drinker. Often? Yes. Little? Depends on your interpretation. She likes a glass or two of red wine. Fortunately, I think, she has developed her taste in beers to include bitter/real ale. In fact she would say she prefers real ale, and her choices would bear this out. This is especially handy in Spoons who, whatever you think of them, normally have an extremely varied stock of real ales. Agnes likes beer or wine at home but never to excess. So I now drink regularly at home without visitors. To balance this I no longer, or very rarely drink heavily for two reasons: I no longer work and I normally stop when Agnes does. I gave up smoking as soon as the ban was announced on smoking in pubs, etc.. After all, they were the only times I smoked normally. I am proud to say I have not had one hangover since I've been with Agnes. Felt a bit rough a few times and on two occasions (one being New Year's Eve in Poland) just got to McDonald's in time to prevent a full-blown hangover.

At times I have seen Agnes drink quite a lot, and mix her drinks but she says she doesn't like to feel drunk, so knows when to stop/slow down. On the other hand, I've always enjoyed being drunk, or mellow. It doesn't have a bad effect on my mood or behaviour except that I may be inclined to dance (and I am a truly awful dancer, so it is very rare indeed that that happens) and I may repeat myself more often than sober. If I digress I have very little chance of reverting to the original conversation.

You may very well be thinking what the hell does this have to do with airport collecting or any other collection for that matter. I agree but isn't alcohol the number one addiction, probably followed by cigarettes? And as I see collecting as an addiction then it's relevant in my opinion, and even if it isn't so what? I have a lot of empathy with anyone who is a regular smoker and wants to give up. I didn't have another cigarette once I decided to stop. It wasn't hugely difficult but I would say that for 3 or 4 years there was a craving when someone else lit up and I had a drink in my hand. Now, and for a number of years, I am back to where I was before I smoked anything. I can't stand the slightest trace of it. Sometimes I would smoke in a smoky pub just because I wasn't then disturbed by other people's smoke.

I don't think I would have become an alcoholic if I didn't get sick so easily but it was certainly a deterrent if I had been heading in that direction. Maybe my inability to have just one drink shows a very, very limited addiction but I can certainly last without, as India undoubtedly proved. Again, I empathise with any alcoholic although we all have different levels of willpower. Hopefully my addictions are not as damaging as those two!

Back to the Spoon collection. Agnes had actually worked in a Wetherspoon (since closed) and we had both been to a few individually, some still open, some closed but this collection would start from scratch. After all, it's a joint collection, and would only involve the sacrifice of one or two previously visited and now closed pubs. In my case Derry has been closed a while. It's not like me sacrificing nearly 700 airports, not that this was ever remotely asked of me. We laid down our criteria which we have stuck to, initially 95+% of the time and since a new addition to that criteria, 100%.

This latter criteria can actually be attributed to Sweaty Pete. Agnes would occasionally share a commute with Peter. Only 10-15 minutes normally, depending on how Southern were performing. One morning Peter proudly showed Agnes a book one of his sons had bought him for his birthday, "Wetherspoons carpets". Agnes says she then ordered a copy for me but I'm convinced it was a present to herself. We had been to a number of Spoons prior to this purchase but this created an altogether different angle: Supposedly every Spoons has a different carpet design. Actually there are one or two, out of around 900 or so, that are the same and some others that can be very similar but, in general, they are all very different. The book only shows around 100 of these carpets, accompanied by some normally fairly witty trivia on the carpet, locality and pub itself. Now, if we didn't partake in an alcoholic drink to tick off the pub we could just take a picture of the carpet. We don't stoop to this level very often. Only if we are doing 5 or more pubs in a day and a pub is either uninteresting or just a dump, or very crowded and noisy.

We know we are not the first to attempt to visit all Spoons. There are many examples of those who have been to all of them or many more than us. Many of these people we have read about are also very partial to trains. Sweaty Pete says that there is a definite connection between pubs and railways. Clearly there are plenty of "Railway Taverns" in this country but I think he's looking into it more deeply than that. Of course, a lot of the towns lucky enough to have a Spoon no longer have a train station since the 1960s culling. It's a constant mystery to us why Sweaty Pete is not also collecting Spoons. He claims that he can't remember all the ones he has been to. This man has an unbelievable memory when it comes to buses, railway and Leeds United matches. Invariably, any Spoon visit by him would be accompanied by at least 2 of the above. He steadfastly refuses to make Spoons a collection no matter how many times we try to encourage him.

What he does do with barely believable accuracy is guess which pub we are in by the carpet photo. In fact, that is unfair on him. He doesn't guess which pub we are in, he knows! And he knows just by the carpet. I am only just starting to remember the carpet of our local Spoon, The Oxted Inn. Whether he has been to the pub himself or not his accuracy of telling us which pub we are in is around 99%. Rather than give you examples of how uncanny this is now, I'll do it when I go back to some of our pub visits.

CHAPTER EIGHT

Well as things stand it's a bloody good job we have another UK based, quite time consuming, collection. Again, unlike airports, I imagine some other people may be attempting it, although maybe not? It is certainly finite.

Agnes and I knew we shared a love of walking. Nothing too strenuous but anything up to 20 miles in a day. This was mainly restricted to utilising fancyfreewalks.org which provides a comprehensive number of circular walks in south east England. I had a desire to do some long-distance walking but felt I should put it to the test locally before going further afield. During the period that Agnes and I were quite distant I decided I would walk the North Downs Way. 126 miles from Farnham to Dover. I managed to do this in 5 days, not consecutive, and realised that I did indeed like long distance walking and could branch out further. At the same time, I would like to say inspired by me, but probably not, Agnes had started to walk the same path but, with friends and at a much more leisurely pace. By the time we got back together I think she had got about a third of the way. So I then joined her on the remaining distance, at the leisurely pace, with as many pub stops as possible. I think this took about 18 months!

In the meantime we had decided we would like to start another long-distance walk and chose The Thames Path. 186 miles. When and where would we start and how would we manage the transport in between? Agnes had been on a work trip to Jamaica and was arriving home on a Saturday, late morning. Would she like to walk rather than head home? For sure. "Just bring my boots and some clothes". What a girl! Straight off a night flight from Miami. What she hadn't reckoned with was the mileage I intended to complete that first day! With virtually no planning and certainly no overnight accommodation arranged we set off from Heathrow around 12.30. I think I was planning for us to walk up to 30 miles. This, Agnes, quite rightly, dismissed. Not just because she had only slept 4-5 hours on the plane but it was already 12.30 and we would not be at the start point until 3pm earliest.

We needed to replan whilst driving. A quick call to Sweaty Pete to work out the logistics resulted in a drive to Lechlade, a bus to Swindon and a train to Kemble, the latter two being a rare species but fortunately quite conveniently timed. We then walked to the source of The Thames, allegedly, but undoubtedly the start of the walk. It was now 4.30 and whilst it was the height of summer, quite literally summer solstice, time was not on our side to reach our revised overnight destination, Cricklade.

Around 9pm and still a way from Cricklade we thought it may be prudent to try and find somewhere to stay. Long story short, it was the weekend of the Cricklade summer fete. There was nowhere to stay. Everywhere was full. Finally we found a pub in South Cerney which had rooms but was around 3 miles off the path. We finally arrived at the pub around 10pm and were very grateful to the landlord for knocking up some sarnies for us. Another thing we hadn't factored into our afternoon was food!

The collection was not yet born but our long distancing walking was. Clearly it was slightly insane of me to think that we could walk 30 miles on arrival, even if we had arrived a few hours earlier. A fact Agnes likes to remind me of. The next day after the boring bit of returning to the path from our overnight we reached Cricklade, where the fete was in full swing and proceeded onto Lechlade where we had left the car. In total we probably walked around 30 miles. A huge positive about a riverside walk, well at least this one, is that it is, unsurprisingly, devoid of any hills, in case you hadn't figured it for yourself. Another one you would probably work out is that there's quite a few pubs on a riverside route. If you are not a long-distance walker but fancy the idea, The Thames Path may be a perfect starter. It's not as difficult to plan the overnights, or start and finish points, once you get past the first 50+ miles.

The source of The Thames is apparently somewhat disputed and, compared to many river sources, pretty underwhelming. Depending on the time of year it is just a slight circular dip in a nondescript field. There is a monument to Father Thames which at least confirms you're in the right spot to start the walk to London. As I've mentioned already and, being a bit of a repeater, will no doubt do with annoyingly regularity, I'm not writing a travel book but would like to inspire where possible: The Thames Path is a lovely walk. The contrast between what starts as a barely visible stream into the world-famous stretches in London is fascinating. Stretches in the countryside can be walked in solitude for hours on end and then a mile or so either side of a town or village the day trippers appear. That isn't me being condescending on folk who have no desire to walk for more than an hour. In fact I'm glad that's all many people want to do or the path would be pretty crowded.

It was on The Thames Path that we were first able to combine walking with adding to the Spoon collection. We didn't get off to an auspicious start as I recall: when passing through Maidenhead we decided to veer a couple of miles off route to visit this town's 2 Spoons. Wait, I hear you ask, "how do you know where all the Spoons are?".

Good question. There used to be a pub and hotel directory produced annually. I have a copy for 2015, 2017 and 2018. I believe the latter may have been the last as, believe me, we have been in plenty of Spoons since 2018 and I've never seen a 2019 or 2020 vintage. I'm convinced my 2018 copy could become a very highly desirable and, consequently, valuable collectors' item.

The modern way of finding a Spoon is, of course, via an app. I'm sure this would've been around in 2015 but I reckon we were on the paper version and I'll tell you why: on arrival at the first Spoon, a couple of miles from the Thames, the service was provided by one solitary barman. Not ideal on a warmish Sunday afternoon. We agreed we couldn't be bothered to wait indefinitely to get a pint so decided we would have a free glass of water from the bar and add that to our criteria of what constituted a visit to a Spoon (this was pre carpet days. Not for the pubs but for our criteria you understand). I think this may be the only time we resorted to this flaky ticking exercise and on this occasion justified it by thinking we would have a pint in the other Spoon just a few hundred yards away. Imagine our horror when we approached The Greyhound, I think, and the bugger was closed. Not just for the afternoon, for good! 4 extra bloody miles we'd walked to get a pint and we still didn't have one.

We should've gone back to the original Spoon to

see if the queue had died down but Agi was thirsty, so we dipped into the first pub we came to. Well, actually it had a beer garden of sorts at the front of the pedestrianised street which made it more appealing. One drawback in our early Spoon career was the lack of outside drinking areas which meant that, on a sunny day, our visits would be quite short. Happily the vast majority of Spoons now have some kind of outdoor area and more and more seem to have nice gardens. Maybe these always did and it was because many of our first few hundred Spoons were in Greater London that we, initially, thought of them as a rarity.

This wasn't our only shattering disappointment in finding a shut Spoon, temporary or otherwise. The problem with the app is that they don't appear to update it if a pub is closed for renovation. Or maybe they do and we were still working on the directory. We did find a permanently closed pub in Lancaster last August still on the app. Fortunately that rather pleasant town/city was blessed with two so all was not lost. I don't know how recently it had closed down to be able to judge how quickly the app is updated. Street and Andover have both necessitated return visits due to renovation closures, whilst Retford and, most recently, one of the many in the Birmingham area will require a tick at a later date being closed "due to unforeseen circumstances".

Whilst the vast majority of you are likely thinking

what sad bastards we are, wasting our time and money going to Wetherspoons let me enlighten you. We have already been to many towns we would have never thought of visiting and I consider myself very well-travelled in the UK without wishing to sound big-headed. Some I had never heard of and I think we can say, without exception, almost all have been well worth it. Even most cities I had previously considered to be a bit shit, based on football experiences only, have actually inevitably shocked me as to the pleasantness they provide. Granted there is the occasional destination that it is really quite a challenge to find a positive within but they are few and far between.

Then there are the pubs themselves. A small number do conform to the uninitiated opinion of a J D Wetherspoon establishment - a less than bang average pub with little atmosphere (I think most would just call it a shithole but how dare they!) with a clientele that they would choose not to mix with - how judgemental. However, the vast majority we have visited so far, I would say in excess of 80%, are either charming buildings (think converted fire stations, tram stations, theatres, opera houses, banks, churches and so on) or have very welcoming interiors and the walls are adorned with local history including famous residents (of the area, not the pub itself).

I don't intend to list all 535 we have visited so

far you'll be pleased to hear but you could do far worse than sample a real ale or enjoy free Lavazza coffee refills at your nearest Spoon one day. Unless you live in Thornton Heath. Truly only memorable because it did fit the preconceived notion of what a Wetherspoon can offer. It was awful, and I think it is now shut anyway. Spoons do seem to close down and new ones appear quite regularly. Sadly it seems the former far more frequently than the latter and, of course, they're all bloody shut at the moment!! It is a constant worry as to how many will reopen if we are ever virus free.

Unlike football grounds where I sometimes don't welcome the opportunity to attempt to add to the collection (because of the difficulty of obtaining a ticket maybe as well as not necessarily being over the moon about going back to Barrow!) the knowledge of a Spoon closure that we haven't yet made it to is always a disappointment. I know there have been well over 1000 Spoons, many of which we will never get to visit due to their closure, and the current total seems to wobble, but we just want our final total to be as high as possible and it is not a collection that we want to finish any time soon (just as well currently!).

We look forward to visiting new Spoons with relish. Alright, so you may think we are sad but really after all the positives I've listed? I haven't even mentioned how cheap the beer is. Talking of which, my cheapest pint in modern times was in 2018 in Sheerness Spoon. A pint of Abbott Reserve, a beautiful beer so much more so than a standard Abbott and not frequently found, £1.35! Surely there was some mistake? And there was. The friendly bar maid informed me that they had ordered the wrong size barrel so, very sensibly, rather than chuck away what they hadn't sold before it went off had made it a manager's special. Discount that further by a 50p Spoon voucher left over from my best Christmas present and you've got yourself a pint of finest ale for 85p!! Two, in fact with change from a £2 coin. Aggers wasn't going to miss out on that one.

What the Wetherspoon app does enable you to do is mark a pub as visited. You can also add a pub to your favourites. The logic being that you would only do that if you had visited the pub. In the top right corner of the pub listing you can click on a small triangle and it turns green, immediately letting us know that we have visited the pub without having to scroll down to the "mark pub as visited" box or scroll through the visited pubs section. I've just realised that I sound like a complete knob/nerd for writing all this paragraph (yeah, I know, and many other paragraphs you're thinking) but there is a reason......

On returning on a flight from Luton a couple of years ago we decided to visit a few Spoons in the area before heading home. By the way, Luton is one of those towns which sadly has no redeeming features whatsoever on closer inspection. Sorry Luton, but from what we've seen it really is a dump, as is the football ground. At least my son, Callum, remembers it as the walk into the away end literally passes on a raised walkway between terraced houses. The Spoon in Luton isn't particularly memorable but it is probably one of Luton's more redeeming features. Maybe we missed something in Luton so I apologise to its proud residents if we did. Even the airport is truly horrible and, like Stansted, has the gall to charge just to drop someone off. Anyway, we both agreed that Hemel Hempstead wasn't too far away so we would start there. Only on arrival outside did we both realise that we had already been there! And probably within the last 6 months. So, my point is, lost as points invariably are by digressing, that the app is very useful and worth checking for a green box before visiting a pub.

To be fair that is the only time it has happened, so far. At least it was on our way to Berkhamsted, our next pub and it is also a very nice pub, a converted cinema. Berkhamsted being one of those towns that fall into the category (for us) of "why would you go there, if it didn't have a Spoon?" and giving us a pleasant surprise. Nice pub too. The weird thing is we had only been to a few hundred Spoons when this happened so no excuses really.

I think the only time we would need to check now if we have been to a pub is in the example of Birmingham. For Agnes this trip satisfied 3 collections and for me 2. Agnes flew back from a work trip to Birmingham airport, a new one for her. I met her there and we realised we had a problem: Birmingham has an airside Spoon so we will both need to do the airport again to do the Spoon in the departure lounge. This mistake was repeated a few weeks ago when Agnes booked her flight back from Poland to Doncaster/Sheffield (Robin Hood) airport to tick that one off. Only when I started looking for pubs we could visit nearby did I realise it also has a Spoon in the departure lounge! When will I learn!? Another schoolboy error. In the post Coronavirus era will this airport even exist? I guess if it doesn't we won't need to visit the Spoon as clearly it won't be there either. Maybe that's being over pessimistic.

Another problem with Birmingham is the NEC. It has 2 Spoons within. As it was late in the day and anyone visiting The Wedding Show wouldn't be arriving at 5pm the car park attendant very kindly let us off the £16 parking charge - that would've made for a very expensive pint! However, to our horror, only one of them was open for this event. If you want to be cynical about marriage, or more specifically weddings, you could opine that a minimum of two pub choices within the show would be respectable. So, if we are taking this collection seriously, which we bloody well are, we are going to have to be very careful about when we go back to the NEC, double check which one it is we have been to and whether the other one will be open.

If you check on the Spoon app you will see Birmingham is blessed with many Spoons, in the centre and in the suburbs. So we picked on a few on the way into the city and then I performed what I can proudly describe as the best bit of parking in my 42 year driving career. You need to see the pictures to believe it, and if I decide to include some pictures in this book I will include one of this remarkable feat. It's that bloody impressive. I still wonder how the hell I managed it when I look back at the pictures. Street parking in Birmingham city centre is at a premium on a Friday night. It's likely it is on any night or day. As we were overnighting in a Spoon hotel, bear with me a minute.....

We are not counting Spoons hotels separately. After all they all come with a pub. And, I don't know why I feel the need to big them up to you, as they are all small and if you take my advice will be more likely to be full, but they are bloody good. If you don't trust me they were voted in a Which survey in 2019 as best UK hotel chain, along with Premier Inn. We have spent a very comfortable night in Newbury, Kings Lynn, Doncaster and Bedford, to name a few.

Back to the parking. The pictures provide proof that there is literally no more than an inch, both back and front, between our car and those

I sandwiched it between. I probably manoeuvred back and forth 20 or more times to get a good distance from the kerb and be parallel, all under Agnes's guidance from outside and, obviously touched the other cars each time and, sorry for being boasting about it, but it was bloody brilliant. Overnight both other cars disappeared and didn't leave a rude note, or a key scratch down the side, so I can only assume they were equally as impressed as I with what I had achieved or, more likely, they didn't give a toss.

In case you are wondering what the third element of the collection that weekend was for Agnes, and second for me, it was walking orientated. Pretty obvious maybe and I'll get back to that in a minute. The point of mentioning Birmingham was that when we went back in December 2019, a couple of years on, that's when we needed to check the app to see which ones we had been to previously so as to avoid repetition. There is a little story with that last Birmingham trip I'm going to share. I haven't pushed the, "Darling, shall we go and do some Spoons on Saturday?" line too often followed quickly by "and whilst we are there I'll just pop off to footy for a few hours and leave you in your favourite one". But Birmingham, albeit on a Sunday, in December 2019 was one of them. The plan on such an occasion is to get to the destination for breakfast in the first Spoon. Agnes came up with a great idea for when we would visit 3 Spoons early: split a breakfast wrap in 2 pubs and have a coffee in a third, unless it was then time for a beer. We have got used to the odd looks from the staff when they come to the table with one breakfast wrap to find two people looking longingly at it. I'm sure they think we are poor, tight or both.

On this occasion we had the customary half a breakfast wrap each in the first pub. Now, I'll really try and keep this as short as possible, for my standards: we both have an Amex/British Airways credit card. If you spend £20k on it in a year you get a free companion flight voucher (obviously, usual con, not free, as you pay the taxes which make up most of the cost). What it effectively means is you only have to use 50% of your Avios points (I'm trying to keep it short so you'll have to google it if you don't know what Avios points are). Worthwhile for us. So we had been trying all year to stick everything we could on Agnes's card, her year ending on 07 Jan. In October and November until Xmas it looked like we would be a couple of grand short but when we booked the India flights and cruise we realised that somehow we only needed to spend another £80 and we were in! No problem!

As Agnes was otherwise occupied I borrowed her card to pay and then kept it for our next pub. Only just as we were pulling up to our next pub so was a coach load of travelling Leeds fans.

Agnes didn't fancy the idea of sharing the second half of her wrap with some of Elland Road's finest even though I assured her it would be their first pint and that they would stay there until just before kick-off. So we took a seat briefly, a carpet picture followed by the rest of Agnes's now polished routine (menu photo, posting of visit on Instagram, my reading from the app of the pub history, ticking the favourites triangle and marking the pub as visited - all sounds a bit nerdy but helps with the memory!). By the way, the carpet photo has to include one foot of each person on the visit. Believe it or not, we are not always alone on these visits.

So off we head to the next pub. I head to the bar to order the second breakfast wrap. You can, and we often do, order from your table on another Spoon app, a godsend in a busy pub. On this occasion I headed to the bar to order the wrap. No Amex card! Shit! You know the feeling when you've lost something like your wallet or your phone or keys? How many times you check your pocket, look in the most unlikely of places etc. One bloody year we'd been trying to spend £20k and we've spent £19, 927 and I've royally screwed up. Back to the pub with the Leeds fans, back to the first pub, back again to the Leeds fans' pub, back to the third one. We can't cancel the card as we know we won't get a replacement in time to spend £73. We leave for India on 02 January. It's 29 December. Bollocks!

Agnes is rightly not happy with me. She's not shouting at me, she never does, but she's upset. She has been far more into trying to reach the goal than me. Secretly I'm more concerned about the goal(s) Leeds better score so this doesn't turn into a really mucked up day.

I may have said this already but if I haven't let me just say that I am fully aware that any issues/upsets/disappointments I have had in life so far have all been insignificant compared to what many people suffer. I believe I always keep things in perspective and recognise the bigger picture. However, for example, if you don't get royally pissed off when your footy team loses you won't experience the unfathomable elation when they pull off the unexpected win. If you don't get fed up when the weather misbehaves and ruins a day you won't marvel at a glorious day. I was annoyed with the loss of the card and the resultant "free" flight but as we had looked six times now for the card it was time to cancel it.

We still hadn't had our second wrap and kick off was approaching. Our next planned pub on our way back towards Birmingham City's ground would need to be a quick visit as we still had to get to the nearest one for Agnes to hole up in for a few hours. We parked up and headed over to the Bottle of Sack. For no apparent reason it was closed! This was going really well. Hungry, we headed off to The Hornet for a quick lunch and pint then I left Agnes there to mull over my punishment for denying her goal. I thought Leeds would probably hand out my punishment but after half an hour we were 0-2 to the good. Knowing Leeds that didn't mean we were sorted but even in 50 years of supporting what followed was quite remarkable: 1-2, 2-2, 2-3, 3-3, 3-4, 4-4, 4-5. If you're a real supporter you'll get that, if not, your loss.

How was I to keep from Agnes that my day had turned out so wonderfully as this result would mean nothing to her other than she would be happy for me. She also always keeps things in perspective so, whilst my carelessness wasn't forgotten, she didn't allow it to dampen my euphoria over a thoroughly mental game of footy. Two more Spoons on the way home, providing a respectable 6 for the day.

The call to Amex to report the lost card had been as expected: no the replacement card would not arrive before 02 January due to the holiday period and no they couldn't extend our free flight period. The free flight would not exist. Imagine the unbridled joy when on the morning of 31 December a letter from Amex plopped through the letterbox. A New Year's Day family farewell curry took care of the remaining £73. The voucher arrived in Agnes's inbox on the 8th of January. How ironic that, after all that, who knows if or when we will ever get to use that voucher?

Right, back to the 4th collection, I promise. As I

said and you no doubt gathered, if I haven't lost you completely and utterly, it's about walking but let us get down to the specifics. As we were only walking at weekends it took us a while to complete the Thames Path. Over a year. In the meantime, for something a little closer to home, we had embarked on our next long-distance walk, The South Downs Way. It was on this walk that we, well Agnes really, to be honest, realised what the Acorn symbol on the footpath signs signified. We were walking National trails. How the hell had we not noticed!?

CHAPTER NINE

"Why don't we do all the National Trails?" Agnes suggests, before checking the mileage involved. I agree as hastily as I did to the Spoon collection. We both love walking and this sounds like a fairly normal idea to me. Not that the latter comes into consideration. If anything, the opposite would attract. After all, doing the 3 peaks is far too common. Walking from John O'Groats to Land's End? Climbing all the Munros? Less so. We are just talking UK ventures here.

We quickly learned that there are 15 National Trails in England and Wales. We haven't found out why none of the long-distance trails in Scotland are included. Maybe that will be a blessing if we are to achieve our goal. Particularly since plans are afoot to create the world's longest coastal path, naturally to become the 16th National Trail. This for some bizarre reason will be the England Coast Path. Missing out a rather large chunk of the UK coast, ie. Wales. Seeing as Scotland doesn't feature in UK National Trails, nor Northern Ireland, for that matter, we understand why these splendid coasts will not feature. Wales already has the Wales Coast Path but it is not a National Trail. So why will this not be included and named as the England and Wales Coast Path? Again, maybe a blessing for us. No Acorn, not part of our collection.

This baby will be approximately 2700 miles short when completed. Judging by the time taken to open some of the trails we have walked I will be long dead, in a wheelchair or a home before this monstrous beauty is officially opened.

I admit to currently being quite obsessed with the National Trails. Bit tricky seeing as we are currently in Silesia, Poland on an extended visit. It is August 2020. As history will show foreign travel is royally knackered (I'm still trying to avoid swearing but it really is upsetting) at the moment. So, when we leave Poland, we will maybe walk at the time of year when we normally would be planning to head to warmer climes. Let's see. For now, I can proudly state that we have completed 60% of the National Trails. However, to quantify that I don't mean that we have walked roughly 1700 miles of the roughly 2600 miles the 15 consist of. I mean that we have walked 9 out of 15. We have started the biggy and nearly finished the daunting one. By biggy I mean the South West Coast Path, not the England as this is not yet part of the collection. The daunting is our most recent effort - The Pennine Way. What a beauty!

I would just like to say: this writing lark; well you really have to put your mind to it, and I have failed miserably at that so far, but since returning from the Pennine Way we have read "Father, Son and the Pennine Way" by Mark Richards and are now on "Father, Son and return to the Pennine Way", unsurprisingly by the same author. Put this down and read those. Maybe they are so amusing because the walk is so fresh in our minds but, honestly, that would do the author a disservice. Clearly, he writes for a living. I would be very hungry if I did! However, notwithstanding his very unfortunate heart attack - on his birthday and just after birthday sex (I'm sure that's not libellous as it is in his book) - 10 years earlier, Agnes and I are clearly more accomplished walkers, so far.

Walking gives you a lot of time to think, and, in my case, talk. So, it would clearly be wrong not to digress whilst talking National Trails: during our Pennine Way adventure Leeds finally achieved promotion back to the top division. Media and most football fans describe it as "back where they belong". I'm not so sure about that. Having now supported them for 51 years they have now spent 24 of those in the second and third divisions. If you take away the last 16 then they were a top division side in 27 of the first 35 seasons I have been addicted to them. It's playing with figures really, isn't it? It doesn't matter what division they are in to me. In fact, their dropping down to the third division enabled me to watch them whilst getting back up to 92 football league grounds. Maybe I would have just dropped further down in the current numbers, I think I dropped as low as 77 at one point, if they had carried on with annual visits to Everton etc.

As it was Cheltenham, Macclesfield, Yeovil, Salford City, to name a few, were all ticked off with a visit from the Mighty Whites. And plenty others where I had not seen Leeds play, not that that constitutes another collection as such. So, will fans be allowed in, and if so, how many? Will I get a ticket or will I be in the country when we play at Tottenham's new ground? So sad that Brentford missed out on promotion. Do I wait for Leeds to get relegated before adding their new ground to the total? When will Harrogate be permitted to play at their own ground, with fans and not at Doncaster? But most pressingly, our Under 23s have been drawn away to Barrow in the EFL Trophy. The fixture will either be played in early September (no fans = no decision), October or November.

The reason I mention this is because, much as I was pleased to see Barrow finally return to the Football League (I remember their demotion in the early 70s) it must be the biggest ball ache of a ground to visit from the south east. Normally this would be no barrier in pursuit of the current 92 but...... we went to Barrow last year for only one reason without the football ground counting. Yes, you've got it, the Spoon. And.... whilst we were there (it was August so I had no idea that Barrow would be promoted) I even went into the ground as I didn't imagine I would ever be back there. So, getting paired with Leeds reserves gives a glimmer of a reason, other than obsession, addiction and collecting, to return to Barrow-in-Furness, to give it its full title. Aren't I so lucky that currently this is my biggest worry in life!!?

To be fair to Barrow it is a local beauty spot compared to Workington. To be realistic, Workington are unlikely to become part of the 92 again in the near future. To appear sane, the only reason we visited either, and Whitehaven, was because it was leathering it down in the Lake District so why not tick off those far off Spoons rather than get soaked through on a non National Trail (therefore, somewhat meaningless) walk? Obviously, any walk in the Lakes isn't meaningless but it doesn't add to any collection unless you plan to walk round every lake - not currently on our radar- but a worthwhile collection to be considered when a new one is needed.

The Cumbria coast, or what we have seen of it, is quite a contrast to the interior of the county. Blessed with probably the best scenery in England inland, the coast and its towns are bleak in comparison. The same can be said of the Spoons. Keswick boasts an extremely interesting and attractive variety - former law courts, whereas Workington, Whitehaven and Barrow Spoons also fit in well with their surroundings, the latter rightly being the best of the three.

Combining Spoons and football grounds has been a recent option. The former being a recent collection and the latter being all but complete. Harrogate does offer a mouth-watering opportunity, pandemic permitting! In contrast, a few opportunities presented themselves with new airports and football grounds simultaneously. As I don't collect football grounds outside of the 92 any overseas football would be more appealing with a new airport in the vicinity but would only satisfy one collection. The same with overseas cricket too.

Actually, I think I may have mentioned somewhere that I have 5 collections. I guess I do, although as this one was/is small and I don't ever envisage it changing I'm not sure if it fits in with the other 4 obsessions. The fact that it took me 45 years to complete and there are only 18 to do (there were only 17 at one point) certainly indicates a lack of commitment on my behalf. I think I decided that I would like to complete the 18 in around 2011 when I realised that I only had 3 left to do. Cricket is my first love, sports wise. Football is a fantastically simple game and can be beautiful but it has been marred so much by those who play it and attend matches. Those who run it have done a pretty good job at fouling it up too. In general, you can only accuse the latter of trying to ruin cricket. I love Leeds United. I don't always like them and I certainly don't always like all those who play for them or manage them or support them. But I don't love football. I love cricket. I think of The Oval more as my spiritual home than I do Elland Road.

I'm feeling more in love with Leeds at the moment than for a long, long time. Not because we have just been promoted but because for the last 2 seasons we have been privileged to have Marcelo Bielsa as our manager. I love Marcelo. I am not alone and I know it. Without checking the populations of Argentina and Chile, Bilbao and Marseille I estimate that at least more than 10 million people feel the same way as I. He is quite simply a beautiful man and he has inspired us to play some of the best football I have seen us play, ever. He is clearly a bit weird but he has none of those despicable traits of Ferguson, Mourinho, Wenger et al. It is quite refreshing to discover a hero at 58 years old.

Back to the cricket. For those not interested in the best sport ever, there are 18 professional counties playing in England and Wales. Counties do not always play at the same ground. In fact, when I first started attending cricket matches regularly, back in the mid-70s, all counties played at at least 2 grounds and it was not uncommon for them to play at 3 or 4 each season. So, in some counties I had already been to 3 or 4 grounds, some only 1 or 2 but I hadn't been to a ground in all 18 counties. This was not too challenging to rectify with a lovely trip to Cardiff (Glamorgan) in 2012 - lovely because Aggers accompanied me to Cardiff, although not the cricket. It was in a cafe in Cardiff before the game that I realised that I loved her. We weren't a couple at the time but it only took me 2 years to rectify that!

In 2013 Durham was number 17. This was lovely because it was day 4 England v Australia and we won. It was also the only time I would imagine I have camped before and after a sports fixture. I had actually driven up to Scotland for a wedding on the first day of the match. I listened nervously in the car, hoping that the match wouldn't progress too quickly and that there wouldn't be a day 4. The reason I camped in Durham was because I had left it too late to book any accommodation for the wedding. It probably isn't a particularly regular occurrence for fellow campers to witness someone emerging from a 2-man tent in a suit but there I was and within stumbling distance of the venue so no concerns about driving or hailing a cab after the event.

The match was going to plan on the wedding day: day 2. Well, my plan anyway. The drive down to Durham from Scotland on day 3 was tense. Would England suffer an all-too-common collapse? Fortunately not. In spite of the rain on day 4, for a couple of hours, it was a wonderful day of cricket. It would not have mattered if it had gone to day 5 as I had planned to attend, if need be, but, if, as it could have, it had ended on day 3, well, I was now set on completing the 18 so I would have to return to Durham one day. Now that the Spoons is up and running that will hopefully happen now anyway but back then? Durham is a really lovely city but I would have now been twice so cricket would have been my only need to return.

The 18 were completed in May 2014 at Taunton (Somerset). Wetherspoon now providing a reason to return there, one day. The cricket was fine. Surrey won. I support Surrey, always have. I am very happy when they win and sometimes quite disappointed if they don't. But the highs and lows do not bear comparison with those caused by Leeds' results. What was a significant low on the way to the match was receiving a phone call to tell me that I was being made redundant and could I clear my desk and office before 9 am the following morning!? No, I couldn't, but I would do so before 9 am Tuesday morning.

It is probably fair to say that the pleasure in completing this mini collection, and Surrey's victory, was somewhat overshadowed by my concerns over who the hell was going to employ me and what was I going to do for money. I had had 2 jobs over 36 years, 22 of which I had been self-employed. I needn't have worried. I never worked full-time again. Most of my colleagues, in particular, friends and family would argue that I never did. In a conventional sense I would find it difficult to disagree with them.

Anyway!! Before I get back to where I

was, wherever that was, there is one slight problem with the 18. The only ground I have seen Northamptonshire play at is Tring, which is actually in Hertfordshire! So, I haven't actually seen professional cricket played in Northamptonshire, or any other cricket for that matter. For many years Northamptonshire shared their ground with Northampton Town FC and this formed part of my original 92 football grounds. I went and had a look in the cricket ground last year, as well, after doing the Northampton Spoon. I don't think there's an official "18" club for cricket like there is a "92" for footy but my rules. I've seen Northamptonshire play a home cricket match. Not my fault that Tring is in Hertfordshire. However, should I ever be passing and Northamptonshire are playing somewhere in Northamptonshire I may just pop in.

One, well actually three, anecdotes regarding the combination of new football grounds and new airports: the last of my original 92 grounds was Blackpool. I needed to go out with a bang. Gatwick - Belfast Aldergrove (now International)/ Belfast Harbour (now City/George Best) - Isle of Man - Blackpool/Birmingham - Heathrow. 5 new airports for one new footy ground. You might not be impressed but I was. What I wasn't so impressed with was the raging hangover I suffered with on the trip from Belfast to Blackpool and having not learnt my lesson, another one by car, on the way home, from Manchester to Birmingham.

Previously I had managed 2 new airports on a day trip to Plymouth Argyle FC. Not without some frayed nerves. The flight to Plymouth only made it as far as Newquay (onwards by bus) due to fog in Plymouth. As I ran up the cul de sac which led to Plymouth airport after the match it still seemed pretty foggy to me but to my eternal relief the plane had managed to land at some stage during the day and was there to whisk me back to Gatwick. The timing was such that I was back in Croydon by 7pm. Should any of the away fans have decided to make the journey, which some diehards would have undoubtedly done, they would have been back an awful lot later - a road journey of nearly 400 miles to Darlington, unless they had also been lucky enough to fly!

The third occasion I managed to achieve this delightful combi was at Coventry City's new ground, and it was against Leeds. Not a route I imagine any other fans took to the game - Stansted - Tours/ Paris Orly - Coventry. What were Thomsonfly doing flying from Paris to Coventry on a Saturday morning? Was there a Leeds supporters club branch I was unaware of in Paris? Highly unlikely after Leeds' infamous visit in 1975. Anyway, they did and it felt quite novel to fly from Europe to watch Leeds rather than fly from UK to watch Leeds in Europe.

Actually, that's just reminded me, sorry. There's a fourth example. I had booked myself a little overnight trip to Poitiers with a return from La Rochelle the next day. This, at a time when Ryanair would have an offer of £1 on certain flights ex UK and 0.10 euro to fly back to UK. Yes that is 10 cents, a little under 10 pence!! Who needed staff concessions if you could stomach Ryanair!? Then, after I booked the flights, the draw was made for the next round of the League Cup. Leeds was drawn away to Rotherham. Rotherham were between old and new grounds and lodging at the Don Valley Stadium, Sheffield for a few seasons. What to do? A new ground, albeit temporary, but a chance to add to the numbers with Leeds. Clearly finance didn't come into it but could I negate the loss of the 2 new airports for which I had already splashed out on and fly to the match? Doncaster/Sheffield had recently become a commercial airport. Where could I fly into there from on the day of the match and where could I fly near to that place the previous day? Easy. Well not really that easy, but with a heavy heart I consigned my Poitiers and La Rochelle tickets to the bin and booked myself from Stansted - Bydgoszcz/ Poznan - Doncaster/Sheffield. Bydgoszcz!? How did you pronounce that!? Where was it? Well Poland obviously but why did Ryanair fly there, and for a £1?

On arrival it appeared that Bydgoszcz had yet

to learn that Poland was no longer under Soviet control, let alone that it was in the EU. I didn't hang around, but jumped on a very ancient bus, on a very uneven road to a very lovely town called Toruń. My spirits lifted, not that they were particularly down anyway but yet again my airport addiction had taken me to yet another place I had never heard of. Even better, the next day, I broke my train journey to Poznan at a much smaller but equally delightful town unknown to me, the name of which I can't be certain I'm afraid.

Via bus, train and tram I made it quite literally to the match in Sheffield just as it was about to kick off. My European adventures with Leeds were continuing, even if they weren't playing in Europe anymore. Several years later I enjoyed a lovely trip to Poitiers and La Rochelle with Aggers. It was during the very last days of just being friends. Maybe it was the clincher which finally got her to back down. I think it was becoming apparent that our days of sharing a room with no intimacy were numbered. If she wanted to visit any more new airports with me things were going to have to change!

Looking back, what makes the visits to Blackpool, Plymouth and Coventry airports more pleasing is that none of them currently have any commercial flights. In fact, Plymouth airport is "mothballed" at this time, having survived attempts to turn it into a housing estate. (You have to love Wikipedia).

How did I get from combining football grounds with airports and cricket grounds in general? Believe it or not there is always a flow in my head, a connection. In this case as I'm thinking of the National Trails it reminded me of how we arrived to do Hadrian's Wall. Would you like to know? Rhetorical question of course. Having driven from Luton airport via John O'Groats and many other beautiful parts of our wonderful nation to Glasgow airport we then headed off to Northern Ireland. Well, if you've been to John, you'll know it's not beautiful but the north coast of Scotland certainly is and possibly even more so is the north coast of Northern Ireland.

One for Aggers as we flew into Belfast International, managed between the rain to admire the utter weirdness of Giant's Causeway, and, for both of us, visited the 4 remaining Spoons in Northern Ireland. I say 4 remaining, not because we had previously done any there but because, for some reason, pro rata, Spoons are closing more frequently than they are in the rest of UK. As they open a new one in Eire they seem to close one in the North. The real reason I had come up with the trip to N Ireland on our way home from Glasgow was because Carlisle airport was reopening to commercial flights for the first time in 25 years.

Something told me that these services might not last too long so an opportunity not to be missed.

Although there were flights from London, they were much cheaper from Belfast and we needed (and wanted) to go there to do the Spoons and most definitely wanted to go to the Giants Causeway. I'd been banging on about it for so long, having taken my mum and sister there on my mum's last holiday before she succumbed to cancer. Maybe it is worth mentioning that, even when planning a trip for my mum, which we knew would be her last as her diagnosis was terminal and her cancer advanced, I could not control my addiction.

Actually, to be fair, I had suggested a journey through the Highlands of Scotland on an Orient Express luxury train. Whilst the money was not an issue my mum felt that the £500pp for 3 nights could be better spent. I couldn't agree more. I could buy a few airports for the 3 of us and still have plenty for beds and food! I didn't think there was any need to burden them with the details but we were going to Eire. Who knew you could fly to Donegal and Sligo from London via Dublin? I didn't but you could and we did, well almost. We flew Gatwick - Dublin - Donegal, had a wonderful few days exploring the north of both Eire and N Ireland, in beautiful autumn sunshine, and flew from Sligo back to Dublin. However, we then had a diversion as we hired a car and drove through the majestic Wicklow mountains down to Waterford where we picked up a flight to Luton. To my mum's credit she only questioned our routing whilst enduring the shitty old Thameslink service back to Gatwick. It was a lovely trip, a fitting final time together for the 3 of us and my quest for 3 new airports causing us to travel more, and, therefore, see more than if I was normal? Why am I always trying to justify myself or explain my madness? Maybe because the burial of my mum's ashes could not be performed without feeding my addiction.

My mum wanted her remains to be buried with my dad at his parents' grave in Inverness. That had long been ticked off a few times. However, I had incurred the ultimate frustration a few years earlier of trying to finish off the Hebrides airports. Oh God, if I digress to those and other Scottish airports this will be one mother of a chapter and I will definitely have forgotten I'm meant to be talking about National Trails. So.... for now, I'll just tell you about the Islay attempt and save Barra and the rest of them for another chapter.

It was the longest and hottest heatwave since 1976. The summer of 2003. I've actually just checked something and it was 2006 that this happened. I'm sure the heatwave was 2003 but, whatever, it was a lovely warm spell. I had had the plan for a while. I would fly from Gatwick to Glasgow and then onto Campbeltown, still on the mainland. A bus could then take me the 30 miles to Kennacraig, from where I could catch a ferry to Islay, fly back to Glasgow and home. All in less than

36 hours - I had 3 kids under 10 to consider (they weren't coming with me!) and a business that "required" me to travel frequently. Well, let's be honest, paid me to feed my addiction. Whatever, it would be a quick trip, and, undertaking it during such stunning weather in our south east climate bubble I didn't want to miss too much of that.

The reason this trip had been a plan without it happening so far was because there was a slight problem. The flight from Glasgow to Campbeltown was normally operated by a 10-seater aircraft. Each time I checked the passenger loads (I still travelled frequently on staff standby tickets) the flight showed full. I really didn't fancy getting to Glasgow and no further so was keeping a regular eye on the flights each time workload and childcare duties offered a window. And, so it was on this check the flight to Campbeltown was wide open. How strange, but time to go! 2 problems, could I really leave this sensational weather behind and, out of my control? Anyway the flight from Gatwick to Glasgow was showing overbooked!

After an all too regular period of total indecision, I thought, "sod it, I'll go to Gatwick. If I get on, it's clearly meant to be". It was quite refreshing to be standing by for a flight and not really being that fussed if I got on or not. Not a frequent experience, but certainly how I felt on my first long haul solo holiday many years earlier. It's difficult to comprehend now but there was a time, about 30 years ago, where spending 2 weeks totally on my own on a non-English speaking island seemed more daunting than it did exciting. Maybe it's just as well I got the last seat on that flight and put those fears well and truly behind me. There's a story from that trip too but even I have a limit on how much I can digress.

This time it would turn out to be a bit of a shame I took the last seat to Glasgow. Although, I quite soon saw the funny side of it. Particularly a few years later. Sure enough when I arrived in Glasgow it was overcast and blustery. I had slept in the garden the previous night for around the 10th consecutive night, so warm and mild it was. It was too cold to have a nap during the day in Glasgow. Anyway, I wasn't here for the weather and I would be back in the garden for a kip the following night if the forecast was to be believed. All was well, the predicted passenger loads were not wrong and I was checked in for the flight to Campbeltown. At the gate it became apparent why I was afforded a seat. There was a group of about 15-20 golfers (this was what I had just been checking, not how many golfers but the aircraft type and capacity, where I realised it was 2006 not 2003). So Loganair had to put a bigger aircraft on to accommodate the golf clubs, let alone the golfers.

We boarded and left on time. It had been worth leaving the warmth behind. Or so I thought. As we taxied out the cheerful captain, or should I say the chirpy captain cheerfully announced that the weather was basically crap in Campbeltown but "we'll go and have a look and if we can't land, I'm afraid we'll have to come back here and stick you on a coach. It's about 3 1/2-4 hours' drive". That's why there's a flight to Campbeltown!

We did "go and have a look". We went and had 3 looks, but each time as it seemed we were so low over the sea if we went any lower, we would be in it, at the last minute we pulled up and went back up into the thick cloud. He'd made a good fist of it but clearly, whilst the sea below us was visible, land, and more importantly the runway ahead obviously weren't.

Naturally there was no point in me taking a bus to Campbeltown and I hope the golfers weren't too inconvenienced - rubbish weather for golf anyway. So, not only was I back in the sunny south east by 1 o'clock but I was in Guildford watching Surrey play cricket in their annual game away from the Oval.

So....... back to the ashes to Inverness. My sister and I – well really me - decided we should make a mini holiday out of what could be a slightly sombre trip. Once it was established that my brother-in-law could not join us as he possessed neither a passport nor a driving licence for identification for the flight, there was only one thing for it (I'm sure there must be another form of identification for a domestic flight that is acceptable to EasyJet but let's just say I wasn't my bro-in-law's biggest fan to put it as mildly as possible)......

Dump the ashes pronto and get our asses off to Campbeltown and Islay! I'd only had 2 years of pain waiting to right this wrong (Puerto Plata and Potosi took over 25!). So, after a 7-hour delay at Gatwick, where EasyJet kindly refused to allow us to change to the Inverness flight, we headed off to Glasgow, and still enjoyed a lovely drive to Inverness. The next morning, with more care and emotion than I just alluded to, we headed off to the cemetery and did the necessary. We then headed down to Glasgow for our 16.00 flight to Campbeltown via the scenic route. It was a lovely sunny day so we stopped for a leisurely stroll around Fort William and enjoyed an ice cream. FUCK!! Sorry but no non swear word will suffice. I had completely and inexplicably lost track of time and totally misjudged our distance to Glasgow airport. It was 13.30. Half past one sounds better actually. We had to drive roughly 100 miles (on one of the most scenic A roads in UK) drop the hire car and check in. Pre Google maps, at least for me, but I reckoned it would be a bare minimum 2-hour drive. There was cutting it fine and then there was cocking it up. I firmly believed I had done the latter. Still, we had to give it a go. We rushed back to the car (I don't think I've ever seen my sister run and I really don't think she grasped the gravity of the situation) and I proceeded to speed down the

A82 just like the kind of boy racer I would curse any other time.

Was Campbeltown airport to remain elusive? I had actually driven to Campbeltown with my mum when we went to Scotland to bury my dad's ashes but didn't know there was an airport there. We actually made good time until we got close to Loch Lomond. I don't consider I drove dangerously but certainly my overtaking took place more frequently than any time since the late 70s. Once we hit Loch Lomond there was simply no chance to overtake and clearly nobody else was rushing to catch the 16.00 to Campbeltown. We finally made it to the car hire drop off at 15.40. Fortunately, it was right next to the airport. I slid the keys across the counter and said, "sorry, gotta dash, it needs petrol" before the clerk could say anything. I ran ahead of my sister in the forlorn hope that a kindly check in agent would accept us 15 minutes before departure. Not only did she, but with a lovely smile said she had been waiting for us and was just about to give up. She helped us rush through security and took us out to the little 10-seater. There was only one other customer, the co-pilot shut the door and we were off, 10 minutes early!

That had been close, way too close. I used to specialise in getting to the airport at the last possible moment back in the day. Something changed drastically around 20 years ago. Since then, I like an excess of time. If I'm honest I don't really remember Campbeltown airport. In fact, there's many airports on the list that I have little or no recollection of. You could opine what's the point then? Well, I don't remember every time I had sex but I don't wonder why I bothered. It was normally good at the time, sometimes very good and landing at Campbeltown had been very good.

Not that I'm comparing sex to ticking off a new airport. Unlike Alan Shearer (I think) who was once quoted as saying scoring a goal was better than sex, I think my priorities are quite normal, even if my addictions aren't!

If I thought Islay would be a doddle after that panic, I was sadly mistaken. After our night in Campbeltown we awoke the next morning to very thick, low cloud and rain. Unperturbed we set off to the ferry. We saw nothing on the journey across to Islay and the island itself was also shrouded in mist. We had made it onto Islay but getting off again, at least by plane, might be an altogether trickier proposition. We picked up a hire car for the day and I thought it may be worth popping by the airport to see what chance there might be of any flights landing that day. There wasn't much point in going sightseeing, that's for sure.

The kind girl at the airport told us that although the morning and lunchtime flights had been cancelled, she was hopeful that it would clear enough for the early evening flight we were booked on to return to Glasgow to land. For some reason I recall not being too phased by the possibility of not only, potentially, having to return to the mainland by ferry and then get that 3-hour bus ride to Glasgow but then missing our EasyJet flight back to Gatwick. Maybe I was still glowing in the drama of our trip to Campbeltown.

She was right. Her optimism beat my pessimism. The Hebrides were completed. Only took 22 years. Sadly, we saw almost nothing of Islay. Sorry but that's just reminded me of my first Hebrides trip. National Trails will have to wait a bit longer. It was 1986, The hand of God World Cup (more like hand of despicable cheating bastard - not fit to be mentioned in the same breath as Pele, Cryuff or Bremner). I had flown in that morning from visiting friends on holiday in Tampa. Florida was not somewhere I had much interest in but with 2 new airports and Richard Branson giving airline staff £5 return standbys to Miami, free accommodation for a week and time on my hands it seemed daft not to. My only hesitation had been that some in-laws had rented a cottage on Tiree for 2 weeks and I didn't want to miss the opportunity to join them. I can honestly say that wherever I find the next airport I will have some level of desire to visit the destination or something nearby. The Hebrides held a strong interest though. By going to Florida it meant I would only get 24 hours on Tiree. A shame but it's pretty small.

After drowning our sorrows, over Engerland being cheated out of the World Cup, jet lag kept me up watching the next game so it was well after midnight before I dropped off, knowing I had a 07.30 flight from Gatwick to Glasgow to get and then onwards to Tiree. I slept straight through my alarm, unsurprisingly, but woke with a start at 6.30. Bugger. Not quite as drastic as the Campbeltown fiasco but I really fancied going to Tiree. 45 minutes to drive from Croydon to Gatwick, then run from the staff car park? 50 if the gate staff were feeling kind. Of course, I made it, just, luckily pre speed cameras.

And it was so worth it. The cottage was located on its own little beach. The water was turquoise blue, just like the nicest Caribbean waters but Jesus! it was unbelievably cold. No trees on Tiree, in fact, not that many in the Hebrides at all I believe but all the islands, at least those with airports, are all starkly beautiful and have stunning beaches - if you didn't know, you actually land on the beach in Barra "timings subject to tide". Barra was next on the list and maybe sometimes they do tell you that they're landing on the beach on purpose but they didn't when I went. Had I not known from the timetable I may have pooped my pants.

Benbecula was next, memorable for one of those, "where were you when you heard..... had died?" moments. This person being Princess Diana and it being more than 36 hours since it had happened.

Such was the remoteness, and maybe illicit nature, of our location we may well have been the last people in Britain to find out!

Next on the list was Stornaway on the Isle of Lewis. Almost unique for me. I was going to say unique but remembered another time. I took my bike to Stornaway and cycled over 200 miles in 48 hours. My only ever long-distance bike ride, so far. We were cycling to Benbecula. I had a crappy old bike and maybe that made the constant headwind seem worse than it was. By golly I ached. I've read some cycling travel books and these dudes can tell you more eloquently about the suffering than I can, but I think the pain in my undercarriage helped me ignore, to a degree, how much I had destroyed my legs.

As we arrived with a good few hours to spare before our flight we cycled on past the airport for a few miles. It was only when we headed back to the airport that I realised how much of a trailing wind we had and how, after 200 miles on this excuse for a bike, it all now seemed so easy. My companion, my 2nd ex father-in-law, was a keen and regular 100 mile a day cyclist. Naturally he not only had a better bike than me but clearly found it a stroll in the park. Notwithstanding when I commented on how my speed seemed to have doubled with the same effort when we headed north, he told me that he had said emphatically that we should cycle south to north to take advantage of the prevailing winds. He figured I had had a very good reason for ignoring him and booking the flights as I had. I didn't know it at the time but when we checked in at Benbecula airport and the agent told us we were in luck, ours would be the first flight to land in 3 days, my reasoning became apparent.

I had noticed when we left Glasgow for Stornaway that that morning's flight to Benbecula was cancelled. When we were told that a sea mist had prevented any flights to the mainland for nearly 72 hours there was clearly no reasoning involved in my route booking but a huge slice of good fortune. It wouldn't have affected the airport count as you can see, but how long would we have been prepared to wait in Glasgow for a flight to Benbecula. Would Loganair have allowed us to change our booking to Stornaway? The whole trip may have been screwed. The news certainly made the memories of that bloody wind more favourable: now remembered fondly with relief rather than regret. Time's a great healer (of the legs much quicker than the undercarriage in a literal sense).

I know you're just dying to know about the other bike experience so, short and sweet: Heathrow to East Midlands, cycle to City Ground, Nottingham Forest 4 Leeds 3 (had to look the result up, I'm no Sweaty Pete), supporters' coach back to London (bike in boot accompanied by puzzled stares from those fans I didn't know). I needn't have bothered. 2 years later, having been requested to attend a meeting with British Midland at their East Midlands base and their Heathrow service discontinued, rather than drive round the M25 and up the M1, my colleague and I flew Gatwick - Amsterdam - East Midlands. What was intended to be a day trip naturally resulted in an unscheduled overnight in Amsterdam. It would have been rude not to!

So ....back to the point! I can actually remember it without having to scroll back up! National Trails. Our 4th and currently most attainable collection.

CHAPTER TEN

As we complete our first half year with coronavirus changing so much about our lives, whilst constantly reminding myself how lucky we are compared to so many, I have become more and more aware how addicted I am to our collections. Is it that, or is it because they just give me a sense of achievement? Or is it because I have too much time on my hands? I'm sure it's not the latter as I was obsessed when work and kids took up a lot of time. Although back then it was only airports and football grounds, wasn't it? So it makes sense that more time available is filled by 875 Wetherspoons and 15 (or 16, one day) National Trails, as well as the oldies.

So which is the most important I hear you ask, or did I imagine it? Well, they all have their merits. The football grounds were the original, so hold a dear place (I was recently reminded that AFC Wimbledon will be off to their new ground in October so 87/92 will nag away at me until it's 92 again). If I had followed in the footsteps of my mentor, Steve "92" Crawley my football ground total would be well in excess of 1,000! Once he had completed the 92 he went non-league and Scottish. For all I know Welsh and Northern

Irish too. What I found out when I last saw him, ironically in 2006 as I flew to Coventry, was that he was restricting himself to UK. If he started on Europe, "it would get out of hand"! This coming after he admitted to having gone to what was basically a playing field in Edinburgh to watch Hibernian schoolboys play, to notch ground 1173, or similar.

Well, I guess so long as he didn't feel it had gotten out of hand..... His other collection had become speedway tracks. For this he did venture to Europe. I had lost touch with him about 10 years previously when I mysteriously received a letter from him, forwarded from a previous address. I thought he maybe needed money or that he had learned of a mutual friend's passing. Neither. He just wanted to re-acquaint. As luck would have it the Coventry v Leeds fixture at Cov's new ground was upcoming. He kindly gave me a lift back. That was the last I saw or heard of him. I did try to track him down via Facebook, but I imagine he's as prolific on there as me. I found someone who looked like him and sent a message, about a year ago, but drew a blank.

I believe I either owe 92 a huge debt of gratitude or hold him responsible. It is impossible to say whether I would have gone after the 92 grounds without his prompting. Would I have started a completely different type of collection? Or would I have reached 60 years of age collection free? Of course I don't hold him responsible. I am forever grateful to him. So…… in memory of 92 (I hope he's not dead): January 1983. "Are you busy next Tuesday Mr Groves (that's what he called me)?". No. "Would you fancy driving me to Halifax? I'll cover the petrol". Well, as my first father-in-law had left me his almost new Ford Granada, with a full tank, why not? He'd left it for a week, not in his will. In return for dropping him and picking him up from Heathrow he let me use his company car in the interim. This was a Ghia 2.8, top of the range. 92 was in luck. Not only would I take him but it wouldn't cost him much either.

On the journey up I asked him why he needed to go to Halifax on a Tuesday night and didn't just go on a Saturday afternoon on the train (he didn't drive back then). Well he had been on a Saturday, to the same match. It was abandoned due to fog after 78 minutes, so he couldn't count it. Why not just go to another complete 90 minutes of a match on another Saturday? For some reason he was compelled to see the rearranged match. Dedication to the collection or the onset of insanity?

If he couldn't find a willing driver would he have treated himself to a night in an hotel in Halifax? I have to share with you…. I thought I would do a very quick search on the history of this match. Can you believe that not only have I remembered the exact minute the match was abandoned correctly (not bad after nearly 40 years) but that on 15

June this year the Halifax Courier ran a fairly extensive article on all Halifax Town's abandoned matches in their history. Funny old world eh? In fact, the match was originally abandoned after 69 minutes but after 13 minutes they tried again but only managed another 9 minutes. I can completely empathise with how 92 must have felt during those 13 agonising minutes. And his utter despair 9 minutes later. To his constant dismay though I had in my collection Bristol City v Leeds abandoned at half time due to fog. This did not count for him. I don't know if he would have counted me as a 92 member, not that it would've bothered me. As I say I do it for myself. I have been back to Bristol City several times since, so, if I ever see 92 again, maybe he will approve of me. 92 was somewhat quirky, as you can imagine. One of his stranger habits was to wear a seatbelt for around 30 minutes, then unstrap himself and repeat throughout the journey. He didn't like being strapped in but figured he was reducing his chances of death or injury by 50%. This was pre inertia reel, so maybe, those as old, or older than me may have some empathy with his habit.

What he certainly would not have appreciated was Jim the pilot's efforts at the 92. More of Jim later I'm sure but, for now; fellow Leeds fan of much later acquaintance – 2000, Jim galvanised me to become 92 current again, as I may have mentioned. After ticking off Brighton's new ground against Leeds on the Friday night, Jim and I headed off to Shrewsbury's new home on the Saturday morning. Jim figured he would have enough time to get back from Shrewsbury for his evening flight to Singapore. Maybe not quite on a par with my Campbeltown miscalculation but, as we headed into hour 4 of our journey TO Shrewsbury, it became obvious that he would not only be late for his check in at Heathrow but that BA would be missing a pilot at departure time if he watched the whole game! Unsurprisingly he was not prepared to put his career on the line in order to appease the nerds of the 92 club, none of whom we knew personally. After approximately 8 minutes of a completely unmemorable encounter between Shrewsbury and Torquay United (I had to look up who they were playing) Jim headed off back to Heathrow. After all, never mind work, he had tickets for the Grand Prix in Singapore the next day. You could argue who was the more dedicated (or mad): 92 heading back to Halifax for 90 minutes of football or Jim the pilot for driving 7 hours for 8 minutes of football. You know though, that when you are collecting the 92, the football is irrelevant. All that matters is that tick next to the ground.

Jim surpassed himself on even this brief attendance. Becoming increasingly frustrated at the elusiveness, to him, of the "92" he confided in me how he had ticked off the Don Valley,

Rotherham's temporary home. In comparison to the lengths I went to via Bydgoszcz, Poznan and Doncaster Sheffield to notch this one Jim was driving back from Heathrow to Leeds when he heard on the radio that a pre-season friendly was taking place at The Don Valley Stadium. He did no more than nip off the M1, park directly outside the ground and run in (the gates were open with only a few minutes remaining). As he recounted to me: "Oi pal, you can't leave your car there!". Come on! Hurry up and take that bloody throw in. Jim's rule for the 92 - see a ball kicked in the ground. No sooner than that had happened he was back in his motor to continue his journey home. Fine by me, you do it for yourself, but 92? He would be appalled at the audacity of it.

On the subject of abandoned or, in this instance, postponed football matches I was unsure at the time, and still am, whether I appreciated learning that my longest journey to watch Leeds in Europe (at the time) was in vain or was a disappointment. I certainly wasn't desolate or inconsolable. Why? Let me explain. Quite simply I have never felt so cold in my life. Leeds had already played Lokomotiv Moscow but I was already committed to other travels. Unlike Rotherham where Poitiers and La Rochelle could wait, Phoenix and Sarasota took preference over Moscow. Fear not. Having overcome Lokomotiv, Spartak Moscow awaited us. Of Moscow's 3 airports at this time it was only possible to fly to Sheremetyevo from London. It was inconceivable to me to go and watch Leeds in Russia and not add to the airport collection. There is, though, a limit to even my madness. I wasn't going to the extreme to fly to either Domodedovo or Vnukovo via wherever in Europe, if even it was possible back then. But what I was going to do was catch a night train to St Petersburg after the match, enjoy a brief visit to the city and fly back from there.

I was fortunate that I could arrange a visa though work. Well, I say fortunate, but it involved a bit of pretence that I was planning to send tourists to Moscow. After a meeting with a ground handler and The Sheraton, Moscow Sales Manager, at London's World Travel Market I was set. I wouldn't be staying at The Sheraton. I'm not sure the lady I met with from aforementioned hotel had smiled in a decade or more and she seemed remarkably underwhelmed when I enthusiastically informed her that I would be travelling to Moscow and would come and have a look at her hotel. She looked like she wondered why on earth I would do that so I decided I may as well come clean and added that my visit would coincide with Spartak Moscow v Leeds United. If this news was intended to change her facial expression it failed miserably.

Undeterred, obviously, by the lack of enthusiasm from her (the business aspect of the trip was solely a means to an end) I finalised plans with the ground handler. A very handy, and empty, BA flight from Gatwick to Moscow Sheremetyevo (the merest mention sends the proverbial shiver down my spine but, man up, it was over 16 years ago and at the moment that's just way too much of a digression, even for me) took me on my way to the 3000 room Rossiya Hotel. I've never ceased to be impressed by Leeds fans who pay the going rate and more to follow our team all over UK, Europe and further. There was a good dozen or more on this flight. Not only had they already travelled down from Yorkshire to start with but no doubt they had also been in Moscow 3 weeks ago for our Lokomotiv encounter. I probably paid around £60 for my entire trip. I imagine they blew more like 600(£).

I checked into the hotel with my friends Marion and Andy and arranged to meet them in the lobby in 10 minutes. As soon as I entered my room the phone rang: "You want sex?". The voice, whilst laced with a hint of Eastern European sexiness, may as well have been asking me if I needed any laundry service. Her enthusiasm matched Mrs Grumpy from The Sheraton. Maybe it was her. Perhaps she had a secondary job. Needless to say I replied with a polite, "no thank you". When I met Marion and Andy I asked if they had had any calls from "room service". They hadn't. So at least they were targeting the solo male traveller.

We headed out to a restaurant that M&A had

enjoyed 3 weeks ago. Bloomin' 'eck it were cold! I'd experienced -37 skiing in France and this was apparently only -29. The Russian football season was already on its winter break but UEFA wouldn't let that little detail prevent them from scheduling a match in Moscow on 25th November. The meal was most pleasant. M&A knew what to recommend from their previous visit. I'm not sure how as the menu was only in Russian and the staff spoke no English. After a few swift vodkas in a vain attempt to warm ourselves from inside we slipped, quite literally, back to the hotel. It seemed the sex offer was on arrival only but I'm sure a quick call to room service would suffice if you were interested. By the way, The Rossiya was the largest hotel in Europe until it was demolished in 2006. I wonder how many ladies of the night they had on the premises or if the provision of service offered wasn't as prompt as the original phone call.

I mentioned to M&A how impressed I was that a good number of the 3000 rooms in The Rossiya seemed to be occupied by Leeds fans, considering the lure of seeing our beloved team in a new city had already been satisfied. How naive of me. They hadn't come back for the love of Leeds United! Just as well.

I arranged to meet M&A at the hotel around 7pm the next evening to head out to the ground as I was being picked up early to go and visit a few other hotels and then have a tour of Moscow. Once the hotel inspections were over I headed off with my guide for a tour of Moscow's main attractions. To my horror the car that had been shuttling us between hotels had gone. It was to be a walking tour. Any other time this would not only be my preference, it would be the only option, but it was just too cold. The more we walked the colder I became. The guide explained that the tour was over, we had a couple of hours to kill before my final hotel visit, so what would I like to do? "Get warm. I don't care where". Normally if I had then been taken to a shopping mall I would have bid my farewells and said I'd do my own thing but this wasn't normal. I'm sure it was for Muscovites, but not for me. I was genuinely concerned, and had been since the previous evening, as to how I was going to survive standing outside in this temperature for at least 90 minutes, watching football.

So....... when I reacquainted with Mrs notso Grumpy at The Sheraton and she looked at me with uncharacteristic sympathy (I know, I was judging her on a 10 minute meeting so how did I know how much sympathy she had at her disposal. She may have volunteered for the Russian version of the Samaritans for all I knew) and she said, "Oh Alan you must be so disappointed!" I think my foremost feeling was relief when she continued, on seeing my quizzical expression: "you don't know? They've called the game off. It's too cold (really!!??). Not for the players but they are concerned for the fans' safety as the terraces are very icy. I'm sorry for you".

Of course, once the news had sunk in I was quite disappointed, but comparing this to previous wasted trips to Arsenal and Leeds (particularly galling as it was New Year's Day) and, since, more recent trips to Doncaster and Hereford, yes, I was 70% relieved I would say. At least I still had the main purpose of the trip to look forward to - St Petersburg airport. That's not really true. I wanted to see more of Moscow than I had previously from the frosted windows of an ambulance, 16 years ago (the suspense not killing you?). I wanted to see some of St Petersburg. I wanted to experience a night train in Russia. I wanted to watch Leeds. Would I have been more disappointed if for some reason I couldn't fly from St Petersburg and returned to UK with no change in the airport total? Yes. Definitely.

I felt sorry for those fans whose reasons for returning so soon to Moscow did not include The Rossiya's room service. Like Marion and Andy. I was still a bit surprised to learn that they had checked out that afternoon and flown home as soon as they heard the game was off, rather than wait to meet me as arranged. But diehards such as these would already be working out how they could afford more time off work for the rearranged fixture. Those, like me, probably only me, would be waiting to hear where the rearranged fixture would take place in case it presented a new airport opportunity perhaps? Others might be waiting on the venue to find out how it compared to The Rossiya room service options before committing. As it was it was to be Sofia a week later. Of course M&A went. The others? I know not. Me? A jaunt from Heathrow via Sofia to Varna and back from Bourgas, again via Sofia to Heathrow, 8 years prior, prevented me from justifying another few days away from kids and work to watch the hastily rearranged fixture in the Bulgarian capital.

What do I remember from that Bulgaria trip I hear you ask? Well, like any trip to Eastern Europe just after the iron curtain fell off its railings, it was a bit odd. Looking back on this and numerous other trips I constantly wonder how things fell into place pre internet and mobile phones. When I arrived at Varna airport in the early evening, of course, I had no plan. Other than to be in Bourgas later the following day. What I remember is standing outside the terminal in Varna wondering where and how I was going to find somewhere to stay when this chap in uniform approached me and asked if he could help me. He spoke just a smidgen of English but understood I needed a bed for the night. "Come, stay me. Wife food cook". What a fine chap. It was a shame my Bulgarian wasn't up to scratch so the meal was mainly taken in silence with lots of smiles.

I did manage to communicate to him that I worked at Gatwick and gave him my extension number. Balkan, his airline employer, operated charters from Varna to Gatwick. A couple of weeks later, imagine my surprise when I'm told, "Forbsie, some bloke on 2765 for you. Doesn't really speak English. Says he's your friend from Varna". Clearly it would be a short conversation so I said I would pop down to his aircraft to say hello. At least then I could give him a firm handshake, a big smile and thank him once again for his hospitality. He looked genuinely chuffed to see me again.

The next morning I made my way to Bourgas, just 80 miles from Varna. What I remember of this journey is stopping briefly at Golden Sands, a Black Sea resort made infamous, some 15 years later in UK, after Scouse football fans misbehaving in Europe. It was certainly very unattractive in 1991. I probably took a bus there from Varna but I then hitched a ride to Bourgas. Unfortunately the car which had stopped to pick me up suffered a puncture. I had a flight to catch. I'm not sure of the code of hitch hikers in this event but I hesitated not and waved goodbye to my kind providers as they facilitated the repair. Let's just say I took their hurling of rocks and abuse in my direction as a sign that they were none too impressed at my abandoning of them.

I made the flight from Bourgas to Sofia somehow. I think I maybe walked the rest of the way or took a bus. What I recall of Sofia is staying in a block of flats somewhere on the outskirts of the city, probably because I arrived in the evening and was leaving in the morning. How did I book this place or how did I find it? I have no recollection. I saw very little of Sofia so it's on my list of places to revisit with no airport addition - well in this instance we will definitely fly either in or out of Plovdiv to add one to my total. If we fly to or from Sofia then it's one more to Agnes's total.

To my shame it took me nearly 30 years to visit Venice after I had ticked off the airport on a quiet night shift (thanks to Ryanair and their version of Venice being Treviso). Tourism has certainly taken its toll on Venice but, my word, what a fantastically interesting place. I would also like to revisit Vienna. My 24 hour trip one January didn't inspire me but many have extolled its virtues so during these vile travel restrictions maybe it's time to return to Austria. It's fair to say as I ticked off Innsbruck, Salzburg, Linz and Klagenfurt airports the only place I actually saw was Zell am See.

Innsbruck is a wonderfully located airport but second in my memory of these additions was ripping my trousers on the flight from Salzburg to Gatwick on a faulty seat. I felt a little guilty claiming £30 from Caledonian Airways for my trousers as I was travelling on a free ticket but.........

Meanwhile, back in Moscow. I needed to eat and I had 4 hours to kill until my train. Back to the same restaurant but how was I to choose my food? I got lucky, my lucky dip was more than edible. I didn't feel as cold as during the day or the previous evening. Could I have suffered those 90 minutes after all?

At the train station I kid you not, there must've been a dozen night trains to St Petersburg within an hour or so of each other. I found mine and my carriage, then my compartment without too much difficulty. I had booked first class which meant just one other person would share my bedroom. All I could think was would they snore? Maybe I would get lucky and have the compartment to myself. After all, how did you fill a dozen sleeper trains every night? This wasn't India. As departure time approached my hopes soared that I would, indeed, have my own room. Just as we pulled out of Moscow central, or whatever it was called, I was joined by a young lady. I would like to tell you that she was as beautiful as the room service ladies from The Rossiya, but I can't. Because I never saw the ladies from Rossiya and, more so, because she was quite simply the plainest female I think I had ever met. She was not an ounce overweight, she wasn't ugly in anyone's eyes, she was just 100% plain but bingo! "I don't suppose for one minute you speak English?" "I am an English teacher". And so she was. Her English was better than mine. I know that that sounds awfully sexist, I apologise. I also know I'm no oil painting and she may well have thought the same of me. I'm just trying to set the scene and I reckon my subjective view on her appearance is relevant.

I found the whole experience of sharing a very, very confined space for 8 hours with a female I'd never met quite unnerving. Well let me quantify that statement: I've never had a one-night stand, two being the minimum but I may have chosen, after not so long, to spend more than 8 hours even closer to a relative female stranger, had it been mine and their choice. In this instance I had neither a choice nor a moment before we were in the confined space. Had she been attractive I would have probably been so scared I would have sought out another cabin. We were expected to lie down together no more than a foot apart. That's less than some married couples I imagine. She told me she made the journey at least once a month so I asked her if she had ever felt uncomfortable with a travelling companion as I felt that this situation of mixed sex sharers would not be acceptable in UK. And not only because we probably only have a couple of sleeper trains per night in the whole country. She told me that only on one occasion had she felt scared: a very drunk guy came into the cabin and proceeded to strip butt naked in front of her. She was worried but he just passed out and that was that.

When it came to bed time and for that matter wake up time, I believe I was the perfect gentleman: I made myself scarce while she readied herself for bed and in the morning, feigned sleep and faced the wall until she disappeared to the bathroom. Altogether a slightly weird experience. At least she didn't snore! St Petersburg looked resplendent in the snow but it also warrants more time, although I'm not sure when I'll be adding to the Russian airport collection.

Now, what was the question again?

CHAPTER ELEVEN

Ah, yes, which is the most important of the collections? Maybe it should be which is the most addictive? I'll try and answer both - by the end of the book at the latest! I struggle with digressing at the best of times with a simple question which requires a yes or no answer. Maybe I'm just bloody good at the art of conversation. Probably not, but writing seems to provide even more opportunities to digress. I've no idea how professional writers manage it but I'm sure self-discipline plays a major role. I'm sure some must have taken courses in writing at some point otherwise they would cease to exist. I'm just trying to do my own thing.

You would have thought that a full-on lockdown would present the perfect opportunity to write. Only being able to leave the house for a walk or a supermarket shop. Not seeing anyone but Aggers. But no, even when the weather was crap I seemed to find excuses. I did finally transfer my flight and football records from their written versions on to Excel. That was time consuming but enjoyable. It reinforced in me that I only want to write when I enjoy it. I don't want it to feel like a chore. Or work. Why give up work to then work?

So the lockdown months were almost completely barren writing wise. Now, back in Poland I wouldn't say I'm flowing through the pages but I enjoy the writing and the memories, so it won't matter if nobody enjoys reading it. Due to my inability/desire to learn Polish I am sometimes in my own self-imposed mental, rather than physical, lockdown. Agnes is great as a translator but sometimes she says the conversations aren't really worth translating. It's a ridiculously difficult language to learn and I just don't seem to have the memory for it. As I'm not doing the Polish football grounds, there's no Spoons (obviously, although there is one in Myanmar, not a kosher JD, so it doesn't count, although we've been, but... never assume), no UK National Trails and I've done all the current commercial airports there is no possibility to add to the collections. The only way to try and appease the addictions is to write about them. Why wasn't that the case in UK when feeding the addictions was impossible, temporarily, too? I dunno.

The airport collection is the only one with no realistic definitive ending. I've looked at mini collections, within the biggy: all commercial airports within a country (easy for some, think Singapore, Luxembourg, or even Andorra! Not so easy for others, even bloody difficult, or nigh on impossible unless we get a sponsor: think USA, Indonesia, Russia, China), all routes by an airline (I'm thinking Ryanair, Wizzair, EasyJet as realistic). I would like to do all airports Dan Air ever flew to. More complex than you might imagine and probably more time needed to research than to write this book!

When we gave up work in March 2019 I decided on my target. I'd never thought of a goal to achieve at any time before this. I didn't even notice milestone airports sometimes, honestly. I can only remember 400 and 700. Little Cayman and Culiacan since you ask. I have never boasted of airport notching achievements. Others have, sometimes, on my behalf and to my embarrassment. I then wondered if I had shared my secret with the wrong person. I would actually say that until about 10 years ago it was almost a closely guarded secret. I didn't want to openly admit to being a bit weird. Sometimes I had to reluctantly come clean as I couldn't think of any other reason to explain my routing or destination when quizzed. "Yeah, that is a bit odd" was normally the response, backing up my feeling.

Something then changed. It was gradual at first. Sod it, I'm quite proud of my addiction. I'm not hurting anyone in the process (well apart from the obvious, but I blame the airlines for dangling the carrot to me in the first place). Jim the pilot often used to introduce me to his mates with, "guess how many airports this fella has been to". My embarrassment was slightly overcome when the guess, if they could be arsed, was always extremely underwhelming; around the 100 mark was a favourite.

I guess the time when I really "came out" was when Agnes joined me and added Spoons. I don't do social media. She does. Our Spoons collecting, therefore, went public. Reactions were varied but even through the cynicism you could always detect amusement. "If you think that's weird here's why it started" Agnes would happily volunteer. Whilst I still have to occasionally explain that, no, I'm not an airplane spotter, I collect airports, the normal response seems genuine interest. Honestly, it's not that tricky is it? I guess everyone has heard of airplane spotters, and certainly train spotters, but I've still to meet an airport collector or meet someone who knows someone who knows an airport collector.

Actually maybe I should rename myself as an airport spotter. After all airplane and train spotters are collecting registrations to add to their list. Doesn't sound right though. Nor does airport visitor, so let's leave it as collector for now. I'm well and truly out now. I will even volunteer the information if asked what I do. After all, I don't have a job but I do have an addiction.

If I could reach 1,000 airports/airfields/landing strips I would retire. Agnes's target would be 500. She hasn't said whether she would carry on. I figured 5 years would be realistic. I feel I need some closure. Why was it so bloody important to me to get a new airport in when it would make the total of let's say, 227? Well, maybe because 500 seemed attainable? But what about 523? 1000 seemed too far away.

Perhaps I should just approach the total like, for example, James Anderson, the cricketer, who has just reached the milestone of 600 test wickets. Just keep going until you can't. I don't think I'll stop at 1,000. Currently I don't think I'll bloody reach it thanks to pandemics, but let's not be too pessimistic. But that's the target I've decided on. When we finished work I was on 790. A year later, almost to the day, I was, and am on 870. So you could say I was well ahead on the 5 year plan. Except there's not too many India type opportunities to boost the numbers. Take away India and that was still about 50 in a year. Only thing is, like collecting football stickers, the more you have the harder it is to get new ones.

It really was such a big deal, and I put in a lot of time researching, just to add one or two to the total. Once I set out on the 1000 mission the self-inflicted pressure reduced, slightly. Time seemed on my side. I could see an end to it all. I have the time to research, the time to travel. If I die on 870, I'm pretty sure I won't spend an eternity feeling suicidal that I didn't reach 1000. In the extremely unlikely event, to an agnostic/atheist, that I did I don't suppose suicide is possible if you're already dead. And don't worry I'm not treating suicide lightly. I wouldn't have been a Samaritan if I did. And I've genuinely felt it, a long time ago thankfully.

So why does it matter so much? Why did it matter so much to finally get the elusive George Best football sticker to complete the collection 50 years ago? If I didn't have the addiction to these collections I'm sure I would feel happier and, certainly, less frustrated than I do at the moment. It's a little like following a football team like Leeds (not that I'm sure there is another team like Leeds): regular frustration and disappointment interspersed with moments of sheer joy. Not that the extremes with the collections are anywhere near as profound as with Leeds. Yes I felt huge disappointment when we overshot Lublin (due to fog) and diverted to Warsaw Chopin, and huge relief, mixed with happiness, when the aircraft landed in very thick fog at Warsaw Modlin for my return journey to UK, ensuring that I hadn't had a complete wasted journey. But no, the disappointment with the former paled into insignificance compared to the utter despair I felt when Leeds lost to Coventry in an FA Cup semi-final or the latter with the pure joy when Leeds beat Man U in the FA Cup 3rd round (on January 3rd (2010), remember the date. Only relevant to Leeds fans, we still sing about it!)

I wasn't expecting that Lublin diversion! In 2013

my employer instructed me to expand their business in Europe. I was to deliver leaflets to the main European airports. They gave me a free rein, within reason. I wanted to act responsibly, within reason. With regard to budget and choice of countries to visit, I certainly did. How I arrived or returned from these destinations was pure self-indulgence: first up, if I had to go to Amsterdam, what an opportunity to drive the 70 miles to Manston (Kent International to some) and back rather than do the obvious and depart from Gatwick or Heathrow. I was particularly keen to notch Manston. During my time at Dan Air it had regularly been a diversion airfield when the equally regular autumnal early morning fog made landing at Gatwick impossible. It seemed to take the crew forever to get back in the taxi. Not surprising when I drove past it one day, much later in life. It's in the middle of nowhere in deepest Kent. Having just returned from what is fast becoming the obligatory reference to Wikipedia to check my facts and memory I now know that the KLM flight to Amsterdam had only just started when I travelled and a year later Manston (KIA) was completely closed. Just in time, eh?

I failed miserably on Copenhagen, it having only one, previously visited airport, but Oslo brought more excitement. Rygge (only open 2008-2016) was only 3 hours by bus from my intended destination Gardamoen (Oslo's main airport) and another bus from Oslo to Gothenburg enabled me to sneak in Gothenburg City airport (closed to commercial flights in 2015!). Stockholm, another winner. Not once but 3 times. Stockholm, thanks to Ryanair was now served by both Vasteras and Skavsta (both between 60-70 miles from Stockholm!). A wonderful opportunity as I didn't see any more trips to Stockholm on the horizon, wonderful city that it is.

Helsinki? I saw little point in going there commercially, but a rare intervention from my employers meant otherwise. For some reason the folk in Texas were certain that their product would be in demand in Finland. If I had to go, there must surely be a way, there or back or both, to add to the tally. So it was that the 4th Stockholm airport, which I didn't even know existed was an added bonus. Bromma, is Stockholm's answer to London City. And a very short flight from Helsinki was conveniently scheduled to give me time to throw the leaflets in the bin, get a bus from Bromma to Arlanda (Stockholm's main airport) and be home in time for tea. All in a day's work of adding one more to the list!

Frankfurt, at least gave the chance to fly on the then new (to BA) A380, if no new airports. A trip undertaken with more glee by my fire engine, aircraft identifying (not spotting!) friend, Nigel than me. Munich? Memmingen, another Ryanair invention (70 miles from Munich). Berlin?

Nothing doing. I think we always think of the Germans as being rather efficient but if you think Crossrail are a bit out with their estimates, then the boys and girls in charge of building and opening the new Berlin airport are giving them a good run for their money: it was due to open in October 2011! It is currently touted to open in October 2020!!

I fear I'm going into a bit too much depth here for anyone but myself. I blame it on my flirtation with OCD (another matter I do not take lightly). I've started telling you about the new airports that my employer, unknowingly, paid for me to go to. I was "out" but not out enough to share my weirdness with my employers. They didn't question my receipts as my arrangements were always cheaper than those a normal person would've undertaken. So I feel compelled to recall all of them. At least I've avoided diverting to any initial visits to any of them, which I am quite proud of.

Switzerland was a non-starter for any new airports but I still wasn't prepared to just drop the leaflets and run. Just to remind you. I don't travel to visit airports. They are a result of my insatiable desire to roam. I like all forms of travel. I still like flying, sometimes I still love it, when I'm comfortable or the views are memorable. A flight from Stansted (a horrible airport and a pain to get to and from) to Rodez is a means to an end but when you then stumble across the beauty of Carcasonne, for example, on your return, it becomes completely worthwhile. A flight from Mestia to Natakhtari (both in Georgia) neither comfortable nor uncomfortable, too short to matter, was as scenic as could be: the mountains not only seemed below us but close enough to reach out and touch. A flight regularly cancelled due to weather restrictions such is the proximity to the mountain terrain. An oft repeated business class flight from UK to Malaysia: very comfortable, nice food, fine wine and a few good films. The 12 hours pass in no time but no new airports.

Where's this going? I like train travel. We both really like it actually. I always enjoyed going on the train to footy back in the day, but foreign train travel is probably considered by most travellers to be the ultimate. If I didn't collect airports I would choose the train first. At least always wanting to fly into one and out of another provides the opportunity for a train ride in between. So, Switzerland. What an absolutely stunning country for train travel. And the lovely Swiss provide a rail pass, that I have been lucky enough to utilise for free and at a very reduced rate, covering unlimited travel on the whole network. The reason I mention this is because, if you like mountains and lake scenery, and travelling by train, you really, really should take a Swiss rail pass. That's how I made my enforced trip to Switzerland worthwhile: by taking 3 days to go the long way round from Geneva to Zurich to Basel by train via the most wonderful scenery. I was even happy to do a similar but more in-depth return trip, with no new airports again, when Agnes expressed her wish to do Switzerland by train. Some of the journeys are simply stunning. Do it!

The boys from Texas also figured they knew best when it came to Poland. Seriously I didn't imagine that they would attract one customer from Warsaw with their overpriced, bland offerings but they envisaged plenty. So, finally back to where this little digression started. Lublin, a very manageable 2-3 hours from Warsaw. Thanks again to Ryanair there was a new opportunity in Warsaw, Modlin. I didn't really give a flying whether the Poles wanted to line the Texans' wallets but I was now happy to make the trip.

When we diverted to Warsaw Chopin, due to the aforementioned fog in Lublin I was gutted. In a bizarre lack of health and safety consideration we milled about on the tarmac whilst the powers that be decided whether we would travel by bus to Lublin or would wait for the fog to clear and fly. What made it bizarre was the number of passengers who decided that this was a good opportunity to have a cigarette. I'm not sure what surprised me the most: the general public's lack of understanding that cigarette ash and petrol aren't a great mix, or the airline and airport staff's complete indifference to those puffing away. I'm not a great fan of the over zealous H&S rules that frequently imply that we are all idiots but maybe this demonstrated why they are in place.

Decision made, it was to be a bus to Lublin. I wandered off, dejected, to rid myself of my leaflets in Warsaw much earlier than I anticipated. I also had a chance to have another look round Warsaw, almost 25 years after my first visit. Considering the Germans tried their best to completely obliterate it I think it's a slightly underrated city. Unsure of when I would be back to tick off Lublin (I was not even in my friends stage with Aggers) I consoled myself with the addition of the second Warsaw airport in the morning. I was pretty anxious as we left Warsaw on the bus and the fog just got thicker and thicker as we got closer to Modlin. The arrival and departure boards told a sorry tale: 'Diverted to Chopin, please enquire'. Well at least when I came back to Lublin I could easily make the journey originally planned from Warsaw. Then, to my joy and utter surprise, a gate number came up for our flight. You couldn't even see a plane at the gate let alone on the runway. Then the beautiful blue and white of Ryanair started to appear through the mist. I hadn't heard or seen anything land. It was weird. But the first plane to land was mine. The trip hadn't been a complete waste.

As for Lublin I only had to wait a couple of years until a holiday in Poland with Aggers where it just happened to be the nearest airport for our departure back to UK. No matter that the only flight on that day was to Skavsta. I was happy to return there for Aggers' sake and it was a small inconvenience in order to add Lublin to the collection, even with a 6-hour connection to Stansted. To boot, Lublin was actually a very pleasant city indeed. All I would have seen if the original flight had gone to plan would've been the train station. So all's well that ends well, as seems to normally be the way in my very fortunate life - so far.

So....... I think I have come to the conclusion that the airport collection is the most important to me. The lengths involved to add to it, compared to the other 3, probably means it is also the most addictive. The numbers involved, as well, put it at number 1. The longevity both in terms of years collecting and flying hours spent mean that all the others are babies in comparison. Yet, I so enjoy walking: reaching the end of a trail provokes mixed feelings of pleasure in the achievement and sadness in the fact that it's over. Planting a foot on a new Spoons carpet after a few months' absence, or just the charm of an historical building that has become a pub, still retaining some of its original identity - a pleasure that I'm sure only fellow Spoons collectors can identify with. A new football ground? Well, I don't know what to say really. How to explain it. Why do I still do it? After all, it's just a collection. What does it matter? It's an addiction that can't be explained, or at least I can't explain it. It doesn't taste nice. It doesn't alter my physical or mental state. I just know that, currently, being on 87 out of 92 bugs me. It doesn't keep me awake at night. I don't have the shakes. I'm not suffering weight loss or gain, but I want to be 92 out of 92 again.

Do I want it more than 1000 airports? If I have to choose, no. But I want both. I want to walk every mile of every National Trail. I want to visit every Spoons which is open. I want, I want, I want, I want. What a selfish bastard I am. Or just another hopeless, helpless addict?

CHAPTER TWELVE

There are currently 875 Spoons. I believe the figure was at over 1000 at some stage. Or at least some heroes have visited more than 1000. I don't know what the highest number of Spoons at any one time was.

I actually wrote that nearly 4 months ago. It's now the end of 2020 and most of the Spoons are closed. How many will open and stay open in 2021? The target could, and probably will, be severely reduced. It may become another 92 to complete!! God I hope it's not that desperate. So what have I been doing in the last 4 months I hear you ask!? Well, not writing that's for sure but I have managed to add 9 airports to the collection.

Greece: I would probably now opine that it is my favourite country in Europe. We were lucky enough to find ourselves on a very last-minute sailing trip around the Cyclades which, when I was outed to our fellow sailors, inevitably prompted the suggestion to start collecting ports! Wonderful as the sailing trip was, my first, ports will not become yet another obsession. Of course, I had to start, and now maintain, a tally of Greek Islands visited. I'm not quite so sad to say that the 8 new

Greek airports were the highlight of the trip but, for sure, the collecting desire shaped our itinerary. I won't say plans, because we didn't really have any.

In fact, we were in Greece nearly 2 weeks before a new airport was ticked off. Plenty of time for me to bore Aggers with all the visits during Dan Air days and one short trip a few years back where I notched a few. Crete: I always dismissed it as being too big. All those smaller islands held more appeal. However, that little airport in the far east of the island, Sitia, provided ample reason to return. Coupled with the fact that we were a little uncertain how easy it would be to travel around Greece, we surmised that it would be better to be stuck on Crete than in Athens.

How pleasantly we were surprised. I was delighted that my airport needs had allowed me to overcome/correct my embarrassingly narrow-minded attitude towards Crete. For sure I already appreciated what a fine city Chania is. I knew how Malia had degenerated from a pleasant fishing village on my first trip to a man-made hell hole to be passed through as quick as possible on my last. What I was unaware of was how, in general, the south coast has remained largely totally unspoilt. Whilst it might not be blessed with stunning beaches, the landscape, villages and sheer beauty of much of the coast line was very unexpected. The walking opportunities plentiful and stunning. It pains me to say that I had shunned the Samarai

Gorge on previous visits. In my defence they had all been very short and, if I was to say that I was familiar with this gorge, or indeed, any other of Crete's gorges, it would be stretching the truth somewhat.

So, if you haven't been, don't leave it as long as I did to really see some of Crete, but do leave it, as we did, to go out of season. For sure, I was counting down the days before we reached Sitia. It's fair to say that this particular airport was a little disappointing as it boasted a very new and rather unnecessarily large terminal. OK, so when the occasional direct charter plonks down from Northern Europe it's required but I didn't know that they existed so I was expecting and hoping for a quaint little terminal.

I didn't have to wait long for that experience. We were heading to the north of the mainland after an overnight in Athens. The "new" Athens airport itself, built for the 2004 Olympics, is a vastly improved experience on the old one. However, like most new build airports and football grounds, and Spoons, for that matter, its location is far inferior to that which it has replaced. New build Spoons, don't replace old Spoons but what I mean there, is that they are purpose-built pubs which lack the interest of converted banks, churches, tram depots etc. They are still normally in convenient town/city centre locations whereas new football grounds and airports aren't. 1-0 Spoons.

We were heading north to tick off a double drop, a rarity it seems these days in most locations, of Kozani and Kastoria and then return from Ioannina. We had booked the flight to Kozani via Kastoria. Ideally we would have liked to end up in Kastoria as research indicated that, with its lakeside setting and history, this was of infinitely more interest than Kozani. The flight, however, stopped in Kastoria first before continuing to Kozani and returning to Athens. No biggy as the towns and airports are only about 45 minutes apart by road, begging the question why the flight operates to both in the first place. How many airports do you know that are more than 45 minutes away from the town/city that they serve? A bunch, and a bunch more since Ryanair reinvented Bratislava airport as Vienna etc..

We planned to head to the north of Greece for maybe a week or more, so hadn't booked our flight back from Ioannina. Then, by the wonders of modern communication, the opportunity to sail presented itself. If we were to accept, this would mean that we would need to return to Athens the next day. The opportunity was too good to miss though. 14 days sailing for 300 euros each. We had identified one must do in the north: Meteora. Apparently Greece's most visited/famous tourist attraction. Forget The Acropolis or Knossos. But, to my shame I'd never heard of it, so I'm not sure I agree with its claim. So, whilst we were a little disappointed to curtail our trip north to little more than 24 hours we would get to see Meteora and snap up our bargain sail through the Cyclades.

"How will we get from Kozani to Meteora and back to Ioannina in that time?" Aggers asked not unreasonably. "Well, we'll just sort it when we get there" was my nonchalant and predictable reply. I still occasionally surprise myself at my naivety, stupidity, carefree abandon, call it what you will, but as we taxied towards the terminal at Kastoria it dawned on me that my notion that we'd compare car hire prices on arrival at Kozani airport was fanciful at best. The terminal building at Kastoria was no bigger than the average living room and, at least, finally, this prompted a reality check on the facilities that would await us in Kozani. What was I thinking? Why would an airport that has one flight per day to Athens with a maximum 40-70 passengers provide facilities comparable to Southampton, for example? Of course, it would be more on a par with Papa Westray or Barra. Nothing but a toilet and a check in desk. In fact, to be fair, Barra maybe had more but it was 30 years since my visit.

Fortunately, having been prone to moments of delusion and lack of planning through much of my travelling days, I seem to be able to readjust my expectations quite quickly and rescue the situation. As Aggers disappeared to the Ladies' I noted that there was only one taxi outside the 'living room'. Luckily the driver spoke very good English. He did think that my idea of a one-way car hire to Ioannina was a little far-fetched but happily agreed to try the only option he thought had any legs. Failing that he would drop us at Kozani bus station where, he thought, there would be a bus to Ioannina before too long. We stopped at a Skoda showroom on the outskirts of town. Unsurprisingly, not only did they not offer one way car hire, they didn't offer car hire at all. Our friendly and helpful driver suggested we try Toyota. I figured we'd cut our losses and head into town. Our driver kindly facilitated the purchase of our bus tickets and we only had to wait 20 minutes before we were on our way.

Two hours later, after a beautifully scenic drive we were in Ioannina. Annoyingly our coach driver refused to stop as we passed the airport, with several car hire companies in close proximity, so we ended up walking through town to finally avail ourselves of the much sought after car to take us to Meteora. After we retraced our journey from Kozani for about an hour, which was a little frustrating considering our self-imposed time limits, we headed off on a lovely drive to Meteora. My goodness was it worth it! What a stunning place. There was a handful of tourists about but we pretty much had the place to ourselves. My objective is not to describe any place we have been lucky enough to stumble across in detail.

However, if you happen to be influenced to visit somewhere, whether you've heard of it or not, by my recommendation and are then equally as blown away as we were in this instance, I will feel a reasonable level of satisfaction.

It annoys me when football commentators/ pundits overuse words such as sensational, brilliant, amazing, etc.. Mainly because what they are describing is quite often just what you could normally expect of a professional footballer. So, not to be hypocritical, I will try and keep my superlatives in check. Meteora is, in my humble opinion, all of the above. I'm sure it is a little less brilliant if there are hordes of tourists milling around. It would be a little less sensational if the sun wasn't illuminating the wonderful landscape and buildings but it would still be amazing.

Suitably chuffed that we had, yet again, been lucky or clever enough to feast our eyes on another natural and man-made wonder we headed back to tick off a very pleasant Ioannina airport. I know that normal people visit all different parts of the world without the lure of a new airport to add to their collection but, if I'm honest, I'm not sure how drawn we would have been to this part of Greece over other islands. So, although, I'm long past having to justify our routings to Agnes, I'm very happy when they take us to somewhere as otherworldly as Meteora.

I was very happy that our sailing trip

predominately featured islands with no airports. In fact, Santorini was the only island we visited where I had previously flown to. It is a stunning island but pick your time carefully. It is a mass tourism destination for sure, albeit void of large hotels. We also visited much underrated, at least by me, Milos. As I had not flown in or out on my previous visit it was clear that we would visit again at some point.

Whilst the sailing trip had been wonderful it was time to get down to business and tick off some of the remaining Greek airports while we still could. When I joined Dan Air in the late 70s it was only possible to fly directly to the islands of Corfu, Kos, Crete (Heraklion) and Rhodes. Otherwise it was a ferry or maybe a domestic flight from Athens. I've never been back to Corfu since my only visit around 1984. Back then it was known as the island blighted by mass tourism. To be fair, it was only a small minority of the island that suffered, similarly parts of the others. Corfu was very pretty, I'm sure it still is, and I would be happy to return, out of season, for Aggers to notch it.

I wanted to say that I had only visited Kos airport on a mad post pub thought shortly after joining Dan Air. I can't remember if I've told that story earlier, but if not it's in the other book! However, I went back mid-80s, to visit a friend on holiday there. I have no recollection of the trip or the island so, again, it won't be too much of a hardship to revisit with Agnes one day. It would've happened on this trip but for a chance conversation but more of that later.

Gradually as the Greek aviation authorities extended some of their island runways Dan Air expanded their portfolio of Greek airports and so did I. In no particular order, Mykonos, Skiathos, Zakynthos , Kefallonia, Lesbos, Santorini and Chania became reachable without the need to pass through Athens. Other islands were also added with domestic flights over the years. A particularly memorable trip with Aggers for my birthday a couple of years ago led to one of my more bizarre travel experiences: I had found a flight from Thessaloniki to Luton for £12 on 26 June. All that remained was to find a flight to somewhere in Greece, tick off a few new airports if possible and get to Thessaloniki by 26th.

After a fair bit of time planning we were off to Rhodes. Not a hardship to revisit but a means to an end: Kastellorizo had fascinated me for a while. It is so close to Turkey, as are several Greek Islands, but it is by some distance the furthest east and it ain't very big at all. After a couple of very pleasant days in Rhodes we took the ferry to Kastellorizo. It did not disappoint. The tiny harbour and main town were to die for. We enjoyed a lunch in the most delightful setting with huge turtles swimming around us, found exceedingly pleasant lodgings and set off to explore the island. As we headed to higher ground what concerned me was how seriously windy it was. A quick refresh of the Lonely Planet confirmed my increasing anxiety: "flight and ferry cancellations are not uncommon year round due to strong winds".

There would certainly be worse places to get stuck but we had a connecting flight from Rhodes to Limnos via Samos, Chios and Lesbos to catch. From Limnos we had a flight to Thessaloniki so if it was too windy it would screw us up a bit, let alone if we ended up leaving by ferry back to Rhodes with Kastellorizo airport still just a vision. We walked up to the airport the next morning trying to convince ourselves that the wind had dropped. It had but I wasn't totally convinced it had dropped enough. It was still very windy. Fear not, it landed and later that day we were in Limnos - not the most inspiring Greek island for sure. Therefore, we were considering nipping over to a little island called Agios Efstratios for my birthday. Only problem was the weather was still misbehaving. Not only was it still rather windy it wasn't very warm, particularly not for the end of June. Some of the ferries to Agios Efstratios had been cancelled so we decided to leave it until the morning of my birthday to make a decision.

Having been reassured by the booking agent that she was confident that the morning ferry would operate the next day, allowing us to get back for our flight to Thessaloniki we chose to set off that afternoon. It was windy but the sun was out. We had phoned ahead and booked a little taverna for the night. Unusual for us but with an island population of roughly 250 we would not be spoilt for choice! We left our hire car in the port and boarded the pretty large ferry. Extraordinarily large for a visit to such a small island. We settled down up the front of the ship to enjoy the sun for the next couple of hours.

As we approached the tiny little harbour an announcement advised any passengers wishing to disembark to make their way to the back of the ship. So we did. "Do I have time for a quick visit to the loo?" Agnes asked. "Yeah, of course" I replied nonchalantly. We hadn't even docked. Just as she was coming back I became ever so vaguely aware that the ship actually seemed to be heading very slowly away from the harbour. No! Fuck!! (sorry but it really was worthy of the word). To try and set the scene this was a ferry with probably 4 or 5 decks. We were still on the top deck and needed to be at the back on the bottom to get off. Suddenly the ship had become a maze. I couldn't find the stairs. When I did I couldn't find the next set and found myself running round a car deck in a blind panic. I had long lost Aggers. I needed to get the ship to stop and go back and certainly wasn't going to achieve this at her leisurely pace.

You really needed to be there to appreciate the ludicrousness of the situation. A few moments previously we had been congratulating ourselves on our decision to leave Limnos for the night and admiring the cute setting of Agios Efstratios. At this stage I knew where our ship was heading next. Agnes was blissfully unaware, hence, when we finally found each other she was more concerned as to my whereabouts than the ship's and our next destination. By this time I had given up trying to find the exit at the back of the ship. That sounds pathetic but it was clear that even if I had, we were now several 100 metres from the harbour. I had found a chap in a very convincing looking sailor's outfit and I was imploring, almost literally begging, him to slam the bitch into reverse and let us off. I'm sure he'd have taken me more seriously if I didn't look such a wimp.

"Why are you sooo upset Alan, let's just get off at the next island. I know it's your birthday but it can't be far so we can just get the next boat back". "Agi, there is no next island. Next stop, Athens! In 8 hours!". "Ah, do you think we should ask them again if they would turn back?"

By now the sailor had started to take pity on us. Having first told us it was our fault for not listening to the announcements, he did admit that they failed to mention that we would be stopping for less than a minute. Rather than charge us the extra 45 euros each for the fare to Athens he gave us a cabin to utilise, gratis. The ship was empty, the sun was out. Aggers had not only nipped off to the cabin to put her glam rags on, she had managed to conjure up a very tasty meal from the limited offerings from the cafeteria, followed miraculously by a birthday cake. Life could have been a lot worse. So could my birthday.

Having seen this particular ship arrive in Limnos an hour before we departed and our ferry to Kastellorizo from Rhodes spending a similar amount of time in port pre departure and on arrival, Agnes rightly had absolutely no idea our turnaround in Agios Efstratios would barely be 60 seconds let alone 60 minutes. It was only on reflection that I recalled a similar experience about 5 years previously. Back then, I remember thinking that we seemed to have left Patmos before we had even arrived, so quick had it happened.

We made the most of our unexpectedly lengthy time at sea but we did have the small matter of working out how we were going to get to Thessaloniki from Athens. We weren't actually even heading for the main port, Piraeus, but a much smaller port on the east coast about 60kms from Athens: Lavrio. This was more convenient for the airport, but significantly less so for the bus or train stations.

Once I had convinced Agnes that us having the keys to the hire car with us was the least of our problems I set about trying to turn a big negative into a small positive (she wasn't convinced that giving the keys to the ferry crew to pass back to the car hire rep when they returned to Limnos the next day was the best idea but I phoned the car hire firm and they were more than happy with that arrangement - I don't think they could quite comprehend we had missed our stop!). I was also very relieved that Agnes had not agreed with me to leave the majority of our gear in the car and just take a toothbrush for our overnight!

Long story short, rather than a bus or train to Thessaloniki I found an early morning flight to Alexandroupolis about 4 hours east. Our flight to UK wasn't until 11pm so we had all day to get to Thessaloniki and could have a nose around Alexandroupolis too. Not the most conventional way to add one more to the total but, in spite of our disappointment on swapping our romantic birthday night on a tiny island for 4 hours in a characterless town hotel with complimentary cockroaches, I'd got more for my birthday than I expected!

Why did I bother with that story? Well, I thought it was quite funny and it leads me onto another unexpected airport addition on our latest Greek trip. As our fellow sailors despondently headed off back to chilly Poland we smugly chose Naxos as the first step on the continuation of our Greek adventures. What a lovely island and a classic Greek island airport setting with a terminal that looked like it hadn't seen so much as a lick of paint this century let alone any other modernisation.

We spent another blissful 2 weeks in Naxos, Amorgos and Koufonissi, the latter two offering no airport opportunities but were too close and delightful sounding to let that stop us. We took a ferry to Paros where we would overnight before catching another ferry to Milos. We were flying back to Athens for a few days to meet the kids (rather than us returning to UK for that sole reason). Fortunately we had made no onward plans after their planned return as we learnt before we left Naxos that their trip was cancelled due to a new UK lockdown. So, sad as this was, what we needed to do was find a flight straight back out of Athens. Clearly we were not going to abandon the addition of Milos airport. Although it did seem a little irrational to stubbornly go to Athens to now immediately leave again, you ain't gonna get to 1000 airports if you don't even visit the ones you've paid for a ticket for are you!?

The best connection was to fly back to Paros. I was prepared to do this for Aggers but she actually found Paros to be the least to her liking of the islands we had visited so far. So it looked like a rather expensive flight to Kos, from where we would find our way to Kasos. Then....... this happened. I don't expect anyone to share my enthusiasm and excitement I felt when the response to my question to our host for the evening "So, do you think Paros has changed much in the last 30 years?" was, "well it's certainly got a little busier since the new airport". Hold up! "Sorry, do you mean new terminal or actual new airport?". "Oh yeah, new airport. They couldn't get permission to extend the runway at the old one so they built a new one a couple of kilometres down the hill".

Thank you very much. Sorry Aggers but we're going back to Paros after all. We headed off on the ferry to Milos the next day. We had treated ourselves for our overnight in Milos. What transpired was one of the most charming places we have ever had the pleasure to stay in: a luxuriously converted windmill in the middle of nowhere overlooking the airport and sea. Not that we would be troubled by any aircraft noise. Ours was the next flight the next day. Our only fellow inhabitants were cats, rabbits and birds. A recurring theme, you may get bored of but we certainly would never have had this pleasure had we/I not been determined to add Milos to our collection. Fortunately Milos airport was incredibly similar to Naxos and not modern like Sitia.

Our flight left only 10 minutes late despite the best efforts of the staff doing their utmost to delay it further. We only had a 50-minute connection in Athens so it was incredibly frustrating that, having seen the aircraft (the one flight of the day) arrive 20 minutes early, they didn't even start security checks until 10 minutes before departure. They didn't start boarding until everyone had crammed into the tiny departure lounge. Inexplicably what was scheduled as a 20-minute turnaround had taken nearly an hour. Obviously nobody else would be catching an immediate connection back to Paros. Any normal person would take the ferry. Hang on, wasn't that what we had just done!? What was the hurry?

Minor panic over we were landing on the lovely new runway in Paros just under 2 hours after we left Milos. What was strange was that the new terminal at Paros was the same tiny size as those of Naxos and Milos. Just a newer version. Yet the runway was long enough to accommodate jets from Europe. We planned to stay a couple of nights on Antiparos and then head over to Syros to fly down to Karpathos via Athens. Just as well we hadn't made any further plans. Our 2 nights in The Sunset Rooms on Antiparos turned into 5 weeks!

My digression is now turning into a diary of our current travels in case you hadn't noticed. It has solved a dilemma as to whether to write a diary of our travels as well as a book on our addictions. The strangest of changes to our world brought about by the Covid pandemic have thrown any future travel plans into disarray. So, as there may not be that much to write about new travels for a long time why not combine the two? I realise no publisher would ever accept a complete change of direction half way, or who knows how far, into a book but as I'm going to be the publisher.......

I thought I should explain as our 5 weeks in Antiparos has nothing to do with addiction to collecting. Well, actually we did achieve one collection. We walked all the documented Antiparos walking trails. Not too difficult on an island 10kms long, roughly. An Antiparos lockdown, as you would imagine, is a completely different experience to a UK one. Once you've accepted that you are not going to leave the island you can go wherever you want. In fact you could leave the island and chances would be that you wouldn't be questioned, as we weren't when we finally left with lockdown still in force.

It had long been a wish of mine to spend a considerable amount of time on one Greek island out of season. Most likely we wouldn't have done so if we could have continued on our merry way. So, for us, a positive of lockdown. We didn't initially rate Antiparos, as one of our favourite islands. Yet, it grew on us quite rapidly to the point that we really felt quite sad to leave. I'm pretty sure, in fact, that it is the longest time either of us has spent in one spot outside of the UK and Poland. It certainly helped that the sun was out nearly every day and that it was still warm enough to venture into the sea in early December. The wind could be strong and cold but we nearly always managed to find a sheltered spot in the sun.

We did manage to add a couple of new airports on our journey back to Poland. We spent a few days on Syros, another very fine, if completely different island, before ticking that one off to fly to Athens. We did book a connecting flight from Syros to Athens and onwards to Berlin but we bottled it basically: with thunderstorms forecast for the morning of our departure we decided not to risk missing our connection. My main concern was that we would end up taking a ferry from Syros to Athens if the flight was cancelled. Agnes rightly saw the bigger picture (as I obviously did, if I'm honest) in that we would probably have to end up spending 3 or 4 days in Athens before the next flight to Germany or Poland.

It would have been unthinkable a year earlier that there would be no direct flight from Greece to Poland and only a few per week from Greece to Germany. So, for two incredibly indecisive people, at times, we made a snap decision to head up to Athens a day early. I'd like to mention the attitude of Sky Express, the airline for most of our Greek flights. When the lockdown started they gave us credit for a year for the flights we had booked to Karpathos, even though they were still operating. In addition, for our inconvenience, they offered us a free flight anywhere on their network. Yet any local we spoke to, and also reviews we read, were far from complimentary. We disagreed strongly. How kind of them. Ryanair, Wizz, BA, EasyJet etc take note!

We had utilised their free flight offer for our Syros to Athens booking. Bizarrely Syros prices never seemed to change and were always more expensive than other Cyclades flights so this was a result even if they did have the audacity to charge us 25p tax each! On top of all this when we turned up at Syros airport a day earlier than booked and said we were pussies (in light of us not being prepared to risk the connection the next day) so could we get on the flight in an hour they were more than happy to change the free flight they had given us for no fee. Thanks to Sky Express we have a monetary incentive to ensure we go back to Greece within a year and hopefully tick off the remaining three island airports and, if they restart services, the four mainland ones.

Off topic, but as our final experience of Greek hospitality, of which we had received plenty, we were offered free accommodation by the lady we had stayed with on our previous overnight near to Athens airport! She couldn't come and pick us up this time because of lockdown so said that, if, with the taxi fares, it was too expensive for us we didn't need to pay her. How kind (we did pay her though and had a rental car from those horrible people at Goldcar for £8 to get us there and back)!

On topic, we were to fly to the new Berlin Brandenburg airport. Only just over 8 years late opening, astonishing by German perceived efficiency standards, it had only opened 6 weeks earlier. Good to get it in so early on I thought. However, when looking to see where the new airport was located in order to work out how to get into the city for our train to Poland, my enthusiasm waned: one of the two runways at Brandenburg was actually the old Schonefeld runway! To make matters worse some airlines were still using the old Schonefeld airport terminal, renamed Brandenburg T5. Of course Ryanair were using the old facilities, and, of course, we landed on the same runway that we would have landed on previously called Schonefeld. What to do!? Count it or not? Probably shouldn't but, it does have a different code and is no longer Schonefeld airport and I'm desperate. I'm sure we will go back one day before too long and use the other runway and new terminal.

That leads me nicely onto other contentious numbers I've included. My reasoning has probably not been consistent. I've included Redhill aerodrome, Blackbushe airport and Paris heliport, for example, all visited by helicopter. I've included Penzance and Scilly Isles heliports, commercial flights. Popham airfield by hot air balloon also features as does a glider flight from some airfield in Wales, which I looked up 8 weeks ago when I was writing this but now..........

I can't remember, 8 weeks later. Just to finish on this subject, I don't count private charter seaplane flights in the Maldives, for example, that just land in the water next to the islands, but I have counted a couple of schedule service seaplanes in US Virgin Islands. I was, and still am, getting desperate and figured as the terminal buildings were more significant than some solid airfields and that they possess IATA codes, they're fair game.

I've decided that as the world has changed so dramatically and drastically, massively with regard to travel, and in the year since I started writing I am going to change my writing too......

CHAPTER THIRTEEN

As I said before, you would think that "lockdown" would have provided the ultimate opportunity to write, but it just hasn't. I've just been too busy!! I would have liked to have made more progress in a year but I haven't. I think it's just the one change really. I still intend to witter on, digress, and generally write a load of inane nonsense about our addictions and collections. But what I'm also going to do is also write a kind of diary, in addition to India at the start, at the same time. Why?

Well, when we quit work just over 2 years ago to travel, that is what we thought we would be doing. We were lucky. We got almost a year in, going pretty much where we pleased, when we felt like it. Now travel is more restricted than we could ever have imagined. Yes we know we are lucky, so far, and people have suffered so much in the last year. We both know we have lived extremely fortunate lives but that doesn't mean we shouldn't still have the drive to complete our collections, satisfy our addictions and generally have a ruddy good time.

So this book is now going to evolve, I hope, with a mixture of any additions to our collections we may manage, catch up in a little detail on our 10 months prior to India, and delve back into the past, reminisce and may even touch on our hopes for the future. The last is unlikely: if I continue to write so infrequently the future will always be in the past!

So, to bring you up to date with what has happened since we rather guiltily added Berlin Brandenburg to our airport list? Well regarding airports: Aggers 2 Me 0. Spoons and National Trails: an honourable 0-0. Along with many 1000s of Leeds fans I've missed the opportunity to add Tottenham's highly thought of new stadium to my list. Probably a few 1000 less would have wanted to make the trip to newly promoted Barrow to watch our Under 23s play them in the EFL Trophy, but that was also played behind closed doors.

I was more gutted about the latter for one obvious reason: we've already done the Spoons there! In addition, it's a bloody long way from Woldingham, the place is a royal dump and I actually had a look in the ground when we were there to knock off the Spoon, as I, yet again, have, previously mentioned. I have a soft spot for Barrow though. Along with Workington, Southport and Bradford Park Avenue they were in the league when I was a very young boy and doing the 92 was not even a distant dream. Like the other 3 they all failed to be re-elected to the Football League, as was the procedure back then, and have never returned since. I have felt guilty and selfish to think that

I hoped Barrow would be relegated this season, therefore negating the need to go there. It seemed for a while that that may happen but now, along with Harrogate, the Spoon of which we have not done, and which is a rather fine town, a visit will hopefully happen before 2021 is done.

Getting ahead of myself but it looks like Sutton United will get promoted to the league this year. Not only is Sutton very close to home, but I've already done it a couple of years ago when Leeds embarrassed themselves there in the FA Cup. Talking of Leeds embarrassing themselves in the FA Cup, in the exceedingly unlikely event that either Kettering or Histon get themselves into the football league and haven't moved from their homes where I watched further Leeds humiliation, they're already done. I'm sure a 92 geek would insist that you have to do the ground when the club is one of the 92 but not for me. To my shame, I did miss out on Boston and Kidderminster (and maybe others) when they were in the football league but you could argue that I had more sense of perspective back then.

In addition to Spurs, Harrogate and Barrow, Brentford and AFC Wimbledon have both moved to new grounds. In sharp contrast to my gloomy fear of how many Spoons would never open after lockdown, our Messiah, Mr Martin, recently outlined plans to open 15 new Spoons (and upgrade 50 more). Music to our ears!!

Actually, I must just tell you about how we came to be in Barrow. It is part of the travels of 2019, so, part of the diary, but not in chronological order, as if anything is in here!

During 2018, Agnes's mum was unfortunately diagnosed with cancer. Fortunately her treatment until now (April 2021) has been hugely successful and pain free. Between treatments in August 2019 we wanted to take her away for a break. Her choice. What did she want to do? She wanted to see heather, in Scotland. OK. Good shout really. I had wanted to visit more of Scotland with Aggers and set, enthusiastically, about a broad plan.

This is how that particular trip materialised. We flew into Luton, and on our way up to Scotland, merrily ticked off Spoons along the way, stopping the first night just north of Lincoln. This was to facilitate yet another attempt to use the microlight flight voucher I had bought for Aggers some years ago. I had decided that if we ever managed it, that that airfield was going to count. The morning got off to a bad start: Retford Spoon, where we had decided to breakfast, was unexpectedly closed at 8 am due to "an incident". There was a police car outside but we never did find out what the incident was, and Retford Spoon remains on the "to do" list. Off we went to Netherthorpe airfield and the weather, at last, was looking in our favour, just.

We were keen to meet David, the microlight

instructor, whose recorded voice I had listened to so many times, drearily informing us that, "there will be no flying today due to the weather. Please rebook". He sounded such a grump and so fed up. The reality was that he was a lovely gentle giant of a man. Agnes asked if she could go first. Well, of course, she could. Off she went with giant Dave, disappearing into the yonder. Agnes's mum and I both remarked that it was quite windy but when they returned half an hour later coming into land at a fair old rate of knots it didn't cross my mind that that would be it for the day. "How was it?" I asked Agnes from a distance. On reflection her reply was a kind of muted and guilty, "yeah good thanks" followed swiftly with a barely audible, "but there's no more flying today". Yeah, right. Ha ha ha. And then the all too familiar answerphone voice kicked in, live! "Yep, I'm not going back up there. We have a saying here: better to be looking up, wishing you were up there than looking down and wishing you were down there".

Dave was quite apologetic. Not his fault obviously. He was fed up as he was cancelling so often these days and therefore, not making any money. He told us he was trying to sell the business. "Can you wait until I've been please?". We tried a couple of days later for me and again at the end of August. Nope. Same old recording. In September it seemed my luck was in. We were returning from Ireland into Luton so planned to head up to Leicester and overnight before heading north for the flight the next day. The forecast looked ideal. However, the day before we were due to fly we received a warning text message from Dave. He'd got food poisoning and his description of it was rather too graphic for my liking!

He advised against us heading north but when I told him we would be in Luton anyway, he backtracked and said he should be ok. So we headed up to Leicester. You'll know what we did that evening. About 6 of them I think. Then, around 10.30, we received the shattering news from Big Dave that he was still spending more time on the toilet than would permit him to sit in a microlight for 30 minutes. Gutted but what can you do?

When I finally checked back last summer, rather predictably Dave's message wasn't just cancelling flights for that day. He was done for good. The line is now dead. Yes I dialled it the other day for some obscure reason. Line no longer in use! I felt more sorry for Dave than I did for myself and I'm happy for Agnieszka!!

After Agnes's flight we continued on our merry way visiting Spoons in Chesterfield amongst others, on our way to overnight in Manchester. Why Manchester? Well, whilst in Poland, Leeds had been drawn against newly promoted to the football league, Salford. This was too good an opportunity to be missed. Although I knew it may be extremely difficult to get hold of a ticket I had to give myself a chance by being in the vicinity. Our departure date from Poland and route north from Luton were, understandably then based around this fixture. I did get a ticket, Leeds won and, at that point I was current on 91 of 92.

We planned to stay a couple of nights in the Lake District- another place I was keen to return to with Aggers. Via Lancaster and Morecambe (Spoons) we reached the lakes in rather rubbish weather. (Actually one of the 2 Lancaster Spoons featured on the app was closed down, as I mentioned earlier, so we missed one for the total there.) So we decided that, as the forecast was better for the next few days we would take this opportunity to visit the delights of Whitehaven, Workington and Barrow. It is really quite striking how stark the grimness of these towns are in comparison to the beauty of the lakes. Barrow was the least bad of the three and actually does have an airport of sorts. Somehow we will have to find a way of flying to the football ground then. At least the Spoon there is an hotel.

I am now aware that I have already told part of the Barrow-in-Furness story and slagged off Workington and Whitehaven too. I could have removed either this, or the earlier reference. However, I think that Workington and Whitehaven are so grim they warrant a second warning. That, and I can't really be arsed to rewrite it, together with the fact that repetition is kind of inevitable when one digresses so much.

After admiring the lakes and mountains (and Keswick Spoon) we continued north via Penrith and Hawick to treat Mrs Czekanska to a traditional British B&B and what a delight it was too. Onwards via one brief Spoon visit in Edinburgh whilst Mrs C visited a cousin, to Dundee (a couple more Spoons) to overnight in Blairgowrie and breakfast in the Spoon the following morning.

Bogusia, mother of Agnes, had already feasted somewhat unexpectedly on heather in several parts of Northern England but she wasn't done yet. The furthest north Spoon is in Wick. It was currently for sale. I, to my shame, had mixed feelings about trekking up to a Spoon that may soon no longer have existed but Aggers, to her credit, was in no doubt. Besides, would Bogusia have another chance to reach John O'Groats? I took no convincing in reality and after an overnight close to Inverness (obviously we ventured into town!!) we reached Wick in time for afternoon tea. It's a fine pub and is actually no longer on the for sale list.

Bizarrely we overnighted in a static caravan (via Airbnb) west of John O'Groats, on the north coast in the middle of nowhere. I just love that north and the west coast of Scotland. I hadn't been to John O'Groats or the north coast since 1978 so it was lovely to revisit, even if the static caravan didn't feel that static such was the strength of the wind and rain.

We slowly made our way back to drop off Bogusia at Glasgow airport, via Stirling for the end of her 12-day Spoons tour. I think she got off quite lightly really, around 30 Spoons in total, I recall. Predictably Sweaty Pete had somehow guessed every pub we sent him a carpet picture of, whether he had been there or not. But I reckoned even his uncanny knack would be foiled with our next plan. After overnighting in a grotty pub close to Glasgow airport we took a very early flight to Belfast International so that we were in the only remaining Belfast Spoon for 8 o'clock opening and a hearty breakfast (sorry, another bit of repetition).

Now, seeing as Sweaty had correctly guessed Stirling around 6.30pm the previous evening we surely had him with this one. How naive could I be. Quick as a flash, "Well that looks suspiciously like Belfast (followed by the date on which he had visited). You did well to get there that quickly from Stirling. I guess you'll be heading south to Dublin, once you've finished with Northern Ireland". Ha, got him! Our purpose of visiting Northern Ireland was primarily for Agnes to visit Giant's Causeway. It didn't disappoint, in spite of the huge visitor centre that had appeared since my visit 10 years previously. What a truly weird and wonderful place. We dodged any crowds as it had pissed down all day and we headed out in the early evening to marvel at its splendour (more repetition!).

As Ireland was opening new Spoons, so they'd been closing others in the North. I had actually been to the (London)Derry one around 15 or so years previously, long since closed. It is my first memory of being aware of Wetherspoon because the breakfast was so cheap - £1.49 for a full English/Irish. Derry was actually a second attempt for the airport. Leeds played a pre-season friendly in Galway so, having already ticked Galway off many years previously I booked to fly into Knock and out of Derry. A few days before departure Ryanair informed me that the Derry flight was cancelled due to a fireman's strike. I had little option but to return home from Knock. In the event a nice little Derry day trip was had for a fiver return, not so long after the failed trip.

We did visit the other 3 remaining NI Spoons and as we did the final one just a few hours before flying back to UK mainland I, once again, was confident I would beat Sweaty Pete. Time to admit why the NI trip manifested itself in the first place. Well, a few months previous it was announced that Loganair would commence flights to Carlisle airport from Stansted, Dublin and, yep, Belfast City. It was the first schedule services for Carlisle for more than 25 years. Even before Covid I didn't reckon they'd last long. This was a must.

As much as I love far flung, remote airstrips the other side of the world I am equally keen to visit as many as I can in UK. This also meant Agnes would do both Belfast airports. Win, win and more win.

As a promotion, Carlisle airport was providing a free taxi to the city for the first 5 passengers to book. As it was about a £30-40 cab ride with no public transport we were keen to avail ourselves of this offer. How? I called the airport. The duty officer answered, from his home, and informed me that we couldn't book. Just head out to the taxi rank. As there was about 25 passengers we dashed out to find the taxi before anyone else beat us to it. Strangely, Special Branch were checking everyone's passport/ID. This seemed rather odd. Were they expecting an IRA attack via this route onto the mainland!?

The taxi driver informed us that the airport hadn't paid him for any of the free rides and currently owed him around £800. I couldn't understand why he would still provide the service but we were grateful nonetheless. After checking into our latest Airbnb in downtown Carlisle we hotfooted it to the first of the 2 Spoons and sent Sweaty the carpet shot. I knew he'd been to the pubs but struggled to think that he could work out how we would have got from NI to Carlisle in just a few hours. Mere detail to him. He knows his carpets and how we had managed to get there was irrelevant. He's a buses and trains encyclopaedia but clueless on airports and planes.

Carlisle was yet another example of my negative experience created by only a football visit, being redressed. What a pleasant city, even if it was still a bit chilly in August. We had decided to keep an eye on the weather and if it looked reasonable we would tackle the Hadrian's Wall Path. This National Trail runs from the coast east of Newcastle to the coast west of Carlisle. We left all but a few changes of underwear in our Airbnb and took the scenic train ride over to Newcastle. Plenty of Spoons to be done, of course, and a chance to see Newcastle, other than the football ground, with the same result as Carlisle.

As is not difficult to imagine it's a damn fine walk. We did it in 5 days, 4 of which were in beautiful weather and headed south on the lovely rail line from Carlisle to Leeds. Our purpose of visiting Leeds was 5-fold: one more attempt to do the microlight, visit some friends, do some Spoons, attend Leeds v Swansea and get a cheap Megabus back to London (we had dropped the car in Glasgow as you may have gathered). As the microlight was, unsurprisingly, cancelled again we spooned our way around Halifax, Dewsbury, Batley and Huddersfield amongst others of Yorkshire's finest which allowed us to make our 500th Spoon in Leeds prior to kick off at Elland Road.

You may wonder as a Leeds fan why I hadn't

already done all the Leeds Spoons. Well it's a joint collection and Aggers usually has better things to do than follow me to Leeds. What a trip: numerous Spoons, another National Trail completed, new airport (3 for Aggers) and a new footy ground. A Full House in my little world. A happy heather hunter and a chance to enjoy the splendour of the British Isles.

Meanwhile back in Madeira.......

During a lunchtime chat one day in Funchal which came about via an ex-work colleague of Aggers', we explained why we would only be taking the ferry one way to Porto Santo and flying back. If you've got this far you will not need to be told why. Our host seemed quite intrigued and proceeded to tell us about a woman he had met once who was visiting as many cemeteries as she could. Unfortunately he couldn't provide any details on how many she had visited, what her aspirations were and if she distinguished between graveyards and cemeteries. Come to think of it, is there a difference? He had met her in that fabulous cemetery in Buenos Aires. Should I ever decide that that collection is for me, at least I've ticked off that beauty.

We have now been away from Blighty for nearly 9 months. Never our intention in one stretch, and more than 3 times longer than any other time I have spent away previously. Homesick? Not really. But missing family, friends and Spoons, in that order, or maybe in reverse, most definitely.

Our plans to return on Dec 26th last year thwarted and our options unbelievably limited we headed off to Madeira to do some walking. We figured we may stay a couple of weeks and then we would be allowed back home. It didn't quite work out like that. We either needed to head back pretty quickly and spend 3 months locked up in Woldingham or see the winter out in Madeira. If I didn't have 3 kids to see it would be a no brainer. After not inconsiderable heartache we decided that, as any contact with them would be so limited, we would stay and explore Madeira.

I had made 2 brief trips to Madeira, firstly mid to late 80s, to finally tick off the infamous Funchal airport and its neighbour, Porto Santo and secondly, late 90s to watch Leeds. To my shame I remember absolutely nothing about the first trip. This doesn't make it exclusive in that regard but what is odd is that Funchal was, and still to a lesser degree, is one of the more, or most, interesting airports in political Europe (sorry, if I'm being a bit anal but geographically it's in the African continent, innit!?). And quite famous for it too. I'm surprised it took me about 8 years to get there after joining Dan Air.

The island, as we now know, has unfairly always seemed to have a reputation for the older generation. That is drivel, if you like walking! Even if you just like nature it's a bloody stunner.

One of the few benefits to us of the pandemic is we have had no choice but to stay put on our revised travels. Selfishly, I had no reason to return to Madeira but we would have hopefully gone for a few days at some point for Agnes to add the airport. What we most certainly would not have planned would have been to spend 11 weeks there!

Once we had decided not to return to UK we didn't really know how long we would end up staying but we had a new collection to complete!!! The first 10 days we were there the weather royally sucked. We despised the wind and rain but for a couple of sun lovers were quite relaxed about it as we knew we had plenty of time to get on one.

Let me just explain what sun loving means to us. We don't want to lie endlessly sunbathing, obviously, but having both lived all our lives, and specifically, all bar 2 for me, winters in Northern Europe we both get a right old hit from feeling the sun on our backs, and other parts of our bodies. We don't need extreme heat. The colours and brightness that come with the sunshine and the blue sky are what we crave. We realise we are not alone in this but one reason for "retiring" was to avoid the worst of the UK winter. It may not have been particularly warm for the latter part of our Greek extravaganza but for the vast majority of the time the skies were idyllically clear and, therefore, the colour of the Mediterranean: just dreamy.

As the locals got very excited about the snow

in the mountains, back in Madeira, not Greece, returning to the lower levels with snowmen built on their car bonnets we shivered away in various accommodations waiting for the weather to improve. I was extremely grateful I had included some long johns and slipper socks in my miserly hand luggage allowance. Whilst we had flown from Warsaw on a charter, new airline for me/us, Smartwings (yes I do keep a note/collection of them but it's not addictive and I don't go out of my way to add to it. Aircraft types as well, in case you wondered) which afforded us a full "normal person" baggage allowance, we figured we would be returning on Wizzair and, whilst I am very grateful to them (and Ryanair) for taking me to so many airports I never knew existed I steadfastly refuse to pay them a penny more than I have to in order to sit 20 rows away from Aggers. Therefore, which I may have mentioned in a previous chapter, apologies if I have, we are hand luggage only. And, since they all introduced two types of hand luggage we go for the free version.

Bloody good effort for me, let alone a well turned-out young lady. How Agnieszka manages it I still don't know. Her bag simply must have Tardis qualities. At some point many weeks into a trip she never fails to produce a dress I've not seen before. We did have the bigger style hand luggage for India but on a couple of the more restrictive airlines this did necessitate us wearing a few more of our clothes than we would have liked and filling our pockets with electrical appliances.

Anyway, what I didn't expect to be doing in Madeira was wearing the 4 T-shirts I had taken all at the same time, day after day. Together with my only fleece and jacket. And that was indoors! Fortunately, I'm not a smelly person and we did have a washing machine available almost the whole time. I did manage to stay in shorts outdoors for virtually the whole duration.

Let me give you a brief report on Madeira: it is an absolute must visit island.

There you are. I can be brief. Some of you, if you've been, will already know this. As I said at the outset, I don't intend to give detail on our destinations - the travel books can do that - but, bloody hell, this little island packs in an unbelievable variety of scenery.

I am gonna contradict myself just a little bit seeing as we spent longer there than I have ever spent anywhere in one hit and longer than many, if not most, places I've visited multiple times, combined. Firstly, what a hospitable island in current times: the government paid for our Covid test on arrival, our food and 2 night's accommodation while we waited for the results. Stark contrast to what we have to pay to re-enter our own country!

I felt sure that on my first visit I would have left the capital, at some point. Maybe not, as back then none of the amazing tunnel and bridge network existed. It took the local bus an incredible 8 hours to cover the 80-kilometre journey to Porto Moniz in the North West of the island. The same journey can be done in 50 minutes now by car! I don't even remember the landing at the infamous airport. Back then the runway was a very short 1600m. This necessitated the jets returning to Northern Europe to hop over to Porto Santo, just 15 minutes away, to fuel up, so short was the runway. The runway extension that had been completed by the time I returned just over 10 years later is nothing short of spectacular when viewed from either the ocean, the nearby hills or, indeed, underneath it.

I do remember on that second trip thinking how quick the journey to the city was in comparison and how the new road, tunnels and bridges must have changed things quite dramatically for the locals. They are still building tunnels and bridges on the north and south west coasts so there are still some examples of how the roads used to be - scary!!

Whilst we spent 2 nights in the coldest and only unpleasant place of the whole trip Agnes took note of a walking book on the coffee table which was to undoubtedly make our stay as pleasant as it was. "Madeira: The finest levada and mountain walks" by Rolf Goetz - 60 of the buggers. We had never heard of a levada before we left Warsaw. I think we can now say we are aficionados. Agnes rightly suggested that it would be 12 euros well spent in the supermarket to have our own copy. The fact that we could also download the walks onto the GPX on my phone, we were sorted.

Rolf, we salute you. Out of 60 walks we would class 55 as spectacular. We were so fortunate to complete the mountain walks in beautiful sunshine with the added novelty, to us, of being above the clouds for the most part. Truly jaw-dropping at times. You gave us a structure to the majority of our extended stay. We were momentarily lost after Walk 60 was completed, not in numerical order, I hasten to add. We are indebted in the most part to you for the variety of the 700+ kms we walked in Madeira.

Tania Ribeiro, how can we repay you for providing us with such a beautiful house to spend the majority of our time in? Well, I suppose we did pay you, so we don't need to repay you, but crikey, what a palace for the price of a bedsit! And thank you to all those other folks whose homes we enjoyed for lesser time. Stunning locations and views all bar Sao Vicente, but that gave us the walks collection.

Lastly, thank you Driving Madeira - £50 a week for a convertible! It has to be said that a Fiat 500 isn't ideal for some of those hills but, then again, it is for plenty of the tight squeezes! What a bargain.

We did have some fabulous sunny days but

let's just say Madeira's weather is anything but predictable and that the contrasts between north and south, and mountains and coasts, as well documented, are peculiar. The clouds are definitely attracted to this island and, although a pain in the ass at times, just add to the dramatic landscape. That is until they completely obscure it, which, in some places is all too common. It was more indoors though that we needed the layers of clothing rather than walking.

CHAPTER FOURTEEN

Well, maybe everyone does have a book in them but how many start it, let alone finish it? How many are happy with their work? What I've realised is that writing a chapter every 4-6 months, which currently seems to be my output, has 2 major issues: I can't remember what I've written and can't fathom out a defined structure.

Should I get much further I may have to amend the purpose of the book to include the trials and tribulations of writing a book. Having reread, for the first time what I have written so far, I was pretty pleased that I got as far as the last chapter before the inevitable repetition appeared. Trouble is I seem to have told the same anecdote in two quite different ways. What to do, other than scrap one and rewrite the other. Another time. Should I ever feel that I'm done and can try to make some sense of it all.

Anyway, enough of my whingeing. What have I been doing I hear you asking? How are the collections/addictions faring? Or, come on, tell us another nonsensical anecdote... please! OK, so in trying to keep a little to the original theme, since you ask, two of the four collections haven't been going too badly at all, thanks. Of the other two, one is predictably stuck and one has not moved on too far but, dear reader (I've stolen that from an amusing book we are currently reading) has it not moved on in some style!

We finally returned to UK via Madeira and Poland some 5 months later than intended, and, having behaved very well during our required 10-day quarantine, decided to get married. How could we make our special day even more special than so many other fabulous days we had enjoyed together? How could we make it different? I know. It should just be all about the fact that one is getting wed, shouldn't it? But seriously, these days how many folk settle for 12.30 in the local registry office, quick pint in the local and back to work in the afternoon? Not many I reckon. I mention that style because that is, in fact, exactly what a very good friend of a very good friend did, albeit a few years back.

The standstill in the airport collecting had been keeping me awake most weekday evenings. I allowed myself to worry about Leeds' results at the weekend. So, being my 60th year, I came up with an idea of how to treat ourselves to a nice big fat birthday present. I contacted Snorter Porter, otherwise known as Ralph, Rudd, Rod, Ross and even occasionally by his real name Russ; Porter that is, not Snorter-Porter. Russ guested for us as a Centre Back for my Sunday football team, Upper

Norwood, a few times and fellow veteran Centre Back 'Tel boy' Jardine could never remember his name, hence why he gained four.

Russ is a long-standing friend from Dan Air days, currently partly employed by that 'orrible orange lot. Whilst at Dan Air he seemed to be permanently trying to gain his private pilot's licence. Therefore, I enquired if he still had one, in addition to his commercial pilot's licence. No he didn't, but he knew just the man, Stinky Penguin. Stinky was a fellow A320 pilot colleague of Ralph/Rudd/Rod/Ross and he did, indeed, hold a PPL. "Here's the situation Russ. I can't die on 879 airports. Would Stinky like to fly us around collecting as many new airfields as possible in UK?"

The fact that Stinky, real name Pete but who would want to be called Pete when they could be called Stinky, replied to my first message to him by return indicated his willingness to become embroiled in our airport collecting fest. I had no idea how much this would cost but, having got this tricky subject out of the way early doors, we were clear to move on with this little gem of an idea.

Stinky would be delighted to fly us from Shoreham by Sea, or Brighton International if you prefer, to a good number of airfields such as Biggin Hill, Rochester, Oxford, Bembridge, Cambridge, Kemble, Duxford, Dunsfold and many other lesser-known beauties. And that was just in one day and in the south. The possibilities seemed endless. If only we were a bit richer, carefree or careless, Stinky could get us to the dreamland of 1000 singlehandedly.

When I mentioned to Stinky that maybe we could get married along the way he seemed a little nervous about that idea. We were to find out why later but were not dissuaded at all by his lack of enthusiasm. I won't bore you with all the permutations but after much back and forth from Land's End to, not John O'Groats, but not much farther south, we settled on the Isle of Wight for the wedding and Tewkesbury Wetherspoon for the wedding night. Well, what do you expect!? We would have undoubtedly wed in a Spoon but only one in London, has a licence sadly. One of the two Spoons on Isle of Wight (IOW from now on) is a fabulous pub, boringly called The Man in the Moon. It is an old church building, not that we remotely wanted to marry in a church, but getting married in a Wetherspoon church? Now that's a different story altogether. They even still had the original organ pipes and many other features.

Alas, no licence for marriage and, on a previous last minute fabulous weekend in IOW, we had visited the pub so it would not be featuring in our itinerary. Not so with the delightful Royal Hop Pole in Tewkesbury. Having been thwarted in our attempt to stay there on the night of my 60th the previous year with my kids, and completely unknown to me about 25 friends, what better celebration to mark our visit to this particular pub/hotel than a wedding night. We were so excited! And we were to fly there! We were blissfully happy but still had 4 weeks to wait until the happy day.

We needed to do something to make sure those 4 weeks didn't feel like 4 months. We had successfully completed the final 50 or so miles of The Pennine Way at the end of April........well, actually not so successfully. Here's my chance to see if I can write! I mentioned earlier, dear reader, that I had stolen that phrase. I would prefer to say I've borrowed it. I'll try not to overuse it. If it seems that I am I'll give it back. Now, this chap we are reading, I say we, that's because, very occasionally, I will read a book to Agnes. Just because we are an old married couple now, why should that change? As we have taken to walking laps of the sports ground in Agnes's home village to keep fit I am reading to her to relieve the boredom of the walking. Inspired by a couple of books by Mark Richards who amusingly recalls two separate Pennine Way walks he did with his teenage son, we moved onto, "Just off for a Walk" by Stephen Reynolds. I heartily recommend all 3 of these books. Now, these two dudes clearly write for a living and have decided to give long distance walking a go for more material. Clearly I can't claim the opposite, that I walk for a living and have decided to write about my walks, but you get my drift. Hopefully. I know it's very subjective but we like the way they write and their humour. So what I am going to try and do now is recall an incident on our return to The Pennine Way that has, to my knowledge, not befallen on either of these two chaps, as far as we've read, and at the same time sound like a bloke who has written before:

Just 56 miles to go. 5 days booked in the campervan. We could potentially finish in 3 days, certainly 4. Weather forecast set pretty fair. What could go wrong? After all we had successfully negotiated over 200 miles of the most revered, daunting National Trail. We were only a year older and had just scrambled over the best that Madeira could throw at us. To top it all Spoons were back. Sadly, outside only for now but, at last, we had the chance to sample our first Spoon breakfast in over 9 months. At least we could go into the pub for a pee and snap the obligatory carpet shot even if we did have to eat and drink in the garden. As it was, the weather was such this would have been our choice had it not been forced upon us.

Suitably refreshed from a hearty burger at the Colne Spoon in Lancashire, number 547 since you ask, we headed up to Ponden Reservoir to park the campervan where we had last left it, 9 months previously. We then drove our adored MX5 to Hebden Bridge in order to walk back to Ponden Reservoir. A mere 11 miles. We realised soon after setting off that we had a slight problem: we had completely underestimated the weather. It was warm, really quite warm for the end of April in Northern England. We had ½ litre of water each for what was likely to be nigh on 5 hours walking. Not a problem as it transpired. We passed a house around 1/2 mile into the walk with a tap in view. The owner appeared, as if preordained, as we passed. "Hi, sorry, we're quite stupid. We're walking to Ponden Reservoir and we've already drunk all our water. Please could we fill up from your tap?". Of course we could. After a brief chat about what a lovely place to suffer lockdown we continued.

Not 2 miles in we dropped to Hebble Hole where Colden Water stood in our way. A delightful looking 2 slabbed stone bridge provided our way across. I went onto the bridge whilst Agnes hung back to take a photo of me. I then decided to come back across the bridge so I could get the camera from Agnes and take a picture of her in the delightful river/stream setting.

AGHHHH!!!! FUCK, FUCK, FUCK!!!! JESUS!!!!! HELP!!!!!

I couldn't believe the pain I was in, and I don't think I'm a complete lightweight. What the hell have you done Alan, I hear you, dear reader, asking? Well, I can be a little accident prone which prompts regular "mind your head" and "watch your step" from Aggers but as I had walked across the bridge already I felt little need to look down again as I retraced my steps. Big mistake! There was a gap between two of the stone slabs, maybe two feet long and at one point just, and only just, wide enough for my left leg to disappear through it until it could go no further, just below my knee.

Unlike most of the Pennine Way there was actually a few other people at this local beauty spot, six maybe. I, justifiably in my humble opinion, screamed out in pain. Quite rightly Agnes and the other onlookers wondered what the hell had happened. Agnes immediately realised that I must've been in more trouble than merely having been stung by a wasp or similar regular mishap. As she covered the twenty metres to me in record time, for her, I was trying desperately to extricate my leg from where it was wedged. "No, no, don't move it!" she implored. Not a chance. It couldn't hurt more if I succeeded in getting it out which I did. I was aware I was in shock but I didn't feel great and the sight of the significant amount of skin missing on either side of my knee wasn't helping. I still managed a thought for Aggers, so gallant am I: she had, not too long ago, literally fainted in our kitchen at the thought of me undergoing an angiogram. How was she going to cope with this far more life-threatening situation?

She didn't have to. To my eternal gratitude two of the onlookers came over to the bridge. Now, Agnes and I walk with the bare minimum. If we are walking under 12 miles on a cool day we will carry nothing. On a warmer day, as this, a bottle of water each. Over 12 miles and with no refreshments en route? A sandwich and a bit of chocolate. Overnight stop? The addition of a toothbrush.

These two ladies, however, had more with them for their afternoon stroll than we would take for two months in Asia! In fact, their first aid supplies would've put most minor injuries clinics to shame. One of them remarked, after administering copious amounts of antiseptic, painkillers, energy bars and offerings of all sorts of dressings that I politely declined, that at last she could tell her eternally piss taking friends that her ridiculously meticulous and overstocked rucksack had proved a life saver. Not literally, of course, and not her life but, beyond any doubt I would not have made it to Ponden Reservoir without her painkillers at the very least. The walk would have been over before it barely started.

They, and Agnes, thought I was being foolhardy to even contemplate continuing onwards but I openly admit to being an extremely stubborn bastard at times. Whilst I thought for around 15 minutes that I would need to be carried out by mountain rescue, or similar, maybe even helicoptered, once the original pain had subsided I was certain nothing was broken. I knew also that the real problems would likely start the next morning once the injury had stiffened up. So, after not being able to thank my two saviours sufficiently we set off, with them, and Agnes shaking their heads at my bravado.

As predicted, the 10 miles to Ponden Reservoir would prove the least of my worries. The painkillers the ladies had given me were very strong and the next 8 miles were stomped at a not too dissimilar to normal speed. The last 2 were just a mere taster of what was to be in store in the morning. By the time we made it to the campervan I was in considerable pain but relieved that I hadn't completely written off the whole day.

The next morning, having struggled to get out of bed and put any pressure on my foot I dosed myself up with several of the painkillers our good samaritans had donated to me. After ticking off Todmorden Spoon - coffee in the car park/come beer garden - we continued south in the campervan, past where we'd left Mazda the previous day to walk north back to it. That's how we roll on these walks. We drive south and walk north. Makes sense? We only planned to walk 7 miles today. With my injured leg you would think that even that distance might not be particularly sensible. You'd be right. However, the 7-mile limit wasn't down to my injury. Leeds v Man Utd at 2pm was. As we set off I was literally dragging my knackered left leg behind the working right one. "Alan, darling, this is ridiculous. Whilst I am deriving some pleasure in our role reversal (Agnes waiting for me rather than me slowing to her pace) I really think we need to go back". We'd only gone about 200 metres. At this rate I would not only miss kick off but most likely the first half at least. I was inclined to agree but too stubborn to admit it. "Give me another 10 minutes or so to see if it it'll loosen up and/or the painkillers kick in further".

I can probably count on one hand the number of times I've taken painkillers for anything other than a headache. I was reminded, after not much longer, just how effective they can be. Soon I was walking with barely a limp. Amazing. My leg predictably went rigid again whilst we held Man Utd to 0-0; a vast improvement on our 2-6 hiding in December at Old Trafford. Agnes didn't protest too much when I suggested we went for a 3 ½ mile evening stroll so that we didn't get too far behind our daily target. I figured we would now need all 5 days to finish.

What I hadn't figured on was the news Agnes shared with me the following morning from the Pennine Way Facebook group: there was a fire raging up on the moor that we were due to cross that afternoon. According to those locals posting, the Path was closed and any number of diversions would add what looked like 15 miles to the route. Whilst the Pennines were undoubtedly significantly drier than when we walked last summer were they really dry enough for wildfire to spread as we were reading? Clearly they were.

On our morning walk we could see in the distance, and in our general direction, a particularly unnerving, large cloud of black smoke.

Having done my best to derail our completion of this wonderful walk it now seemed that some careless idiots were going to finish the job for me. We would not have time to add another 15 miles to our route and, whilst I had swiftly settled into a routine of painkillers, patience for them to kick in and gradually working up to an acceptable speed I really didn't fancy an extra 15 miles. What to do? We decided to adopt our standard operating procedure when faced with road closures: see if they really were closed. I reckon that 50% of the time the roads weren't closed. The powers that be were either too lazy to remove the signs or wanted to limit the amount of traffic passing.

We agreed that our best option was to continue on the track and see if the doomsayers on FB were scaremongering or providing invaluable advice. For those of you who haven't traversed any of the Pennine Way, as you would imagine it doesn't go in a straight line. One minute we seemed to be heading directly for the thickest smoke, the next it was to the right or left of us. The suspense was gripping. The fact that we met not a soul on the Path, remarkably unusual for Britain's most popular National Trail, did not bode well as this wasn't the middle of nowhere on the Scottish border but accessible walking not far from some of our major northern cities. We pressed on until we reached a reservoir where the fire brigade appeared to be pumping water to tackle the fire.

Our hopes lifted when we passed them and they didn't shout, "Oi you complete morons, are you completely brain dead?". Fortunately for us, as a small percentage of the Path does, this section benefitted from some kind souls having laid huge stone slabs to enable happy walkers to cross the frequently waterlogged landscape without sinking up to their knees in mud and water. We could now see that our route passed maybe ¼ to ½ mile to the right of the belching black cloud and the fierce orange flames below it. The land to within a metre either side of the stones on which we were traversing was charred black and still smouldering but we were through!

This whole section took us about 2 ½ hours. Our hunch to give it a go had proved correct. The fire must've been over a mile wide and we witnessed all kinds of firefighting equipment that would have got Nigel the plane spotting ex fireman quite aroused. It's so sad that idiots' carelessness and stupidity causes so much damage. We learnt later that this was just one of several fires in the area caused by discarded portable BBQ equipment. There are warning signs everywhere not to light fires of any kind, but clearly this doesn't apply to certain complete and utter wankers, or so they think.

We completed the remainder of the walk with no further dramas. Thanks again to Agnes's FB participation we were able to walk the penultimate day with the lovely Tim and Lynsey whom we had met briefly 18 months previously in Vietnam. They got stuck in Taiwan for the first Covid lockdown and then came home to Bristol for a son's wedding and had been unable to resume their travels. We were puzzled when Lynsey contacted Agnes, and extremely excited to learn that they were currently living just 30 minutes from where we would cross Snake Pass on our way north, after we had driven south! The campervan is pretty comfortable but they insisted we lived it up in their spare room. We didn't take much persuading.

We saved the last mile of the 266 for the morning of Agnes's birthday and completed it just before the skies opened. It's a tough walk and requires considerable planning unless you get one of the many companies, available at a fair old whack, to plan it for you, carry your gear and transport you to and from your overnight accommodation. We have the utmost respect for those who camp along the way and carry all their shit on their backs. Maybe 30 years ago for me. Likely not in this life for Aggers, even if I offered to carry everything. It's a fabulous walk though, it really is. Unlike Mark Richards and his son we only got royally soaked once in the whole 3 weeks it took us in total.

Mark had some mishaps but my biggy dwarfed his minor ailments. Of course we were off to some Spoons to celebrate our success. Only one problem: after a coffee in Macclesfield it rained so the next 2 were restricted to a brief nose around, on our way carpet snapping, to the unnecessary toilet visit. Not how we like to do it but when needs must.....

So, I know I haven't managed the professional storytelling of the aforementioned. I knew I wouldn't. I thought I may be able to introduce a little humour but I couldn't. What I did achieve was that I didn't digress, not once. The temptations were plentiful and not limited to telling you a) that I realised I'd promoted Mark's book already in a previous chapter, b) my injury on our next walk, c) my near fatal accident - seriously and d) the Transfagarasan Highway in Romania really being closed when they said it was and the ensuing inconvenience and missed airport opportunity our stubbornness resulted in. I'll get back to you on the last 3 at some point.

So...... back to the wedding plans or more importantly what we would do in the next 4 weeks.

CHAPTER FIFTEEN

To be honest there wasn't much planning required for the wedding. Getting married on a Monday lunchtime at 4 weeks' notice and advising any potential guests that we would only be there for 3-4 hours maximum understandably reduced the numbers to single figures. With Covid restrictions still in place we couldn't have had many more if we wanted to. There was, though, plenty of back and forwards via WhatsApp and email with Stinky to determine our route. Finally, whilst he stated that it was pretty ambitious, we had a planned routing:

Monday 14th

Shoreham - Goodwood - Lee on Solent - Bembridge - Sandown - Yeovil - Compton Abbas - Andover - Kemble - Gloucester

Tuesday 15th

Gloucester - Oxford (Kidlington) - Wycombe - Denham - Cranfield -

Little Staughton/Bedford - Cambridge - Duxford - Stapleford - Damyn's Hall

There's a reason why I was extremely keen to notch 19 new airfields. This would mean that our honeymoon destination would be my 900th!

I knew it was a long shot but aim high, right!? Agnes also decided a little nearer to the time that she would like our wedding night Spoon to be our 600th. Manageable, just, but might have been better to give me a bit more notice of her intention than what was realistically 7 days to visit 36 Spoons. During which we had over 100 miles to walk! I won't spoil the drama, tension and excitement just yet on whether we achieved either milestone.

First, we were off in the campervan for 3 weeks' hardcore walking. I should explain that we don't own our own campervan. I don't think I have shared this information previously so please allow me to explain how we, well I, if I may be so bold, came up with this dastardly plan. When we finally conceded defeat and came back from Dubai by plane rather than our hugely anticipated cruise through the Suez, lockdown wasn't on the menu. We couldn't really head overseas but we could head off for a walk. We never intended to walk all 630 miles of the South West Coast Path (SWCP) in one go. The official National Trails guides conveniently divided the walk up into four books. If we became incapable of choosing when to break the walk this could help.

For those not in the know the walk starts, or finishes, in Minehead and finishes, or starts in Poole. Actually, it finishes/starts on the other side of the water to Poole, the far end of Studland Bay, where the chain ferry crosses to Sandbanks. I'm not quite sure why the official point is stated as Poole. It's not as if Poole is just over the water. Anyway, that was a very long way off for us. We were heading to Minehead and a night in the Minehead Spoon, after some walking.

We had managed to complete 8 of the National Trails utilising buses, trains and the goodwill of a good few fair folk in Wiltshire, Norfolk, Cumbria and Pembrokeshire who kindly responded to our outstretched thumbs in order to reunite us with our car as we made our merry way along the trails. This did require a fair amount of research to ensure we never got stuck without our car or a bed for the night. As you can imagine buses and trains can be very few and far between as a lot of the walking is out in the sticks. On one occasion on The Peddars Way in Norfolk I could find nothing better than 3 buses to cover a distance of 14 miles in just over 3 hours. We decided to chance our arm, or thumb, with hitching. 30 minutes and 3 lifts later we were ready to walk back to our car. God bless the good folk of Norfolk.

We wouldn't plan to hitch with no public transport alternative available but if the bus option was rather unpalatable then we would see if we could catch a ride and save time. Clearly this wasn't going to be an option with Covid starting to kick in. Rather surprisingly the relatively populated North Devon coast was looking a bit tricky in places. Even worse, the pubs were about to close their doors. Accommodation of all varieties was closing. It was raining. It wasn't a particularly cheerful time. How could we rescue this situation or did we just give up and go home? The government were telling us to only go out if necessary. "Avoid the pub if you can". What a bizarre thing to say. Of course we could avoid them but when would we be in Ilfracombe again!? On day 3 we abandoned our walk and headed back to our room in Ilfracombe to sit it out for the day. "What if we hire a campervan? Sorts out the transport and accommodation in one go". Agnes didn't seem convinced but thought it was worth looking into. Neither of us knew anything whatsoever about campervan life but a few hours later I'd done a bunch of research and it now seemed more than just a possibility.

We had settled on a company in Wellington, near Taunton. £1350 for 3 weeks. Seemed a good deal. We needed bedding and towels amongst other stuff so, bizarre as it sounds we drove home the next morning via a couple of "avoidable" Spoons, picked up the necessary and headed back the next morning via a breakfast at the equally "avoidable" Wellington Spoon. We went to pick up our mobile home. Much later in life I realised that we actually were hiring a motorhome, not a campervan. Unless you're an expert on either, or both, like us, you probably didn't know the difference. This was quite exciting if rather a lot to take in. After having listened carefully to all our instructions we headed off in our vehicles, me in the new toy, whilst Aggers led the way in Mazda, back to Ilfracombe for our first night in the campervan in a car park. This was fun. Why had we never thought of it before? No more endless studying of bus and train timetables. No more searching Booking.com and Airbnb for Aggers.

Sadly though, our adventure was to be over after a week. We managed to get just north of Bude, around 125 miles I think, but the situation was becoming untenable. Basically we were running out of water and options to empty our toilet. One could just empty the toilet at the back of a lay by. After all, many folk seem to think nothing of chucking all sorts. We may have been tempted but we still needed water to wash and cook. Campsites and public toilets were all now closed. We were operating within the government guidelines: "Stay at home, only go for exercise once a day". We were staying indoors, isolating, and only going for one walk a day, albeit a fairly long one. The "Tourists fuck off home" signs that were popping up kind of summed up the mood of some of the locals. A tad unnecessary as there seemed to be hardly any other non-Devonians about. Just a few other hardy campervanners.

We begrudgingly headed home but when we were allowed to hit the trails again we knew how we would be doing it. In fact, that was the plan last July. Our campervan hosts had kindly allowed us to have £900 credit for the 2 weeks we couldn't use. We didn't want to attempt the SWCP in July because of the crowds. It was tricky enough manoeuvring the campervan down the single-track lanes when there was hardly any traffic. Not much fun with plenty of tourists about. So..... we thought we would tackle the Offa's Dyke. Not far from Wellington to its start in Chepstow. Problem. This trail mainly follows the England/ Wales border, quite a lot of it just over the border in Wales. Wales was still in full lockdown and was not welcoming Englishmen. In fact, they were doing more than not welcoming them. We were likely to be arrested if we crossed the border! Seriously. When we finally did this walk in May we wondered how the police would have found us crossing the border and back in fields miles from the nearest road. Surely they had better things to do. We also learnt from a chap on the English side of Chepstow that he had been having to drive 15 miles to his nearest supermarket in England rather than be allowed to go a mile over the border into Wales for his essentials. This farce continued for him for many months.

So we were going to have to head up north if we were to add to our National Trails collection. There was little point in driving to Somerset to pick up the campervan and drive both this and our car up to Yorkshire. I had a little experience in this field now. I found an extremely friendly chap up in Newcastle but unfortunately his vans were unavailable. However, his brother-in-law, Keith, down in Cheshire had a van available. An equally nice chap. Couldn't do enough for us. Off we headed to tackle the Yorkshire Wold Way. We wanted to get started on the Pennine but the weather forecast was horrible. The Yorkshire Wold Way is a very pleasant 80 mile walk from Hull to Filey. Let's just say that the start is none too salubrious on the outskirts of Hull close to a very large industrial estate. We spent our first night sleeping in this industrial estate. It was quite bizarre. Why, you may ask? Well, the next morning the pubs were reopening and we didn't want to waste a second getting back into Spoons.

So keen were we that we were in the centre of Hull by 07.30 waiting for The Admiral of the Humber to spring its doors open. We didn't really know what to expect. Would the pub-starved general public be as keen as the same mustard we were? Not in Hull. We had the queue and the pub to ourselves. There were a few people in the other Hull Spoon when we wandered along for a coffee. It was very good to be back. We managed to tick off a few more Spoons whilst completing the walk. Now we were off to Scotland. We would start at the end and work our way driving south then walking north. It was such a fantastic walk, in spite of the fact that the weather was more like autumn than summer. We knew we wouldn't finish it but we were very proud of how far we got. Only once did we get really wet, very lost and slightly concerned. We spent nearly 3 weeks in the van. I can't recommend this lifestyle highly enough. Some people tend to make for a campsite every night in their van. We don't see the point in that. We loved being able to pull up at the roadside, enjoy a bottle of red, admire the view and then retire for the night. We spent two particularly memorable nights on the border of Scotland and England at the view point on the A68. We ticked off a few Spoons here and there but clearly we were fairly remote at times so opportunities were a little limited.

We dropped the van back with Keith in Knutsford and told him we would be back for sure. Having had a mini trip to finish the Pennine we booked in for another 3 weeks to warm up for our wedding. Now we would get to have a pop at the Offa's Dyke and, time permitting, Glyndwr's Way. Then we would only have a week to wait for our big day. Of course, in true British fashion, it was pissing down as we arrived in Knutsford to collect the van. We headed over to Prestatyn to leave the van, drive south and then start the first/last leg north. On our way we stopped at a Spoon in a place called Shotton in North Wales. We'd never heard of it, unsurprisingly. I think I may have mentioned already that we nearly always find something redeeming in every Spoon location. Not so with Shotton. If, dear reader you hail from this town, my apologies. It probably didn't help that we had to take our breakfast out the front of the pub on a busy main road due to continuing Covid restrictions, in chilly, rain-threatening weather.

The interior of the pub, not one of Spoons' finest, would only have provided temporary respite had we been allowed to sit inside. This town appeared to have absolutely nothing going for it apart from its proximity to more interesting spots. Cwmbran would give Shotton a good run for its money in a few weeks but for now, this was one of the bleaker towns we had come across in recent years. At least we weren't tempted to hang around and the weather did not encourage us to venture to the outdoors of any other Spoon in the vicinity. So we could get on with the first part of this 177 mile magical mystery tour before the predicted rain reached its full potential.

We had decided to break ourselves in gently with a 12-mile stroll back to Prestatyn from Bodfari. I was still suffering a tad from my Pennine Way stumble but that did not account for why both of us felt thoroughly knackered once we finally arrived back in Prestatyn. I say finally because it took us 5 hours to walk those 12 miles but it seemed to take an eternity. Granted it was fairly up and down but not like a Pembrokeshire stretch. Why were we so bushed? OK so we'd left home at 05.30 to get to Keith's at a reasonable hour but that kind of early start wasn't unusual for us. We would normally plan to walk 15-18 miles per day, sometimes 20 but if we were drained after 12......

Finally it dawned on Aggers whilst we gorged on our fish and chips in the van in a residential cul de sac in Prestatyn: we had both had our first Covid jab less than 90 hours ago. 24 hours after it we both felt quite rough. That had to be the cause of our feeble energy levels. Surely enough, normal service was resumed the next day, well at least for the next week or so.

I have already promised that I won't list or go into detail of every Spoon visited. Neither will I for every airport or even each of the 92 (which is now 149) footy grounds. However, there are only 15 National Trails. I won't even go through all of those in detail but I think that they probably hold the most interest for normal people. Having read a good few walking themed books they tend to, probably quite naturally, consist of tales of adversity, misery and joy, not necessarily in equal proportions. I would say that prior to the Pennine incident and what I am about to tell you, our walks pretty much only consisted of the latter, apart from the "misery" of having to give up and go home from the SWCP which wasn't exactly the walk's fault. Obviously some days one's feet are rather sore, legs tired, the weather a pain in the ass. Before we discovered that we could download the routes on our GPX we even got lost occasionally. We moan from time to time about the frankly quite idiotic, at times, placing of the acorn markers that signify one is indeed on a National Trail. Seriously, the path splits in 2, no sign to indicate which way to go. The path is on a cliff face with an electrified fence the other side and there's an acorn telling you to go straight on rather than take a likely permanent break to practice your cliff diving skills or electrocute yourself.

We have often wondered if those tasked with signing the trails had a certain number of marker posts to get rid of per day and didn't give a damn as to where they put them, so long as they were home by 17.30. Don't get me wrong. We are very grateful that these paths exist in the first place and on the whole are well maintained. It is just a consistent thread, not only in UK. To finish that little moan on a positive: when crossing a moor that may be particularly prone to fog, mist and/or snow and with no discernible path it is very kind of the aforementioned sign-posters to plonk metre high signs at frequent intervals. Thank you.

Isn't the Welsh language a curiosity to us non-Welsh speakers: Coed Llangwyfan, Bwlch Penbarra, Llanwddyn, Machynlleth, Llanidloes, Llidiartywaun, Abbeycwmhir and, best of all, Llanvihangel-Ystern-Llewelyn. Even predictive text can't cope with them! But the Welsh folk?

What a friendly bunch. Well, all bar one, in our experience. We completed the North section of the Offa's Dyke to our fairly non-existent schedule with 2 emphatic Leeds victories and 7 new Spoons along the way, particular mention to Ruthin - lovely little town and equally impressive Spoon. Spoons are very, very rarely on the actual path but within reasonable diversions. We were particularly delighted with our visit to both Wrexham Spoons as it was the first day where we could go back inside!! Almost 10 months to the day for us since our last seat inside a Spoon. Just as well it was peeing down again, hence why we were spooning and not walking.

Don't you just hate parking fines? I don't like paying in the first place, particularly to park on a road for which I already pay £300 a year to drive on (I know, shouldn't have such an environmentally unfriendly Mazda MX5) but these private car park owners are a seriously shifty bunch. When we finally returned home after our Welsh odyssey we were somewhat surprised to find a parking fine of £120 because we had overstayed by 10 minutes the 2 hours we had paid for in Wrexham. It took 3 appeals and over 3 months for justice to prevail and have the fine removed.

Having planned our walking days very much around the rain it seemed possible that we could indeed break off from the Offa's Dyke for a quick 135 miler on the lesser-known Glyndwr's Way.

Lest I forget to mention it, both these walks are an absolute delight, particularly if you like sheep and lambs as we do. Literally thousands upon thousands of them. Clearly not as nice as those we're gonna import from Australia! The human race truly is bonkers. The weather continued to be a royal pain so we settled for a brief 6 mile stretch back into Welshpool as our start on the Glyndwr. Having finished the last 6 miles of the northern section of the Dyke, as divided up by the 2 official guide books, this gave us that rare opportunity to walk 2 different national trails in the same day.

Before continuing, it's worth pointing out that Prestatyn does a very fine job of marking the start/finish of the Offa's Dyke. Many of the start/finish points of the National Trails are pretty underwhelming in varying degrees. Bath, start/finish of the Cotswold Way, possibly being the worst offender. All it warrants is a circular stone in the pavement of a very busy pedestrian area. It took us a while to find it. I don't think we are alone in wanting some kind of ornament or something by which we can document our latest achievement.

Anyway, back to our encounter with one of the most undesirable, miserable human beings it has been our misfortune to come across, or cross to put it more accurately. As I've mentioned it can be a tad tricky at times to find somewhere to dump the Mazda and walk back to the van. On the

Pennine Way I had occasionally left a note in the car stating what we were doing, when we would be back to move the car and my phone number in case somebody needed us to move the car in an emergency. Highly unlikely seeing as we were always as sure as we could be that we would not be in the way of a combine harvester, should one have managed to pass through such narrow roads. This particular "B" road that we wished to leave the Mazda on offered no opportunities near to the path bar one. It was single track with passing places on some stretches. We always observe any gate, no matter how overgrown the field may be, any turning point for farm vehicles, any signs of private property etc.. I would go so far as to say we are meticulous to the point of OCD behaviour in our concerns not to upset or inconvenience any other road users.

Therefore, having scouted this chosen area for any "private" signs and correctly come to the conclusion that 5 or 6 lorries could pass us side by side at the same time, we chose to park against the hedge of a farmhouse. Seriously the area was the size of 2 football pitches. It looked like a lay by on steroids! Just in case the occupier of the farmhouse had any concerns as to how long this little Mazda may be hiding there I decided to leave one of my notes. Off we set back to Welshpool in frankly miserable conditions.

Around half an hour or so later I could feel my

phone vibrating. The caller didn't shout at me, she screamed. I managed to decipher enough to understand that this was somebody who was a little disgruntled that I had dared to come to the conclusion that the land the other side of her fence and hedge was public, as there was absolutely nothing to indicate to the contrary. "Get back here and move it immediately ". "I won't be responsible if it gets damaged". "You're just the sort of person who complains when there's no milk in the supermarkets". Eh? I seriously couldn't get a word in, to start with, which you know is unusual for me. Finally, I managed to convey my apologies for causing her such unbearable suffering about 15 times. Clearly Miss Perfect (surely nobody would have ever married her, surely!?) had never come to an incorrect conclusion in her life. Actually, there was nothing to prove that I was in the wrong but this was one fire that I didn't want to stoke any further.

This conversation literally lasted all of 30 minutes. She simply was unable to accept that I couldn't move the car immediately. I told her we would be about an hour or so and that under no circumstances were we walking back to the car just so that she wouldn't take a sledgehammer to it. Finally she put the phone down on me but not before signing off with "Well I bloody hope you at least have the decency to show your face when you get here". I was really quite keen to see what this piece of work looked like. Aggers wasn't so sure, particularly if it was still raining which it was, but my curiosity was the winner. And by God her appearance was, if possible, even more utterly miserable and devoid of any redeeming feature than her voice. I repeated my apology yet again. She just stared at me. "Bye then, nice to meet you".

The following day in our search for Calor gas (there was a countrywide shortage and poor Keith had driven 50 miles to no avail to try and ensure we left him fully gassed up) we met, not 5 miles or so away from Miss Grumpy, Mr Kindness-Personified. We related our experience to him. "Ah that miserable bitch. I delivered fuel to her for 20 years. What a piece of work". I always try and give the benefit of the doubt, not that it necessarily excuses miserable behaviour. You never know what suffering people are going through. In this case our gut feelings were correct. She was just not very nice.

Now I think I had been as polite as possible to this witch so what followed couldn't be considered karma. The next day we were descending a not very steep but rather slippery slope. Down I went on my backside, and back. I rather winded myself that's for sure but didn't think much more of it until I tried to get out of bed the next morning. This was way more painful than the previous mishap. Certain movements caused me, literally, to yelp in pain. Had I cracked some ribs or worse?

Ruptured an internal organ? Walking was OK but lying down, getting up, sitting up was a different ball game altogether. After 2 nights of this Aggers was having no more. We were suitably close enough to Aberystwyth A&E to get me checked out. It was raining again. We could reacquaint ourselves with the Spoon too.

What a nice nurse. What a nice A&E. Free parking. In and out within 10 minutes, even though the receptionist had said it could be up to 4 hours waiting time (I think he was reading from a script rather than assessing that I was his only customer!). A bunch of complimentary heavy-duty painkillers. This was becoming a habit. We even managed a 7-mile stomp once it had stopped raining and the painkillers had kicked in.

7 days later we were once again doing 2 National Trails in one day as we finished The Glyndwr and started the Offa's Dyke South. We were on schedule to finish our 12th National Trail. We even had time to begin Agnes's fanciful attempt to get to Spoon 599. After a very early start from a blissful overnight on Hay Bluff (highly recommended) due to forecast rain we set off to tick off 6 Spoons in the Welsh valleys, 2 in Cardiff ending up in Barry. To be honest we were more interested in Stacey's house of Gavin & Stacey fame in Barry and the ice cream parlour than yet another Spoon. 4 more Spoons the next morning and then we were back on the Offa's. The contrast between the drab town of

Cwmbran and the isolated hamlet of Llanvihangel-Ystern-Llewern was probably why the expression chalk and cheese was invented.

The next day after a Spoon breakfast in delightful Chepstow the final 15 miles of this rather splendid walk was completed. We had walked approximately 315 miles in 3 weeks. We were, rightly, quite proud of ourselves. What better way to celebrate than visit 23 Spoons on our way home!? Not all in one day you understand. And not before our last overnight in the van in the utterly charming setting of Tintern Abbey. The perfectly located Anchor Inn allowed camper vans to overnight. The sun was out. Life was pretty ruddy good and we had a wedding to look forward to in 9 days.

There's a lot of Spoons in the West Midlands and quite a few in areas which warrant a debatable amount of time to be spent over and above the pub visit. After 14 Spoons in one day, a personal record we have no intention of ever trying to emulate, we overnighted in the delightful George Hotel in Bewdley. I'll say it again. If you haven't Spooned overnight you're missing out. The next day on our way home we could have done more than 4 more but that would take us past 598. The "new" and long-awaited Spoon Clapham Junction would take us to 599. Agnes was happy, very happy.

CHAPTER SIXTEEN

"Have you updated your Spoons spreadsheet recently darling?" I enquired of Agnes once we were back. "Uh, no not recently. Let me check......Actually not since December 2019". "OK great, let's do it now". This is obviously where a diary comes in quite handy. Disaster! Our 4th entry for our Birmingham trip in December 2019, The Pear Tree, was already there. How did that happen? We'd been there a couple of years previously on another Birmingham mission. Clearly when I had changed phones I hadn't updated my app correctly. So Tewkesbury would have to be 599 after all that. Did we care really? Really? Nah! Well, maybe, we did, but not enough to drive a couple of hundred miles to do one Spoon before next Monday. Anyway, temporarily, 599 Spoons total would be the least of our problems.

Whilst Stinky Penguin was quietly managing our expectations of visiting 19 new airfields either side of our change in marital status I had hope that this may be achieved. That hope was, in one WhatsApp message, obliterated:

"Bad bad news this evening. Here is a copy of the text at 22:00.

Admin SCFC

Message: ZE has suffered an electric fuel pump failure. We are planning to source one ASAP and will keep all pilots posted on developments. Apologies to all those who had flights booked. As soon as the aircraft is repaired and repatriated back to Shoreham, we will update you. SCFC Sent to PA28 pilots"

Apologies to all those who had flights booked!! What about those who had weddings booked? Maybe Shoreham Flying Club wasn't accustomed to people chartering their aircraft to transport them to their wedding venue. Even if they were, their plane was broken, and in Swansea, we later learned. It didn't really matter what the purpose of the charter was. If it's broken, it's broken, isn't it?

I had returned home in good spirits around midnight after an afternoon and evening spent in the Twickenham Spoon with a couple of fellow Leeds supporting pals who could more than hold their own with me in the storytelling stakes. I only saw Stinky's message when I was about to retire. Agnes was spending the night with a friend, our first apart in well over a year, due to Covid restrictions. It was kind of a subconscious stab at tradition with a stag and hen do and separation of the betrothed the night before the marriage. Even if it was the night before the night before. There was no point in me sharing this news with Agnes, be she fast asleep or not. I didn't cry myself to sleep. That would've been pathetic. I just didn't sleep. Well, not strictly true. After I had mulled over all the options with Stinky - he was clearly troubled enough to still be up - I did achieve some shut eye.

There was actually only one alternative: Stinky was also a member of a flying club at Redhill. He would call them in the morning to see if their plane was available and, if so, if he could use it. This was the state of play when Aggers returned the next morning. I had surprised myself at how quickly I had adjusted to the loss of our special plan. We often use the popular "worse things happen at sea" and "if that's all we've got to worry about" etc. to put our disappointment into perspective. It works, normally gradually but, on this occasion, I had convinced myself very speedily considering the severity of this upset. We both knew that our plan could be disrupted by Covid or weather but admitted that a technical fault with G-ZE, hadn't crossed our minds.

I had already checked ferry availability to the IOW for Monday morning and this was fine. What was a little more disappointing than not flying to IOW was that we both agreed that we weren't interested in driving from there to Tewkesbury for our wedding night. We were both uncharacteristically phlegmatic. No new airports and now no new Spoons!? What kind of a wedding was this to be?

An update from Stinky: the plane was available.

Great! But only for Monday. Not so great! "I need to take a test in it". What? Surely if you can fly one Piper Cherokee you can fly them all? "True. But it's their plane and they want to see with their own eyes that I can fly it, even if a piece of paper from the CAA says I can. I'll let you know how I get on but I should pass."

To be fair to Stinky we had never even met the dude. He could so easily have said that the plane was knackered, end of. Not his fault after all. Yet, here he was, giving up his Sunday to take a test at his own expense. He had warned us at the outset that he was a little nervous about us planning our wedding day around his flying. With blind optimism we had dismissed his concerns without a second thought.

A good few hours passed before I could contain myself no longer. "Not wishing to stalk you, well I guess I am, but did you pass?" Not only had Stinky passed but he had negotiated to have the plane back at 09.30 the following morning. We were back in business!! Such was the relief that a 75% reduction in proposed new airfields barely caused a murmur. Let me put that into perspective: some years I hadn't even managed to reach double figures in new airports. How I had matured to the extent that I took it in my stride that 19 new airfields had become 5 because of one shitty electric fuel pump failure. We were delighted that our plan had been salvaged to some degree and, more importantly, the weather forecast was utterly and joyously splendid!

09.45 Redhill Monday 14 June. A simply glorious morning. Not a cloud in the sky. Agnieszka looking radiant in her imported from China, map of the world, wedding dress. We should have left at 09.00 sharp but Stinky was taking his time on his pre-flight checks and happily showing us every little detail of the plane. To the point that when he finally got round to starting the little fecker I already had a few butterflies. They weren't down to the impending wedding. I just wanted us to be on our way. For the uninitiated, which I would kind of include myself, the starting of a Piper Cherokee is not dissimilar to that of a pre-80's car - pull the choke out and try and get the right mix for a start.

10.00 Redhill Monday 14 June. Pull the choke out and pray for a start. "Leave it a while so you don't flood the engine" I remember my driving instructor saying in 1977 in his even older bullnose Morris Minor. This was what Stinky was now putting into practice. Now I was more than a little worried. Were we going to miss our own wedding? Well we certainly didn't have time to drive to Portsmouth now and catch a ferry.

10.15 Redhill Monday 14 June. Finally, with Stinky's coaxing the little bugger had realised it was going to have to do some work that day. He had seemed unperplexed by the inability of the engine to cough and splutter into some meaningful action but I reckoned he was concurrently having an internal sweat. "Do you want to go straight to Sandown or call in at Bembridge first folks?" Agnieszka and I both agreed. "Let's get to the wedding venue first, just in case". There's little distance between Bembridge and Sandown but we were both hungry and didn't fancy getting married on an empty stomach. If our Redhill departure was anything to go by speed was not going to feature on the menu.

I would opine that the vast majority of commercial flights I have undertaken are normally only memorable for one or more of take-off, landing, food, booze and in-flight entertainment, the latter not necessarily always from the little screen! Only on rare occasions does the view in the cruise feature highly in the memory. For sure, a day time flight from the Far East to Europe or Europe to North America, depending on the route, can provide some fabulous sights. And it never ceases to intrigue me how few passengers show the slightest interest. Never judge a book by its cover but the majority don't look as if they've had the opportunity to view our world from 6 miles up all that often. The vastness of the Russian landscape, the sheer beauty of the Greenland icebergs, never fail to delight me, I could go on. The Alps, Mount Teide, The Great Wall.

The difference in your little light aircraft is

that you're always low enough to pick out so much more detail. The scenery might not be as spectacular but there's something quite special about seeing that from the air which you've seen from land on numerous occasions. Our route along the south east coast from Eastbourne to IOW fell into this category. It was so much fun. As was getting married. We learned on our return to Sandown as Mr & Mrs that our decision to skip Bembridge and head to Sandown had been a wise one: the plane to land after us didn't manage to stop before the runway ended and closed the airfield for an hour!

I was pleased for Aggers that she had been able to add Redhill to her list. Whilst I've said, quite rightly in my opinion, that it's my collection so my rules, there are a few on my list that I'm not 100% comfortable with. Should I ever reach 1000 I would like to keep going for about another 10ish so that any of those I am not entirely at ease with don't have to feature in the 1000. Let's face it, what milestone can there be after 1000? It will only ever be "over 1000" because I'm never going to get to 1500 am I? I wouldn't even want to think about trying for 1100. So, I was pleased to take Redhill, out of the dodgy list. Why was it there? Because I had only flown by helicopter.

One way to perhaps categorise the collection would be commercial airfields only. But then what about Lasham on a Dan Air B727? OK commercial airfield/airline only. But a nice long runway at Goodwood, Solent or Gloucester in a private aircraft? You can see where this is going dear reader, can't you? Nowhere. Gloucester, or Staverton as it was, did have a Dan Air scheduled flight to Jersey once upon a time. Hang on, does it have to just be commercial or a scheduled service, or a charter? See. It's complicated isn't it? Our own private flight into and out of Solent or a scheduled service into and out of a grass strip in Auki, Malatai Island in the Solomon? I know you think I'm showing off with the latter but there are 2 reasons for picking that particular example which have stuck in my mind. I consider myself very fortunate to have had a free trip to Papua New Guinea and Solomon Islands amongst many others. I certainly had neither the time nor money to undertake my own holiday to either of these countries at the time so I was extremely grateful when the invite came. For sure, spending a total of 6 days in both presented ridiculously limited opportunities to experience much of either but clearly much better, for me anyway, to see something rather than nothing.

I knew I was restricted to two new airports in each before I left. I've just checked Wiki and there are supposedly more than 50 airfields in PNG with schedule services and another 20+ without. Endless possibilities if you had endless time and funds. Solomon Islands boast over 40 airfields.

Now for the reasons I mentioned Auki before I test everyone's patience yet again. Firstly as we waited in Honiara for our flight to Auki there was also a flight to Atoifi. I'm not going to lie. I'd heard of neither, let alone where they were but it seemed to me from the handwritten departure board that it was one flight. We were going to Auki. If it was one flight which one would it go to first? I asked the question of the Solomon Airlines check in agent but he just looked at me blankly. "You go Auki Sir". "Yes I know but does the plane stop at Atoifi first Sir?" "You go Auki Sir".

I would just have to wait and see wouldn't I? None of my fellow passengers would've understood if I had shared my concerns with them. I'm sure they just wanted to get the flight over as quickly as possible. Whilst I'm not going to search for evidence to back it up I imagine the thought of one flight on Solomon Airlines Twin Otter (20 seat, propeller aircraft) would strike fear in most rather than them relish the chance of two. As we approached the airstrip, which one I still didn't know, it was a quite bizarre sight. On the twin otter you can see through the pilots' window as there's no door (in my experience of this aircraft) just a gap between the passenger area. Obviously I'd bagged a front seat to maximise my view. Actually I have no idea if I did or not but what I do remember was the view of the runway in front of us. Or more specifically what was inhabiting the grass clearing amongst the dense jungle that we were going to land on. I exaggerate not, dear reader. I could see cows and naked kids, the latter running around, where we should be landing. Clearly this was nothing out of the norm for the pilots. They carried on their approach and skilfully pulled up just short of the kids and cows. Maybe they also knew exactly where the plane landed. But where were we? Would I get an unexpected extra in?

I didn't have to wait long. A few boxes were offloaded and a couple of locals disembarked but our host for the trip made no movement. She had been to Auki before maybe or she just knew anyway. This was Atoifi. Was I happy!? It was a fascinating experience. I actually can't remember Auki airstrip but I do remember the fish market.

Clearly whether we landed in Auki first or not was beyond my control but a similar unexpected double drop many years earlier in Venezuela wasn't. Me and my mate Nail (obviously he was Neil but he'd been Nail for some unknown reason for a very long time, and still is   he was also obsessed with unpacking and repacking his rucksack every day) had taken advantage of the ridiculous offer from Iberia of a standby service charge of £28 to anywhere on their network. I'd done likewise a couple of years previously with another Dan Air pal, Finchy, to Peru. There's a story there too but I need to tell you about the honeymoon before I digress too much further at this juncture.

Nail and I had done a few internal flights in Venezuela already into some interesting spots and decided to head to the coast for the last couple of days of our trip. We caught a flight to Cumana from Caracas. When we landed the crew announced for those passengers travelling onto Porlamar to remain on board. We hadn't realised that the flight was continuing rather than going straight back to Caracas. We didn't particularly want to go to Margarita Island as we knew it was known to be quite touristy but, more than anything, for some reason, well obviously one reason - to get another airport in - I was interested to see if we could remain on board without a ticket or boarding pass to Porlamar. This was 1990 but I thought they might at least do a head count or something. They would have two passengers too many. We would, of course, own up and plead ignorance.

Nothing of the sort. We were taxiing out before long and felt like a couple of stowaways. Stupid stowaways really. We didn't want to go where the plane was headed. Maybe you had to be there but it was quite funny. Margarita Island was touristy and not very interesting but at least there were boats back to the mainland which we kind of hoped there would be. I wonder if things have tightened up at all in troubled Venezuela these days.

Sorry, back to the wedding day. No Shoreham as you see. That amongst many others on that fanciful itinerary would have to wait for another day but we were quite content with 4 (5 for Aggers) new airfields on our wedding day and so enjoyed the flying that we will head off with Stinky again to do the other 15 and hopefully more at some point. We also had a new Spoon on our wedding day, albeit number 599. I know you won't believe me unless you have had the pleasure of staying in a Spoon hotel but our room really was befitting of a special occasion. Wooden beams everywhere, spacious and a lovely big, comfortable bed.

A quick breakfast wrap the next morning and we were off for our sightseeing trip from Gloucester to Redhill. We had picked up Russ (Ralph, Rudd etc.) at Goodwood on our way from IOW to Gloucester so together with Stinky, my ageing aunt, who lives near Tewkesbury and 2 friends from Worcester we had had a Spoon wedding reception for 7. No speeches, no family upsets just some fine ales and good company. Now it was time for a honeymoon.

Clearly covid severely restricted where we could consider going, particularly as we didn't want to be away for too long. Aggers had bought me a flight from London to Dundee and a stay in Spoon Fraserburgh for my 60th. The airline had kindly agreed to give us a year to use the flight as we couldn't travel to Scotland a year previous, so Scotland it was. I love Scotland and am rather proud of my Scottish heritage so I was more than happy with this idea and so was Aggers. Dundee was the only mainland commercial airfield in UK currently served by a scheduled service that I was still to visit. But we couldn't just do one airport and one Spoon on a honeymoon obviously.

"I want to do that shortest flight. You're always banging on about it". Not strictly true, Aggers, but I may have mentioned it a few times. There are 7 commercial airports in Orkney Islands. I had done 6 of them on a very brief trip 30+ years ago. Anyway how could I deny Mrs Czekanska (no name changing for us although we did briefly entertain Forbes-Czekanska until I realised my initials would be AFC - no thank you!) her honeymoon wish. So, after a brief tour of North East Scotland to tick off a good bunch of Spoons it was the ferry from Aberdeen to Kirkwall. Arbroath had been our 600th Spoon after all that. A very nice pub but quite a strange place to spend the first night of a honeymoon.

The north east coast of Scotland seems to get regularly overlooked - unless you're into golf I suspect. Certainly it doesn't have the dramatic scenery of the west but it was a surprisingly scenic train ride up to Aberdeen. We were sooo lucky with the weather. Aberdeen, bathed in sunshine, was most pleasant but on a cold grey day....... In addition to another fine Spoon hotel, Fraserburgh has the most wonderful beach for a stroll.

For those not in the know Westray to Papa Westray is the world's shortest scheduled service flight. The distance between these two Orkney Island airports is actually shorter than the length of Heathrow's runway. Mental, eh? The flight is scheduled for 2 minutes. It can take less than a minute depending on the wind direction. At least this time I would spend a little time on Papa Westray as we were to take the ferry back to Kirkwall.

The Orkney Islands are wonderful and wonderfully different to mainland Scotland let alone UK. There's not a lot there, even trees don't like it much, but that's part of the attraction. They seem to attract some quite strange folk, or at least the hostel we stayed in did. Not least the owner, but what a splendidly kind and interesting character Malcolm, our host was. He even took us on a day trip to spot puffins. The best birds in our opinion. Just adorable looking little critters. We did stay over on one outer island in order to tick off the final Orkney airport remaining for me; Sanday. A relatively lengthy flight of 5 minutes from Stronsay. I say airport, but that takes me back to the internal and eternal argument of what constitutes an airfield. At least they had paved the Orkney airfields since my last visit 30+ years ago. I distinctly recall Papa Westray being no more than a field with a shed in it. Now it had a tarmac runway but like all the outer islands the fire engine station/garage is bigger than the "terminal". Terminal would be stretching it somewhat in normal times. Not much bigger than a large disabled toilet with baby change facilities but Covid restrictions prevented passengers from entering in any case.

We didn't check in for the flight from Kirkwall to Papa Westray via Westray but at least they did ask for our names before we boarded. In Stronsay they didn't even want to know our names before letting us on board. These planes only carry 8 passengers and I'm sure the regulars know the pilot and vice versa. I asked the Loganair agent if they wanted to know our names and she just told me that the pilot was expecting us. How could he be expecting us if he didn't know us? All quite refreshing in these security conscious times.

5 days in Orkney was enough for us though. The beaches are truly gorgeous as is the turquoise sea but that wind, man. And there's no shelter. Particularly on a Monday when the one potential bar on Sanday, for example, is closed. We were cold in June. What's winter like? We're not keen to find out. Aberdeen felt positively Mediterranean when we flew back there. 2 nights in one of Britain's finest cities, Edinburgh, also home to a couple of the finest Spoons and it was time for a brief return home before our next adventure.

CHAPTER SEVENTEEN

The next adventure? Well that would be too straightforward wouldn't it? The next adventure after the honeymoon or the next adventure moving forward? Well, I guess I should write about things that have happened causing collections to have been added to, addictions to have been momentarily fed. Experiences to have been....well, erm, experienced? Then again, addictions suffer constant disappointments and frustrations. Obviously ours - well, I say ours but I don't think I've ever actually asked Aggers if she feels addicted - aren't life threatening as such. Yes, we could die in a plane crash, get caught up in a landslide, or a pub or footy match brawl.

One such frustration experienced recently was the notification received of a flight cancellation just a few days after, quite literally, 2-3 days of ridiculously complicated planning all in the name of notching the remaining 6 commercial airports in Greece, for me. Finally, I compromised and booked a route that included 5 of the 6. It seems it's always a difficult balance between rushing to the targets or chilling out, taking a bit more time. We clearly have far more time, in theory, but the world seems a more uncertain place than ever, in our life times and, well, stating the obvious, none of us know how much time we have. By the law of averages I should have another 17 years and Aggers 39 - that should certainly be long enough for her to get to 1000 airports!!

I'm not sure why I feel the need to always reiterate about putting things into perspective. Maybe it's because, all too often, folk don't. So, for the last time, and to stave off even more boredom, it's always in perspective. Our favourite Greek airline, Sky Express, much despised by the locals we spoke to, decided, due to Covid, to cancel one of our flights which meant either 3 days in Athens or forego one flight. Deeply affected addicts will go to varying lengths to feed their addiction depending on it and their strength. Everyone we've ever confessed our addictions to opines that we go to ridiculous lengths. Of course, and for the last time as well, I'm not trivialising or comparing our hobby addictions to those better known and life-threatening ones. But, if Sweaty Pete can travel 500 miles round trip to cover 100 yards of previously uncollectible train track, and spend hour upon hour searching for a picture of another bus registration operating the number 64 bus route......?

Anyway, reschedule done, let's see how that trip pans out and how many Greek airports are left. I'd said to Agnes that I felt it would be a good idea to get all the remaining Greek airports out of the way, then we could truly island hop by ferry without any forward planning on our future visits. Unlike flights, ferry prices seem to be static and ships don't fill up like planes do. Time will tell if I can back that up. At least for now we will have at least one mainland and one island to entice me back, maybe more.

On many of our internet era trips I've regularly wondered, as I think I've already mentioned, how we previously got from A to B and onwards without all the information we now have in our phones. I'm sure I'm not alone in thinking this but we did. It certainly helped working in an airline office and having access to the ABC WORLD AIRWAYS GUIDE. This "bible" was produced monthly, A4 size and around 3-4 inches thick of the thinnest paper imaginable - even thinner than that disgusting 60s school bog roll. It had, supposedly, every scheduled service operated worldwide. Schedules changed at short notice naturally but, any planning was also done at relatively short notice, and one could call the airline for confirmation in cases of obscure/ infrequent routes. I also became a regular visitor to other Gatwick based charter airline offices if Dan Air didn't fulfil my needs.

So, immensely grateful as I am to Skyscanner these days flights weren't too much of an issue for me. Once the computer era took over I had constant access to a GDS (Global Distribution

System, I think) through working as a tour operator. The added bonus was that the computer gave you an extremely rough idea of passenger loads for standby travel chances - beware airlines overbooked by huge numbers back in the day: on one standby trip back from New York (one new airport, Bermuda, involved) on check in with Continental Airlines the check in agent cheerfully informed us that we would have no problem as the flight to Gatwick was "ONLY overbooked by 94 tonight". Well I knew airlines overbooked but by more than 100!!? Clearly back then, 1990, my knowledge was not so strong on this policy.

Funnily enough, as we taxied out, settled back into our business class seats on the upper deck, an announcement was made that we would be returning to the gate as we appeared to have 1 passenger standing! Would we be bumped off? Was it possible that another staff passenger had a lower priority than Dan Air staff? Clearly they did as we were not the unfortunate ones in this instance.

This wasn't the first time this had happened to me so I can only assume that it must've been a fairly regular occurrence back in the day for airlines to taxi out before everyone was seated. Many of us will have experienced chaotic air travel in certain countries but, of this variety, mine had been in USA and previously in Portugal. It may have been before vigorous security became a thing but not before computerised check in - to my knowledge.

As a standby passenger we were always advised to take "back up" tickets for the return journey. These would be refunded if not used. The details of the Portugal farce, mentioned above, are as follows: in November 1984 we (Jackie, wife 1 and I) had standby tickets to Tobago. As I couldn't get any back up tickets for this route I had applied for tickets to Rio on TAP Air Portugal. They gave us free standby tickets. So, if we didn't get on the flight to Tobago we would try for Rio instead. Why we chose to go to Tobago over Rio is a mystery to me, particularly as the Tobago tickets weren't free. Anyway, after an aborted take-off on BWIA at Heathrow, a 4-hour delay resulting in us missing our connecting flight from Port of Spain to Tobago, ending in a very uncomfortable night at Port of Spain airport, we spent a distinctly underwhelming week in Tobago. Why underwhelming? Well, because for the first, but certainly never the last time, we heard the immortal line from the locals "weather ain't normally like this at this time of year, man". When it wasn't raining the sky was very black. We barely saw the sun all week.

Standby tickets on scheduled services were generally valid for 3 months. Could we seriously throw 2 free tickets to Rio in the bin? We had until the end of January to use them but Jackie had only 4 weeks precious holiday each year compared to my 12 minimum! Still we couldn't throw these away, could we? So, off we set bravely with no back up tickets. After all we'd been travelling standby successfully for 6 years. What could go wrong?

I'm going to permit myself a brief digression here. Back in 1985 there was little live football on TV but the FA Cup had started to feature live games. Leeds, languishing in the old 2nd division, had been drawn at home to Everton and the game had been chosen for TV on the Friday night. I watched the first half before we set off for Heathrow and duly set the VCR (I doubt anybody under 40 would read this but just in case, the VCR recorded TV programmes pre Sky etc) for the second half. I think Leeds were losing at half time.

We travelled to Lisbon without incident. We stood by for our connecting flight to Rio. Our names were called at the last minute. We were on! As we taxied out to the runway a passenger was wandering up and down the aisle as he had no seat. Here we go I thought. Back to the gate. "Could Mr & Mrs Forbes please make themselves known to the crew". No. Not no we won't, but no the announcement never came. The poor dude who couldn't find a seat was kicked off. We were off to Rio. What a place. Loved it. Not a thought about our standby for the return flight a week later.

Off we headed back to the airport to standby for our return flight to Lisbon. Full! Oh dear. Plenty of flights back to Europe that night but not many of the carriers keen on accepting a free TAP ticket. I won't bore you with the rules and regulations of airlines accepting other airlines' tickets because I never really understood them anyway. Suffice to say that it really did come down to the individual employee back then. The kind man at the Swissair desk would help us out and get us as far as Zurich if TAP would endorse the tickets. That means that TAP couldn't claim any money from Swissair for taking us. But why would they anyway as they were the ones who had given us the free ticket in the first place? The arrogant bastard at TAP bluntly refused to endorse the tickets. "If you wanted to fly Swissair you should have bought a ticket on Swissair". "Well actually sir I want to fly on TAP but you've just told me all flights are overbooked for the next week so how can I fly on TAP?"

Many, many years of standby flights later I've normally been met with helpful check in staff but this bugger was not budging. Off we trudged back into Rio. Most people would think it would be paradise to get "stuck" in Rio. Not so when you have to be back at work. Long story shortened: back to the airport the following evening. No joy. TAP full. No other airline willing to take an unendorsed TAP ticket. Back to Rio for another night. Back to the airport the following evening. TAP full again. Our only hope, a British Caledonian flight to Gatwick. Surely they would help, being fellow Brits and all. Well, if Dan Air would telex a request for a staff rebate ticket to them they would consider it. Time was not on our side. I called my colleagues in our Gatwick office who seemed to find it quite hilarious that I was stuck in Brazil, even though I was due on shift in less than 12 hours!

It always surprised me how few airline staff took advantage of the amazing opportunities we all had to travel the world for next to nothing. I had already built up quite a reputation for myself as the "standby boy". Now I was getting my comeuppance. Once I had convinced Pete Irwin - yes him, who bloody had me on this airport caper in the first place - that it wasn't actually all that much fun being stuck indefinitely in Rio and that I seriously wouldn't mind showing up for work he agreed to send a telex to British Caledonian asking them to help out the standby boy.

As luck would have it, I found out later, the local staff were none too keen to accept his request but it just so happened a senior manager of BCal based at Gatwick was flying back, saw the telex and took pity on us. It cost us an extra £100 each, instead of being a free trip but we were on our way home and I should have been back just in time for my shift at 0800 the next morning. Not so fast. The flight was delayed by about 3 hours so we ended up landing around 1000. I thought I may be due a disciplinary for being late back for my shift. No chance. My manager was just interested to learn of our experience. I loved Dan Air.

Every cloud and all that: the British Caledonian flight operated via Recife to Gatwick so the airport count benefitted at least. I think I could write a book on Dan Air and standby travel but as this one is nearly 2 years old now and seems to have no natural conclusion I better crack on....

Just before I do. What did I have to do before collapsing after my shift that evening? Come on, you know, don't you? Of course, watch the second half of Leeds v Everton. The cloud was not so silver after all. They lost, 0-2 I think. By goodness it wasn't so tough to avoid a footy score back then. I'd lasted 10 days. It's nigh on impossible to last 10 hours these days, unless you do the unthinkable and switch your phone off.

Right, back to Greece. And how happy we were to be back. I think Greece is rapidly becoming our favourite country in Europe and possibly the world. Out of season, which for those islands catering mainly to the domestic market, is unbelievably short, quite literally July and August in some cases, it is just dreamy. We started back in Crete. Why? Because it is the only place you can fly to Volos from at the moment. Oh, and we hadn't seen it all last year. Aggers duly ticked off Heraklion and we had a lovely couple of days in Bali. Typo? No, but I never knew there was a Bali in Crete either. And what a lovely little place it is too.

Off we went to Volos, with no plan, of course, but a flight from Skyros in 6 days. Of course it can't be that difficult to get from Volos to Skyros can it? At least I'd researched where Volos airport was and that there was a bus to the city. Good job too, seeing as it was a 25-mile journey. Whilst you can get nearly all ferry schedules from the Internet we had learnt that there were a few companies who did not appear unless you knew of them already. We had found a ferry from Volos to nearby Skopelos, Skiathos and Alonnisos but the onward service to Skyros seemed to have already disappeared for the winter. We found the tourist office in the city and they confirmed this to be true. "You'll have to go via Athens to Chalkida on Evia". "Err, no. We're not going all the way back to Athens to come back to Chalkida, thanks".

Sometimes people look at you like you're a nutter and dismiss you when you're trying to do something slightly unusual. Occasionally they buy into the weirdness. "Why you fly from Athens to Heraklion just to come to Volos to get to Skyros? Why you not fly Athens to Skyros? Every day flight. Very cheap. Or bus from Athens to Chalkida? Why you come Volos, you not stay Volos?"

"Because we're airport addicts and we can't help ourselves!" "Eh?". We had found a train route that Sweaty Pete would've been proud of but it was going to take 6-8 hours. No need, our local tourist office lady was keen to find us an alternative. She may not have really cottoned onto what an airport addict was but she was certainly keen to find a lesser used route to Evia. So a rare bus to Glyfa and, a previously unknown to us, ferry route to Agiokampos and we were in Northern Evia 3 hours later. Charming place and, once the bizarre sight of 3 coachloads of Serbian tourists had disappeared onto our ferry, utterly deserted. Greek bliss!

So all we had to do now was travel the length of Evia to get the ferry to Skyros. Apart from witnessing the utterly heartbreaking devastation caused to the north of Evia by that summer's forest fire the 4-hour bus ride to Chalkida was pleasant enough. Another 2-hour ride and we were in Kymi on the south east coast of Evia, with Skyros in sight. Another couple of hours and we were in the charming port of Linaria, in time for a sunset beer. Total travel time from Volos roughly 10 hours as opposed to a 30-minute flight from Athens. Let alone if you add in the initial trip to Heraklion from Athens so we could fly to Volos in the first place.

Were we questioning our own logic? Well, it briefly crossed our minds but Bali in Heraklion made it worthwhile on its own. The journey from Volos to Evia was delightful, off the beaten track, spontaneous, easy-going travelling at its best. Skyros was not our favourite island but the Hora and castle were fabulous and there's a couple of nice beaches too.

After a mild, well actually fully blown, panic that the 0600 bus to the airport we had been promised would call past our apartment was not going to appear - it was 0630, no sign of it and the taxi numbers we had taken as a precaution all going into voicemail - we were back to Athens to connect for Kythira. The panic was justified as, if the bus hadn't turned up, we would most certainly have missed our flight and connection. Bear in mind we were in a tiny, deserted village. Where the hell was this bus? Would it actually bother to go from the main town to the airport, let alone pass by us? This was the rearranged flight we had gone out of our way to catch to Kythira and we were extremely close to missing it. We knew there wasn't another flight for 3 days.

Panic over. Skyros ticked. Kythira ticked. We loved Kythira. The colour of the sea where we stayed was even more unbelievably turquoise than what we'd seen last year. We stayed in the main harbour for the boats to the mainland. Everything was shut bar one restaurant which also closed the day before we left. It was charming though. We explored the island by foot and car. Thoroughly delightful.

Kalamata airport had been on the to do list for a while now. Again the journey looked quite straight forward on the map from Neapoli, where our ferry would dock from Kythira, to Kalamata. Not so. Take a bus to Sparta, change, take a bus to Tripoli, change, take a bus to Kalamata. Sparta to Kalamata is only 35 miles. Only one problem. It's a very windy mountain road and clearly the bus companies don't fancy it as there's only 2 buses a week! Hence why you've gotta trek via Tripoli.

Yet again, this actually worked in our favour. Unbeknown to us (we really should do a bit more advanced research) lay the "famous" ruins of Mystra within walking distance of Sparta. I'm trying not to repeat the same superlatives so, in this instance, I'll just say extremely worthwhile to visit. We actually saw some other foreigners/tourists there. Where had they come from I wonder. We saw none in Sparta. Had they braved the mountain route from Kalamata? Or chickened out and gone via Tripoli, the boring route?

Well, when we got to Kalamata the next day, once more we neither saw, nor heard, hardly any non-Greek speakers. Not a bad city, for a port, Kalamata. Stacks of places to stay on the seafront but where was everyone? Yeah, I know, Covid and all that, but that certainly wasn't affecting Crete when we passed through. So it was quite a shock when we took our BA flight to Heathrow a couple of days later. It was full - of Brits. I was one of the youngest, let alone Aggers. Not one kid! Where had they all been? Not Kalamata, unless they hid indoors. Clearly BA had tapped into a market nearby as theirs was the only commercial flight all week! Bizarre.

So, another delightful, if significantly shorter trip to Greece came to an end. We're already looking forward to getting those last 2 airports in next year. The perfect excuse to return again. There is another airport which receives a couple of expensive charters from Germany but even our madness does have a limit. Well, let's see if they operate next year and, if so, just how expensive they are. Now it was time to head back to Blighty before winter truly set in and, if all went to plan, crack on with the Spoons count, walk and maybe even see the family and friends! We got more than we bargained for......

CHAPTER EIGHTEEN

So what was more than we bargained for? I know you're just itching to know but please let me keep the suspense going for a little longer. You'll be pleased to know we managed to reduce our remaining National Trail miles by around 140. I know walking has become increasingly topical in the last 18 months, its benefits during tough times etc. Supposedly 1000s more of us are walking. We've seen no evidence of that on our National Trails mission. We now ONLY have around 270 miles of the South West Coast Path to walk, out of 630 in case you've forgotten.

It's an utterly splendid walk. On this particular section from Exmouth, well the other side of the river Exe to be precise, to Fowey, well, again to be precise, Polruan, the other side of the river Fowey, there was also the opportunity to tick off 10 Spoons. Actually, if you count picking up and dropping off the campervan, 13. Cash back! What more could a Spoons and National Trails collector wish for? Add in another 24 Spoons and you will understand the soon to be revealed, more than we bargained for and why I felt on such a high after our month back in Blighty.

Just so you don't think I am a complete and utter, total weirdo that feeling of elation most certainly encompassed the time spent with family and friends. Maybe the need to do that is an addiction of sorts in itself but let's not go there, for now, if at all. We are not so far off 700 Spoons, so less than 200 left, have less than 400 miles of the current National Trails to walk, and I have 5 football grounds to visit. And, where are we at with airports, you're wondering? Well, just before I get onto that I think it is worth a few lines to encourage you to walk.

It can be argued that visiting pubs, airports and football grounds has little merit. Of course I would beg to differ but I think the argument against lapping up the National Trail miles is weak to non-existent. I cannot, no, do not wish to fight the desire to notch up the aforementioned 3. They are self-indulgent, petty, worthless to some but, for me, well, I'm addicted and I love it. But, who can criticise us for walking? We have chosen to focus our walking in UK. We walk all the time while we are abroad but have no goal, no collection. Whether you choose to walk here or abroad, or both, just get out there. It really is the most pleasurable and rewarding of pursuits.

This particular section of the South West Coast Path was so incredibly varied. What we hadn't appreciated because, of course, we hadn't researched the path in advance, was just how many river crossings were involved. And that some of the ferry services were summer months only. We had credit left on the campervan we had hired for 3 weeks pre lockdown one, way back in March 2020. The further south you go into Devon and Cornwall the less suited it is to campervan travel in our experience. The lanes just seem to become more and more narrow. The Mazda kind of acted as a leader vehicle. Let me explain: Agnes would go ahead in our beautiful MX5 so when she met another car she could inform them that a campervan was behind her. We even checked out the bus timetables to try and avoid meeting them!

We ended up wading across one river at low tide, as advised by the bibles - the National Trail guide books. Quite amusing particularly as it was raining at the time. The beauty of the campervan is the flexibility. Finish walking, wine, food, bed all in one place. No need to look for a pub, restaurant or lodging. The downside is getting the campervan as close to the National Trail as possible so as to avoid any unnecessary additional walking at the end of a long day walking. These Cornish and Devonian folk are a lot less accommodating than their Welsh, Yorkshire and Scottish counterparts. They really don't embrace a bit of overnight parking anywhere other than a campsite in the main. In general, the others don't really care for now. Park up where you wish.

Whilst Aggers likes to innocently describe herself

as a traveller, as she is blissfully unaware of the connotations, we are not travellers in that sense. Not that I'm a fan of that lifestyle but, at times, I almost felt sympathetic. Maybe slightly different wanting to find an overnight for one campervan as opposed to a few weeks/months for a gaggle of Ford Transits and caravans but, nonetheless. Not wishing to be too judgemental but we were maybe slightly more diligent in our desire not to offend/ aggravate the locals than your average modern-day traveller.

Blimey!! That is way off on a tangent even by my loose standards. Just get out there and walk. Please. You really won't regret it. Before we headed back to Greece via Poland we had enjoyed a breathtakingly beautiful 10 days walking in tandem with Keith's campervan. We headed north the day before collecting 6 new Spoons on the way: breakfast being taken in Sutton Coldfield in the pub that was unexpectedly closed in December 2019 during the lost credit card debacle. Managed to right that wrong in under 2 years. It is also worth mentioning 2 fabulous adjoining pubs in Derby. It was actually an unexpected bonus because, as the pubs are literally next door to each other, only one shows up on the app. Delightful, therefore, when you discover there's actually 2 there instead of one.

This day actually being the day that Engerland famously blew yet another chance of footy glory by capitulating in a depressingly familiar manner under the unbelievably overrated Southgate of Crawley (anyone who knows Crawley must be amused that Gareth Southgate is from Crawley which has an area called Southgate (I may very well delete that as it really isn't very interesting but .....)) meant that the pubs and streets were busy with very bullish footy fans. We did watch the match in our overnight stop at the Spoons hotel in Chesterfield - already ticked off on the heather finding expedition with Bogusia - but my times when England football caused me heartache are way gone.

Nothing to do with the collections but prior to heading to watch probably our most glorious defeat in 1990 in Turin, I had only seen England live once, at Wembley in 1977. I grew up more a Scotland fan due to my father's influence but unlike most Scots, always wanted England to win, unless against Scotland. After all, I am more English than Scottish really. It helps that in the 70s Scotland were good and full of Leeds players. Sorry, this isn't a football book is it. Suffice to say the '90 semi-final did get me right into England for a good 10-15 years and took me to a few airports I may well not have visited: Tirana, Baku, Moscow - Domodedovo, Lydd, Lille.

Lydd?? Got you there eh? For those of you without a detailed knowledge of Kent or a very strong interest in aviation I would be very impressed if you have even heard of it. Well, many years ago Dan Air used to operate a service from Lydd to Beauvais. I never made it. It may even have been before my time but I think this is worth a digression: when I was approached by a friend of my ex business partner to organise a private charter to the England v Colombia match in the 1998 World Cup, of course, I didn't hesitate. To be honest this guy was a total twat but I didn't completely dislike him. Anyway, he had something I wanted - a ticket for the match and the opportunity to add 2 airports.

He worked for a sports mag or advertising agency, can't remember but he wanted to take around 10-15 "VIP" clients to the match on a private charter. He told me that he had the match tickets guaranteed. I'm sure I could have arranged him a flight from Biggin Hill, Blackbushe or somewhere else more convenient to London but I secured him a rate he was happy with from Lydd. Fortunately he never questioned me on why Lydd. To be honest he had much bigger problems as the big day grew nearer. I had asked him a couple of times whether he actually had the match tickets in his possession. "No, but the guy is totally legit, Al, don't you worry". I wasn't worried. I'd be getting 2 airports in and the match was a bonus.

I forget the exact timeline but I think it was only a couple of days before when I got a phone call from a very worried Nelson (not his real name but you never know who might read!) "Al, I haven't got any match tickets. The guy's done me. What the f.... am I gonna do? I simply can't lose face on this one". "I'm really sorry Nelson, but I can't help you". I did feel sorry for him and I would absolutely have helped if I could. The next day a very excited Nelson calls me. "Sorted! Fucken sorted man! Get In! Yes!! Dave's got me all the tickets I need and he's gonna meet me at Lille airport. Phew! Close one, Al"

I've no idea what the geezer with the tickets was called or where Nelson found him but we were on and once bitten twice shy Nelson was not. Off we went, Lydd, with no scheduled services, so not easy to tick off in a world before Stinky Penguin, and Lille added to the total. When we arrived at Lille, Nelson was off to find Dave. I offered to join him, not sure what I could offer if it got tasty, but was quite happy he declined when I saw the size of Dave and his mate from a distance. He was large to say the least. Nelson returned jubilant. Not only did he have the tickets but 2 of them were VIP. Who should he give them to? The other tickets were dotted around the ground, in pairs fortunately. I suggested that he and I should have the VIP tickets in case they were duds.

I know Nelson paid a lot of money to Dave but I think Dave could've named his price. Nelson could not lose face on this one. After some deliberation he agreed to my suggestion. As I said, twat he most certainly was but I didn't want to see him humiliated and, for some reason I had a bad vibe about these tickets in general, but particularly the VIPs. Dave was not only very large. He was very scary looking too. Tickets in hand Nelson was off to entertain his clients once our minibus arrived in the match venue, Lens (no airport, hence Lille. Actually it may have an airstrip). I went off to do my own thing and arranged to meet Nelson outside the VIP entrance about an hour before kick off. He thought this was too early but I said we may need time to sort out the tickets should there be a problem.

Nelson finally agreed and when he returned he had clearly imbibed some of his favourite white powder as well as regulation beers. We got through the first security check. "Al mate. No worries. Look it's all good. Relax". I wasn't not relaxed but I fancied seeing the match and Nelson was getting very hyper. We made it into the VIP area which was full, of VIPs. Amongst others, Sir Bobby Charlton who Nelson approached like a long-lost pal. "Come on Nels, let's go and take our seats and soak up the atmosphere" I suggested as much out of avoiding further embarrassment, as Nelson made his way through the other famous faces, as still harbouring a nagging doubt that this was too good to be true. Reluctantly he agreed. I showed our, to be honest, kosher looking tickets to the official who pointed me in the opposite direction.

I questioned him. "Ticket invalid" was all he said. I looked in the direction he was pointing and saw about 15 other chaps looking as out of place as Nelson and me.

A very kind French police lady explained to me that the tickets had originally been valid but, once Prince Charles and/or Prince William had decided to attend, had been voided to allow room for their security team. She told me not to worry, they were prepared for this eventuality. We were escorted out of the ground and then back in to the very front row which was so low down that our eyes were at pitch level. Not the greatest view and the opposite from VIP but we were in, only missed a couple of minutes and England won. My hunch had been correct. The others had no problems with their tickets. Nelson was returning to earth and was happy with how the day turned out.

Jim the pilot sorted out our trip to watch England take on Azerbaijan in Baku. No dramas when Jim was arranging match tickets, ever. Meet the FA official on the bridge in Niigata, he's got your tickets. Meet Kevin Pietersen in his hotel in Bangalore, he's got your tickets. And so on. No problem. I actually can't remember where, or from whom, we picked our Azerbaijan match tickets up but I do remember another 2 airports done, one more of the 3 Moscow ones, Domodedovo and Baku. It took me a while to notch up the last in Moscow. Well, when trying to make sure I spelt it correctly I've just learned from our mates at Google that a fourth one opened in 2016, Zhukovsky! In 2015 Aggers and I embarked on a wonderful little holiday to Georgia and Armenia. You may, or more likely may not, have been wondering if I collect countries. In the unlikely event that you had you would, rightly, have dismissed the notion. Obviously I would have mentioned it. Like anybody with an interest in travel it's always nice to tick off a new country. I am no exception. Neither is Aggers. In fact, she has a very nice and big wall map of the world and loves sticking a new pin in it.

The reason I don't "collect" countries is twofold: I am not interested in putting myself in unnecessary danger. Take your pick over the years but, currently, as an independent tourist I am unlikely to venture to Somalia, Mali, Afghanistan to name a few. So, I don't think I would ever complete what is, compared to Spoons a pretty small list. The other reason is the ambiguity in the list. For example, our very own UK and our dependencies. Scotland, Wales, Northern Ireland and England play football separately but compete as one country in the Olympics as GB. Northern Ireland is not part of GB is it!? It's part of UK so even the Olympic committee is confused let alone those knobs at FIFA! They count Gibraltar and Andorra, amongst others as countries. Most of the world can't make up its mind about Taiwan and

Kosovo. Don't start about Northern Cyprus! And this is just the tip of the iceberg.

Obviously I've had to do a little research, I can't help myself. If you're interested www.onceinalifetimejourney.com/inspiration/ how-many-countries-are-there-in-the-world goes into quite a lot of depth and quotes that country collectors vary the total between 193 and 267!! I rest my case. Actually I've just looked at another one, travelerscentury.org, and I could get seriously lost. So you can join their club if you've visited over 100 countries. Obviously they want some dosh from you for the privilege, but, get this, their list is 329 as of 2019. A quick glance, as otherwise I will never finish, and they count the UAE states individually! Seriously!! That's like me counting New York JFK 7 times because I've been to each of the 7 terminals.

There was me thinking it must've been quite interesting for these country collectors when the Soviet Union and Yugoslavia collapsed. Would you be like, great, more for my list or bugger it, just when I thought I was done. Would you hope that Ethiopia reclaimed Eritrea? Israel to invade Palestine? Anyway, I digress. All I needed to say really was that I do have a list, but it is neither a collection or addiction to be conquered.

Back to Georgia, which we hopefully will do one day as there's at least 2 easily accessible airports to visit. Never mind that it was a fabulous country to travel around. And the best immigration ever. We travelled via Istanbul SAW (Sabina Gokcen) to Tbilisi. Quite an uncomfortable route, involving a 4-hour transit and a 3.30 am arrival, but I don't recall there being a direct service at the time and it meant 2 new airports instead of 1. So, we were queuing for immigration. It was 4.00 am and not only was the immigration officer "serving" us remarkably attractive for that profession but she was smiling. Then, she wasn't the only one! Aggers turned round and was positively beaming, quite unusual for her at that time in the morning. She had a bottle of red wine in her hand! Seriously. I think she thought, momentarily, that this unique, to my knowledge, gesture may not be for every foreigner. No. A couple of minutes later, having received the same warm greeting I also left the area with a bottle of red.

Honestly folks, at least those of you relatively well travelled, please have a think. Have you ever been greeted with a smile at any immigration in the world? OK, so the odd Yank might momentarily forget their role and what is mandatory, i.e. be a grumpy bastard. Even in "The land of smiles", Thailand, they train the natural smile out of them.

Maybe, just maybe, after visiting approximately 190 countries, if you go with Travelers Century, more like 160 if I go with me, I've become cynical about this lot. The "how dare you want to come to my country" and the even less forgivable "how dare you go abroad and want to come home" attitude prevails in my experience.

Once through customs even one of the most annoying taxi drivers I have ever encountered could not dampen our initial enthusiasm. We knew where we wanted to go but he was beyond insistent, and not in a pleasant way, almost somewhat threateningly, that he knew the establishment for us. Clearly he knew the establishment where he was going to earn some extra Lari (brilliant name for a currency). I ended up almost shouting at him to stick to what we, the customers, wished. Unfortunately our first port of call, which to be fair he had warned us would be unsuitable, was just that. Granted it was a hostel but there were literally bodies, and shoes, all over the floor.

He thought he'd got us but we had plan B and we were not going to his plan A, end of. Plan B, admittedly significantly more expensive than his and our plan A, was more on a par with our immigration experience. As the taxi driver literally refused to take us there, we had ended up walking the last part but the young lady on reception may have been related to Miss Immigration 2015. It was 5.30 am but she happily allowed us to check in there and then for the following evening. None of this 1400 check in B.S. The room was empty so, of course, we could go right ahead. "Could we have our breakfast this morning rather than tomorrow morning?". Of course. She didn't even mind us drinking our own wine for breakfast!

I'm sure more intrepid travellers than us (even though many of our friends think we are modern day explorers) would have delighted in navigating their way through the former Soviet Union if permitted. Its collapse had certainly made most of the 'Stans, all the Baltics and those, like Georgia, Armenia etc which don't fit into either of those two categories much more accessible. We loved Georgia and had a bit of a plan. We had booked a night train to Zugdidi to then head into the mountains via Mestia. I had tried to book a flight from Mestia back to Tbilisi before we left. This had to be booked via a tour operator, not direct with the airline, Vanilla Sky - cute name for an airline, eh? Unfortunately the flight was full but we could go on the waitlist.

We were desperately keen to take this flight. Not only because it flew to a different airport on the outskirts of Tbilisi, Natakhtari. It also sounded like a seriously scenic flight and it meant we wouldn't have to take another night train. Not that the sleeper to Zugdidi or the mini bus to Mestia sounded so unpleasant as to make us apprehensive to repeat it in reverse. Consequently, after several months on the waitlist (this trip had been booked way in advance as it was taking place in August peak season) we were over the proverbial moon when, less than a week before our departure from UK, we were confirmed.

Mestia airport is beautifully, no, magnificently located, walking distance, for us, from the town in the valley at approximately 5,000 feet. I've obviously just looked up the elevation and, seeing the pictures of the valley again is why I decided beautiful alone was not an adequate description. I was going to write that the modern terminal was at odds with its surroundings but, again, seeing the picture, that's not enough. As it reminded me it is positively weird. I don't think I'll be having pictures in this book so should probably acknowledge Google and Wiki at some point. Maybe I should say written in conjunction with Google and Wiki. This particular airport really does warrant a look at a picture or two even if, unlike ours, there's no cows wandering around, outside.

Looking back at the pictures of Georgia, it really is a stunning country. Include the food, people, architecture, history - the Stalin museum was fascinating - and the fact that one of the remaining airports is called David the Builder Kutaisi, which is served regularly from Katowice, our local airport for Poland visits, and we have plenty of reasons to return.

The flight from Mestia did not disappoint. At times the mountains seemed so close that you felt you could reach out and touch them if the windows opened! The weather was very kind to us. Apparently another airfield that suffers from regular cancellations due to wind and cloud issues. On top of the fabulous flight, Vanilla Sky provided a limo style transfer for the hour or so journey into downtown Tbilisi, included in the ridiculously cheap price of US$60 each for the flight. When asked for some feedback from the tour operator I suggested that they should really charge a lot more for such an immense experience.

I can't write so glowingly about Armenia because we only saw Yerevan, the capital really. Certainly not an unpleasant city. Clearly we weren't going to return home from Tbilisi so an overnight train to Yerevan with a flight via Vnukovo, the remaining Moscow airport, would take the total for this trip to a healthy 6 new airports. I did question the merits when our scheduled 6-hour transit turned into 9 hours and we couldn't leave the departure lounge. Mind you the fact that the airline in question, Transaero, went bust 2 months later, we probably got off lightly.

Obviously I have digressed somewhat from Chesterfield but there is a chain here, believe it or not. If I don't digress then I'll have to change the title won't I? I've just thought of a circular route to end up back in Chesterfield but I'm not quite there yet. There's a bit of a story about my first visit to Moscow and Sheremetyevo which actually made it into the Croydon Advertiser.......

CHAPTER NINETEEN

February 1983. My first visit to a truly tropical location. First the dilemma of how to get there. KLM would give us a 90% discount on standby to Colombo and back. For the same price Aeroflot would give us confirmed seats. What to do!? USSR was still very much behind the iron curtain but we would only be transiting. Aeroflot had a terrible reputation but we wouldn't get stuck in Moscow like we may in Amsterdam. As we set off for Heathrow we still weren't certain what we would do. Finally we decided the pros and novelty of confirmed seat travel outweighed the cons of flying with Russia's finest.

The rush to get on the plane first at Heathrow surprised us. There were no allocated seats, so we realised soon enough, once on board, the reason for the rush. The first 5 or 6 rows in economy had leg room more associated with business class travel of the time whereas the rest made Dan Air's leg room seem generous. We would make sure we were amongst the first on the next sector. The actual business class seemed to be exclusively reserved for armed military or KGB. The flight from Heathrow to Moscow was uneventful. The Ilyushin IL62 was the closest I would ever get to flying on a VC10. The similarity beginning and ending really with the 4 rear located engines. To my eyes the VC10 was a thing of beauty but I had left it too late to fly on one. What the IL62 did do was run its engines at what seemed full power for what appeared to be an eternity before finally taking off. Again we knew what to expect on the subsequent sectors.

Moscow's Sheremetyevo airport had been newly renovated for the 1980 Olympics so was a very modern affair. The flight to Colombo was via Abu Dhabi, which had, and still has as of Nov '19, one of the nicest ceilings of any airport I've been to. I can still remember the shocking green brightness of the endless rows of coconut trees (slightly more impressive than the shocking green brightness of the Selhurst Park (Crystal Palace FC's home) pitch, although, having mainly watched footy in black and white on TV a 9-year-old me was pretty impressed) as we made our approach into Colombo. Aeroflot? Scary? Piece of cake. We headed to nearby Negombo beach. At that time the prettiest beach I had seen. It went on for miles. We had a private car to take us up to Kandy and on to Sigiriya Rock (site of a Duran Duran video, which had bizarrely influenced first wife, Jackie's choice of destination). It was all very beautiful but was surpassed a few days later as soon as we started our approach on the quick one-hour flight over to Male.

Although I'd not seen anything like Sri Lanka before I felt I knew of it. Maldives I'd never heard of, let alone imagined it. The runway (since lengthened and land reclaimed to vastly increase the size of the terminal) and the tiny terminal took up the whole of one island. Looking around on the approach the colour of the ocean and the tiny specks of Islands were jaw-dropping. The 20-minute boat ride to Embudu was equally captivating. The accommodation and food were very simple. 5-star luxury was a long way off from hitting Maldives. The island, the sand, the Indian Ocean though, were just beyond anything I had imagined. It took about 15-20 minutes to walk around the island which we did several times each day. There wasn't much else to do but admire the sheer unspoilt beauty of our surroundings. One day I was alarmed to see what I thought to be a small oil slick just a few metres from the beach. On closer inspection it was a school of 1000s of tiny black fish. As you walked towards them in knee depth water they spread apart and then encircled you. It was Jackie's birthday while we were there. I was suitably impressed when they produced a cake at breakfast. How did they know? Drrr! They had our passports.

After another few lovely days on the southern beaches of Sri Lanka we headed out to the airport relaxed in the knowledge that we would not be standing by. We had our confirmed seats and we knew the drill with Aeroflot to make our journey as comfortable as possible. We were, therefore, somewhat taken aback when the check in agent told us that we could not travel. As we had not reconfirmed our flights (as was mandatory for normal passengers back then) our reservation had been cancelled. Could he not reinstate it? The problem was the flight from Moscow to London only had one seat left. I think I kind of bullied him into letting us on the flight as far as Moscow. We knew they couldn't leave us stranded there as we had no visa - the whole reason for the flights being confirmed for staff, not standby - so we were unconcerned if we managed to get on this flight.

I had had a bit of a dodgy stomach for the last few days. Nothing serious. The flight to Abu Dhabi passed without incident. Then soon after take-off to Moscow it started. I spent most of the next 5-6 hours in the toilet. I'd never been so sick. When we landed in Moscow I felt I couldn't face the long transit queue without close proximity to a toilet. We informed the crew, who informed the onboard military/KGB who accused me of drinking too much red wine. Right! Finally they agreed to take us to the medical unit. Pretty smart it was too. We had 4 hours until our flight to London. Surprisingly I wasn't sick again and felt ok to continue the journey. Not so fast laddie! I had come from a tropical country so they needed to check what had been the cause of my sickness.

My protests fell on deaf ears. I would be leaving for hospital shortly. What about Jackie? She would be sent to a transit hotel. Could she visit me in hospital? No. Jackie was a little too quick to accept my suggestion that she may as well continue to London for my liking but I didn't blame her.

An ambulance took me to a hospital I knew not where. I was well enough to want to satisfy my curiosity as to what lay behind the iron curtain but the frosted windows made this impossible. I was taken straight from the ambulance into a room with an en-suite. I saw a Nigerian doctor who spoke pidgin English. My understanding from him was that they would take my blood and inject it into a rabbit. If the rabbit survived I could go home. When? 5-6 days! Surely I had misheard him. He said something about cholera. I felt fine, just tired and hungry. The door to the main corridor remained locked, as did the door to the gardens, from which I had entered. I had nothing but the clothes I had arrived in. What the hell was I going to do for 1 or 2 days let alone 5 or 6? This may have been an isolation unit to them but to me it was solitary confinement. Even in pre mobile phone days I had never spent an hour or more doing nothing, let alone a day.

The rest of Friday passed quite quickly. I slept intermittently. My waking hour thoughts were dominated by the fact that I was to miss Carlisle v Leeds the next day. So few new grounds had I done recently that this was a major blow!

There's not much to say about Saturday and Sunday. Apart from inedible meals being delivered I saw nobody, I did nothing. This was a new experience. Doing nothing, saying nothing, listening to nothing. I didn't like it, not one bit. I wasn't scared that I would "disappear". I just wanted something to do and to go home.

By Monday morning I was really hoping I might at least see a doctor. Breakfast came and went, untouched. Then, around midday the exterior door opened. A gentleman entered, motioned to me to get my jacket on and follow him to the ambulance. That was it. My stay was over. The ambulance dropped me kerbside at the terminal. I motioned that I had neither a ticket nor a passport. They kindly escorted me to the Aeroflot office. They had my passport and a boarding pass prepared for a flight at 7pm, in 5 hours. Would they mind awfully to let my family know I would be on the flight. Could I possibly have some food? I had barely eaten for 4 days. They gave me a voucher for the restaurant but let's just say I can't recall feeling that my stomach felt any less empty until I was back in Blighty.

As soon as I boarded the plane the smell hit me. The odour of cheap disinfectant was overpowering to me, so much of it had I inhaled during my time in the bog on the previous flight. Jackie and her dad were at Heathrow to meet me. Clearly the message had got through from Aeroflot. Although Jackie mentioned she wasn't sure if I was coming back as cargo! To be fair to them the whole situation had been handled extremely efficiently, particularly considering I was only a staff passenger to boot. No money changed hands for the hospital stay, so no messy insurance claim needed. On reflection I was pretty well looked after and it wasn't their problem that I spoke no Russian.

One of our friends worked for the local newspaper; Croydon Advertiser and managed to run a story, with picture, of "Croydon boy's Moscow blues". Little more than a year later Jackie and I made it onto the front page of said publication after she had inadvertently disposed of 2 FA Cup final tickets. The headline story was accompanied with a rather flattering picture of her bent over a dustbin whilst receiving a whack on the backside from me! It was still a broadsheet newspaper in those days so it quite dominated the front page.

I have returned 3 times to both Sri Lanka and Maldives and they are certainly still fabulous destinations even if certain aspects have changed considerably, like the size of Male airport and the motorway through the heart of southern Sri Lanka. No great airport opportunities in either but I was delighted to add Gan, an old military airport in southern Maldives and even more delighted when the return flight stopped at Kadhdhoo, another island with an airport. As

I think I mentioned before I don't count the seaplane landings at the Maldives Islands so Gan and Kadhdhoo are quite treasured. Wiki actually shows 17 airports in Maldives but as a recent trip proved they are not always right.

It took me a good few years to return to Russian soil but before we head back to Chesterfield and then to more than we bargained for - I'm sure you've forgotten but I haven't - I'd like to mention one more trip in that direction. I was invited to sample the delights Almaty in Kazakhstan had to offer courtesy of Air Astana. Air Astana would fly us to Almaty. Us being my good friend and then work colleague Greg. I didn't fancy this one without a drinking partner and a very amusing one at that.

I don't like to be too down on ex-Soviet states as they all have something to offer I'm sure and the ones I've been lucky enough to visit certainly do. However, whoever wrote that Almaty was one of the more modern and pleasant cities in the region... well I wonder where they were comparing it to. Ironically our visit was just one month after the first Borat movie. Let's just say his depiction of Kazakhstan was not too unrealistic in our brief experience. The airline was rather archaic and the air hostess seemed unfamiliar with the concept of an after dinner whiskey. On reflection maybe she was familiar and it was tradition to give us half a pint of the stuff each. It was just that she looked bemused firstly at our initial request and then at our reaction when she presented us with the full half pint mugs.

Not wanting to back down from her challenge we proceeded to spend the next few hours drinking said half pint rather than take the more sensible option of grabbing a couple of hours kip. Consequently when we arrived in Almaty the following morning we weren't feeling 100%. The hotel laid on for us was, to put it politely, a dump. And these dudes expected us to return home and promote this place to our customers! We had to request a room change as the numerous bloodstains on the carpet were not helping with our constitutions' efforts to cope with the alcohol, lack of sleep and general demeanour of the place.

We headed down to the breakfast buffet. Were we seriously expected to eat this stuff? It all looked like it had been sitting there untouched since Soviet times. Our guide for the next few days, Rima, came to pick us up for our day tour. She took us to see the highlights of the city and then for some lunch in a yurt. This was also inedible even allowing for some vodka to wash it down. Off we went skiing for a couple of hours. Just what the doctor ordered. Not bad slopes actually but the snow was patchy. We retired to the Irish bar across the road from the hotel for a couple of Irish coffees. Maybe this was the modern element of Almaty.

The following day consisted of some of the more

bizarre hotel site inspections I've experienced. Well, Rima thought they were hotels. In her eyes maybe they were but we would not be selling any of this product. I think many a backpacker would've turned their noses up at what was on offer. We did a little more sightseeing and then were taken to a very pleasant Russian restaurant where the food was actually quite edible. We had an early start home the next morning but decided that it would be best to spend most of the remaining time in the Irish bar as the Irish coffees were excellent.

It's really quite difficult to sleep after about 8 Irish coffees, perhaps some manage it but I didn't, yet remarkably felt ok. Greg was looking a little worse for wear. To be fair to him, in case he reads, he can easily consume a significantly higher amount of beer than I but I seemed to have the edge on him with Irish coffees. Air Astana had kindly given us a ticket to fly back on KLM via Amsterdam. All this way just for one airport?

As we waited in the rather lengthy line up for the KLM flight with Greg looking worse by the minute I ventured "mate? You know I have this airport collection thing going on? Well, would you be awfully offended if I take a different flight and meet you at Heathrow?". "Fill your boots Al. I'll probably be filling mine with sick then going to sleep".

I had sneaked a spare staff ticket into my wallet

to fly back to Heathrow via Ekaterinburg. You see these were and are the lengths I was and am prepared to go to add to the tally. I'd felt slightly guilty even thinking about abandoning my buddy on the way home but when I saw the state of him I figured it may not be such an unreasonable idea after all. No harm done to our friendship. Greg didn't fill his boots with sick but he did fall asleep. I most certainly filled mine and was there waiting for Greg at Heathrow when he finally made it back from Amsterdam. I was lucky enough to be invited to Uzbekistan a few years later. Whilst the airline was on a par with Kazakhstan's flag carrier, what I saw of the country was far more inspiring. I've not seen enough of either to give you a really educated opinion but I would certainly recommend what I saw of Uzbekistan.

I could and maybe should go on to regale you with other stories of the fabulous free trips I was so privileged to experience and the airports that these took me to, but at this rate even I'll forget to return to Chesterfield. So, let's get back to Chesterfield via another little 92 story.

Just to remind you, Steve Crawley is/was Mr 92. He wanted us to go to Chesterfield v Millwall one Tuesday night back in 1982. I was really slow to be adding grounds at this point so figured why not. My little mini was not so keen. Clearly it didn't fancy the return journey since, as we approached the turn off for Chesterfield the temperature gauge burst through the red. I managed to limp it to a lay by on the dual carriageway. I'm no mechanic and I didn't have any breakdown cover. None of this was of any concern to 92. He just wanted to know when the next bus into Chesterfield was. We could sort the car out after the game.

I had no counter argument as I had no idea what we were going to do. I don't remember feeling overly concerned so we abandoned the mini and hopped on a bus to Chesterfield. At some stage 92 must've been thinking of a plan. We had positioned ourselves on the terrace by the players' tunnel on the half way line. At half time as the players came off 92 called out to the Millwall manager "Pete, excuse me, we're Millwall fans and our car has broken down. Any chance of a lift back to London after the game?". Even more surprising than 92's cheeky request was the immediate response from Peter Anderson, the Millwall manager, "yeah, no problem. Meet me at the players' entrance after the game". Not so sure he'd get the same response these days.

Lift sorted I figured I would come back up at the weekend with some help to fix the car and return it to London. It's nigh on 40 years ago so, unsurprisingly, I can't remember exactly why I wasn't comfortable to leave the car on the dual carriageway lay by for 5 days. So, I went ahead on a Millwall supporters' coach to drop me at the lay by, move the car and wait for the team bus to pick me up. Bearing in mind it was gone 10 pm by now I've no idea what possessed me to knock on the door of a nearby farmhouse but I did. "Terribly sorry to bother you but my car won't go more than a mile or so without overheating. Can I leave it on your farm until Sunday when I'll get my mate to come and fix it?". Not a problem. I guess I must've found out that the fan belt was broken at some point.

I trudged back to the lay by and waited for the Millwall team bus to stop and pick me up which it duly did after not too long. All sounds a bit fanciful really doesn't it, but it did happen. Not only that but when we arrived back at the Millwall ground around 2am the manager asked us where we lived and then instructed 2 of his players to give us a lift home. It was only when my driver, Nicky Chatterton, ex Crystal Palace, asked me how long I had followed Millwall that I came clean that I was actually a Leeds fan. He didn't seem to mind, probably because Millwall had won that night and he was part of the Palace team that had a shock FA Cup win at Leeds in 1976, my first ever visit to Elland Road. We did manage to collect the mini on Sunday but not until our farmer/mini minder helped us repair it as well as having offered me 5 days of free parking. Back then the current, general hatred between Millwall and Leeds fans didn't exist. We never played them. Different times, in more than one respect.

Back to modern day Chesterfield, I was a tad

disappointed that we had failed to win the Euro Final v Italy but we were off early the next morning to pick up the Campervan. Only the weather was a downer. So we were in no hurry to start walking. Therefore, having picked up the van we took our time over breakfast in Spoons in Altrincham and Sale before heading across the Pennines to Scarborough. It was truly lashing it down but the forecast was actually for a heatwave in a few days. The Met men weren't wrong. After a dodgy couple of days at the beginning of the Cleveland Way we were blessed with the best possible weather UK can offer.

I would very strongly recommend the Cleveland Way. It's only around 100 miles. It takes you up (or down, depending on which direction you choose, of course) the North Yorkshire Coast from Filey to Saltburn before heading inland to cross the North York Moors and finish in the charming village of Helmsley. We had been to Filey the previous summer as the Yorkshire Wold Way starts/finishes there. It really is a sumptuous (I'm trying to use some alternative descriptions but stunning/ dramatic would really, once more, be more apt) coast line. Whitby and Scarborough are fine towns but the real gems are the villages of Robin Hood's Bay, Staithes and Runswick. I would opine that it's as lovely as anything the South West and Pembrokeshire paths can offer.

There's a couple of Spoons directly on the path

itself in Whitby and Scarborough as well as plenty more not too far off it. When Scarborough had a football league team I managed to get 3 airports in, Norwich, Humberside and Teesside but didn't see too much of Scarborough. We did divert to Middlesbrough to visit the 2 Spoons there for breakfast one morning. Unfortunately this is a town, previously only visited twice for footy, which has very little going for it. Redcar, another Spoons diversion, was similarly lacking but at least it had a beach which provided the bizarre experience of being on the east coast of England but somehow watching the sun set over the sea!

The weather was really so splendid that once we had finished this National Trail we extended the van hire for 4 more days to start the only one we had yet to step on. Well, actually that is not strictly true as the Pennine Bridleway shares 10+ miles of its route with the Pennine Way. So we had already walked 10+ miles of it last year. Or had we? Could we count it as we were walking the Pennine Way at the time? We're not that anal; honestly dear reader. We wouldn't have walked that section again but any nagging doubts over whether we could claim to have walked all of both routes if we didn't do that section twice were dismissed as we couldn't find suitable points either end of it to leave the van and Mazda. It was ultimately going to be quicker to walk it again.

The weather lasted and we continued to enjoy

our breakfasts and evening meals sitting outside the van in glorious locations, when not in a Spoons' garden. We had an opportunity to revel once more in the splendour of the Yorkshire Dales and are seriously looking forward to having a pop at finishing the Pennine Bridleway next year. We know that we won't have the same weather but the scenery is just awesome.

Right. Finally. More than we bargained for. As our return from Greece to UK became more imminent we were keeping an eye on the UK forecast. It actually looked pretty darn good for early October. We knew from our wedding day experience that Stinky Penguin seemed almost as keen as us to do some more of the flying that we had missed out on the day after our wedding. We had arranged a day at the end of July. The weather was so stormy it was a non-starter although Stinky officially didn't call it off until some considerable time after we had already made up our minds that we didn't fancy it.

We had one window of opportunity before we headed off walking and this coincided with Stinky and the plane's availability. We headed off from Shoreham to a mixture of airfields which enabled me to notch up my 900th. Quite a milestone as 800 had been over 2 years previously. There's a good story behind 800 but I'm not going to be sidetracked for once. The 900th will only be memorable for the fact that it was so nondescript.

Henstridge. Never heard of it, but Stinky had. It goes back to that question of what airfields really count but, as I've already addressed it, Henstridge counted. As did the other 12 we managed in a day and a half of flying, as well as 2 Spoons in Worcester, including a night in the hotel.

On our travels, and during planning, I am prone to the occasional "if money was no object" comment. We are happy with how we travel and appreciate our good fortune. However, there are times when either a flight or hotel or both just doesn't seem value for money or fit the budget. Potentially I've failed to appreciate the going rate, having availed myself of so much free or exceedingly reduced travel and accommodation for the best part of 40 years. Yet these days there are some exceptional bargains to be had. For example, we have just flown to Poland for £1.79 each! Proportionally to almost every other commodity air travel seems to get cheaper and cheaper. I have also availed myself of a Megabus from London to Leeds for 50p on more than one occasion. Utterly ridiculous.

Thanks to Couchsurfing you can also find somewhere to lay your head almost anywhere in the world for free if you try hard enough. I'll come back to Couchsurfing shortly as I'm not sure if I've mentioned it yet. Reluctantly, I sometimes have to resign myself to paying more than I wish for a flight, bed or taxi. We have now discovered our "if money was no object" weakness. Yes, it's

Stinky. Well not him exactly you understand, but what he has introduced us to. Of course the initial motivation was airport collecting but it is so much fun flying around at 2000 feet or lower, particularly over ground you're so familiar with.

Stinky flying also takes us to some most interesting airfields that we can't reach by scheduled service: Cotswold/Kemble with all its parked up, out of use, commercial airliners, scenically located Compton Abbas to name a couple. We definitely plan to adopt a couple of "if money was no object" moments with him in the future. There's still plenty of opportunities to add to the collection with him in the south of UK let alone if he joins a flying club in Shrewsbury as he has intimated he will.

"If money was no object" leads me onto our next trip. Having walked, spooned and flown it was time to start avoiding the onset of UK winter.

CHAPTER TWENTY

I'm sure you're wondering if we ever managed to use the American Express/British Airways flight companion voucher that I so, very nearly, managed to screw up in Birmingham back in December 2019. Well, yes we did. As you know, travelling in the early 2020s was a different animal to what we had grown more and more accustomed to over the previous decades. Let's hope it was only the early 2020s but I'm not too confident. Our options were somewhat limited but that did present an opportunity to head for one of the few remaining Caribbean destinations yet to be explored. We weren't totally against the idea of spending a few weeks doing very little on the beach in the warmth even if we would prefer something a little more adventurous ideally. Poor us, eh?

Through a mixture of thinly disguised "business trips" and an early backpacking jaunt I had managed a pretty healthy number of airports in the Caribbean. Yes there were still plenty more in Cuba and the Bahamas in particular to add but in terms of new countries the list was quite thin. Without labouring the point our chosen destination was not a country according to most, apart from our American friends at Century, or whatever they call themselves.

Flights by British Airways were about to resume to Turks & Caicos and this presented the ideal opportunity to use our precious voucher. Well, as those in the know know, it's not that precious is it? But use it we could and did. All it does is save you a bunch of Avios points. I won't get started on one of my pet hates: airline surcharges and taxes. Suffice to say that a "free" return flight to Turks cost £370 each. Still, not a bad price I suppose before you start thinking I really am a moaning, tight old git. I just do not like the way airlines go about their business. Let's just say that I've yet to hear of a fish and chip shop charging a "fish" or for that matter "chip" surcharge. They'll likely charge you extra for a sachet of tartare, fair enough. So why do airlines charge a fuel surcharge amongst others? It's not like the fuel for the plane is an optional extra is it?

I think the main reasons I hadn't been to Turks were that a) it has a reputation for being very, very expensive and b) nobody had offered to take me there! We booked a return ticket for 5 weeks time but our initial research indicated that we may be leaving after 5 days. Our research on Airbnb and booking.com threatened to blow our budget into orbit for just one night. There was virtually nothing which looked slightly enticing on offer for less than £200 per night. There was the odd, very unenticing looking apartment which could potentially be had for £1000 a month. Airbnb actually advertised one apartment for around £150 for a month. It was very clearly a mistake but we decided to book it. I only mention this because of the owner's response once they noticed their error and Airbnb's subsequent offers of "help".

Around 2 weeks after the booking was confirmed the owner indicated that it was our fault that we hadn't brought their cock up to their attention. "How can you possibly think you can stay for a month for £150!?". Well we didn't but we thought it may be a starting point to negotiate a realistic rate. No, the apartment wasn't even ready to rent. Airbnb offered us alternatives in Spain and Morocco!! Seriously, for a man who's trying not to swear, this is pushing all the wrong buttons. I don't think I'm a moron or behave like one but this was, in my humble opinion, a completely moronic response.

Couchsurfing to the rescue. For those not in the know, Couchsurfing is an organisation that links likeminded people to stay for free around the world. Well, that's the theory. In August of 2017 we decided to take advantage of a sadly extremely rare to find nowadays, Air Pass. These used to be very popular back in the 1970/80s (when I had no need for them) a little like a rail pass - unlimited travel for a specific period. Wideroe, Norway's domestic airline offered a pass for travel in July and August, something like 450 euros for 2 weeks unlimited travel. Now Norway has a lot of, very nicely located, airports. I had learnt this nearly 30 years earlier.

Dan Air had quite a long history with Norway. In fact, my first Dan Air flight, another 10 years earlier had been to Bergen. The view from the flight deck into Bergen was stunning and I always wanted to go back to see more of the country despite its renowned expense. Allow me to indulge myself for a moment: Oslo used to have quite a central airport for scheduled services, Fornebu, and another airport, Gardemoen, about 30 miles north for charters. In later years Ryanair decided that Rygge and Torp, 40 and 75 miles south of Oslo respectively, could also count as serving Oslo for them. Not that I'm complaining, obviously, as that's 4 "Oslo" airports for me.

Fornebu closed in 1998, I assume as there was no room to expand it, and Gardemoen became the biggy. Back in 1988 Dan Air had a weekly charter to Gardemoen. As I was on standby I was accepted late for the flight. A delightful young Norwegian girl was running for the flight and we just happened to be seated together. She worked on cruise ships and was going home to visit her father in the north. "Where are you staying in Oslo, Alan?". No idea, of course. "I am staying in my friend's apartment. You are welcome to stay on the sofa". Thanksalot! More than once she came to check on me to see if I was comfortable on aforementioned sofa. What a pussy! Me, not her. I just wasn't cut out for one-night stands. Well, having not tried I didn't know for sure.

Unperturbed by my innocence, naivety, stupidity, chivalry call it what you will my hostess asked the next morning what my plan was. I didn't really have one, only that I was heading north. "Why don't you come and visit me in Stokmarknes? It's really quite nice." Maybe I had another chance to rectify my reticence with this most accommodating young lady. I forget her name. Even if I didn't, which obviously I didn't, no spoiler alert there, at least I could plan out a route, have a bed for a few nights and get on with the important task - airports. I guess the good folk at Wideroe must have let me change whatever tickets I had, if any, as I certainly didn't have a ticket for Stokmarknes. I'd never heard of it. What was so good about Wideroe was that many of their flights were then, and still 30 years later, multi stop routes. Heaven to an airport collector. I won't bore you with the list but my journey to Stokmarknes and back added 15, yes 15 airports to the list. Admittedly, I didn't go the most direct route but still quite impressive.

Being summer there was no night time in Stokmarknes. I don't think that's why we went to bed so late. Let's call her Greta. On reflection I think Greta thought that surely, at some point, I would make a move on her. Truth be told, I am (not that it is relevant any longer) one of those sad blokes who let the fear of rejection get in the way of many a female conquest. In this instance there was maybe a 5% chance that she didn't at least want me to kiss her. I genuinely didn't want to abuse her hospitality. Lame excuse? You decide.

Sorry about that, got a bit sidetracked. Back to the Wideroe airpass some 30 years later. I spent quite literally 3 days planning out a route that would enable us to hit as many airports as possible and see some of Norway from the ground as well as the air. We only had 9 days as leave was too precious back then, for Aggers at least, to use more of it in Norway.

What the hell has all this got to do with Couchsurfing I hear you ask? Bear with. So..... beautiful itinerary planned, 22 new airports for me and 30+ for Aggers on the horizon but what about accommodation? Most likely Turks & Caicos and Norway only have one thing in common: costs! I was so excited about all the airports I hadn't really thought about accommodation costs. "We could camp darling?" Surprisingly Aggers did not dismiss this idea immediately. Au contraire. She likes a bit of research so we were soon the proud owners of a top of the range 2 man tent and sleeping bags. We never did get the mats/pads: way too much choice for a couple of indecisives.

Then it dawned on me. We were, as always,

travelling hand luggage only. We had room for the gear but we had a few early morning departures in our itinerary. How would we get our soaking wet tent into our hand luggage without having soaking wet clothes too? It was obviously going to rain wasn't it. Even if it miraculously didn't I'm sure the tent would have been at best rather damp. I/we hadn't really thought this through. In fact it was only when I ventured to have a trial run in the garden, having not shared a tent together previously, that I realised that camping was not a practical solution.

As a matter of fact we didn't actually do the trial run until 3 years later. It was a complete failure 2 nights running: we ended up back in our bed at 2.30 the first night and only lasted until midnight the second night - cold and uncomfortable. Finally a year later we did use our tent, still no mats. I can proudly say that we camped for 2 nights, quite successfully, on the South West Coast Path.

So, we've got these very cheap flights but this could work out rather expensive in total. When I asked Google about "Cheap accommodation in Norway" one of its answers was "Couchsurfing". Never heard of it but it sounded very interesting if too good to be true. Our second overnight, after a treat in the Hilton Trondheim on arrival at a surprisingly respectable £100, would be in Kirkenes, in the far north on the Russian border. My first Couchsurfing request was an unqualified success. Our host, a Serbian school teacher, Marko, would not only be happy to let us sleep on his couch but he would also pick us up at the airport. Not much going on on a Saturday afternoon in Kirkenes but Marko introduced us to a few of his friends and it was certainly proving a much more satisfying choice than holing up in an expensive, nondescript hotel, let alone camping!

We asked Marko what the deal was, as we were Couchsurfing virgins. He had just cycled from Amsterdam to Budapest and couchsurfed the whole way. He reckoned that it wasn't a bad idea for the surfers to cook for their host. So I treated him to a traditional English roast as best I could. The next morning he took us sightseeing in the surrounding countryside. I think he would have taken us all day if we didn't have a flight to catch, such was his generosity. He told us he was hosting 8 Japanese cyclists the following evening. Where would they sleep I wondered. "Not my problem. They know I have a one bedroom apartment and they're not having my bed."

It just so happened that our Wideroe crew on the flight to Kirkenes were also staying the night and would be on our flight the next afternoon. I only mention this because we got quite chatty with the air hostess. Our flight to Hammerfest would make 5 stops. Heaven! Even if one of them was a repeat from the previous day. When we landed after the first flight the air hostess said the captain wanted to speak with me. What had I done wrong I wondered? (This chain of thought was related to being summoned to the captain's quarters on a cruise ship a couple of years previously and told off, in no uncertain terms - my crime being to slide off the lifeboat being used to shuttle us to shore as my glasses had fallen into the water. This was deemed as a "man overboard" situation, no different from if I'd fallen from the 12th floor of the ship proper! Really!?).

Nothing this time. The air hostess had informed the captain of our travels so he wanted to invite us onto the flight deck for the next few sectors to enjoy the views much better. This was post 9/11. Flight decks were strictly out of bounds for passengers and kept firmly locked in flight. Clearly not up in the Arctic. I had been lucky enough to travel in the flight deck on numerous occasions with Dan Air and other airlines but 9/11 had put paid to that, so it would not only be a novelty for Aggers. We took a couple of turns each. It was a lot of fun. Aggers enjoyed it so much that the next day I asked the air host (never called that I don't think, steward yes) if she could repeat the experience. She could and she did. During a transit in Hammerfest we got talking to another captain and told him how much we were enjoying our Wideroe experience. "What's your next flight?". Quick check on his iPad to see who the captain would be. "Oh, he's a good mate of mine. I'll text him. He'll be happy to have you on the flight deck". And he was. In fact, he was so friendly, he tried to help us with accommodation for the night.

I had booked a flight to Lakselv from Tromso and back. Only problem was it arrived at 11pm and left at 6am. Aggers rightly thought that this was a step too far. I tended to agree. We didn't have any accommodation booked so I challenged Aggers to get help from the captain on the next sector as she would be taking the flight deck seat. If she could get us a bed we would go. If not, one airport less and we would stay the night in Tromso. Unfortunately the crew hotel was full but the delightful captain suggested somewhere nearby to Agnes and said they would drop us off. It just so happened that a couple of young Poles were running this rather bizarre establishment so we didn't get to bed for long but at least we had a lift back to the airport in the morning. The flight to Lakselv was scenic, in the extreme, so we both felt it worthwhile.

Next stop the simply stunning Lofoten Islands. Norway is a fabulously scenic country as you know or imagine but I think this was our favourite spot. After leaving Lofoten we had one more highly enjoyable Couchsurfing experience in Bodo - a single mum with 2 teenage kids, one of whom she shipped off on a sleepover so we could have their bed. Again she picked us up and dropped us at the airport. We would have couchsurfed more in

Norway but our other choices already had guests. We were up and running though and I'm sure I'll treat you to a few other Couchsurfing stories. There's still some very kind, if slightly strange on occasion, folk out there.

We actually managed to find reasonably priced Airbnb for the rest of our Norway trip. It was a wonderful holiday and Aggers had to begrudgingly admit that I had been right to factor in so many airports. The views from the air were simply spectacular. We took a cruise to the fjords the following year and, whilst a completely different experience, it just confirmed what an incredibly beautiful country Norway is.

One issue with Couchsurfing is that information can be quite sketchy. It really depends on how much the member wants to divulge about themselves and their dwellings. There's a lot of drivel to sort through frequently to find a plausible host as there's members on the site who haven't been active for anything up to 10 years. When it works though, it's fab.

Unsurprisingly there weren't so many potential hosts to sift through in Providenciales, Turks and Caicos' main island but not the capital. Provo from now on and T&C, if that's ok. I sent off 3 requests for a couple of nights on arrival. A few days later and Winky Pilgrim; yes we now had Stinky and Winky, came to our rescue. We had a bed for a couple of nights while we acquainted ourselves with any possibilities that may exist for a long-term stay. I'm a firm believer that things will always work out, even if not as you originally planned.

It was difficult to look forward to our trip with any certainty as coupled with taking a Covid test within 2 days prior to arrival we had to prove to T&C authorities that we had, what they deemed, adequate insurance in the event of us needing to be airlifted off the island with Covid. We couldn't do the latter until we had our negative test as we couldn't submit our information without it. We had become accustomed to the uncertainty of travel but, even so, it was quite frustrating to have less than 24 hours' notice that we would be accepted for travel. Most annoyingly I didn't want to risk booking any inter island flights in advance. I know, first world problems blah blah blah.

I'd done my airport research. South Caicos and Grand Turk looked like the only current opportunities. Let's see what the reality would be. In true Couchsurfing tradition Winky, real name Haiden, picked us up at the airport and took us to his humble home. We were his first couchsurfers. He hadn't quite grasped the concept: he gave up his bed to us and took to the couch himself!

Winky was a policeman, originally from St Vincent, and can only be described as one of life's good guys: he got a friend to take us on a tour around Provo, he cooked for us and let us stay an extra night. He would have let us stay longer. He was interesting, thoughtful and it seemed that his current lifestyle did not match his history. We did not wish to outstay our welcome with Winky and, after some pretty extensive research, it was as clear as the gorgeous ocean we were surrounded by that we wouldn't be spending 5 weeks in T&C. We had a potential back up plan in mind before we left UK. Our options were quite limited due to the considerable reduction in inter island flights around the Caribbean compared to pre Covid. At least this made it easier for a couple of indecisives to make a decision.

We wouldn't be coming back to Turks so we needed to tick off those other airports and see a bit more of the islands before we left. In this instance my preconceived perceptions of Turks (sounds better and easier to type than T&C) was fairly accurate: without doubt some of the most beautiful beaches and ocean colours but that was pretty much it. Provo was either touristy, not in Benidorm numbers you understand, or scruffy. It had no soul. It was ridiculously expensive, apart from shared taxis. I openly admit that I can be a bit over conscious price wise at times but I nearly fainted when we went to the local supermarket. Waitrose would put Aldi to shame in comparison. I'm not sure if that makes sense but let's just say that when I saw what the customer in front of us had in her basket for $360 I was scared. When I mentioned to Winky that the supermarket seemed quite expensive (try £1.50 for 1 banana) he said that it was because it was the tourists' supermarket. Well, there was no other supermarket within several miles and the clientele looked 80%+ local. When we stayed with Molly she had a "local" supermarket nearby and the prices seemed the same, just significantly less choice.

Winky's friend, Jacque, who showed us around Provo took us to a local jerk chicken style restaurant for lunch. £8 for 1 piece of chicken! You get the picture. So let's move on. Aggers was very keen to visit North and Middle Caicos. I, less so. Both airports no longer received any flights. She reasoned, with 100% accuracy, that we would never plan to return to Turks so, whether there was a new airport involved or not, we should see as much as we could on our sole visit. It was $55 return each for the 20-minute crossing to North Caicos, similar to a flight to South Caicos or Grand Turk, but this wife of mine is not too demanding and, addictions aside, I was curious to visit. The ferry operator staff advised that they thought there was accommodation for $60 on North Caicos and gave us the details. I was a little taken aback when, on contacting said accommodation, I was quoted $260 for one night. Well, we were hiring a wee car so we could sleep in that for a night if $60 really did become $260, couldn't we darling? I just checked with Aggers and the answer was still an emphatic No!

Off we went to North Caicos. What a contrast to Providenciales. The place was seriously deserted but, by goodness, did it have some of the best beaches I have been lucky enough to see anywhere in the world? Yes. And the colour of the water? Fill your boots son (or daughter, for sexual equality). Simply breathtaking. Although back from the coast the landscape was still uninteresting in the extreme, at least there was no development so it was not messy but as nature intended - barren. We had been met at the ferry (I won't say terminal as it only consisted of a small shelter from the sun and I wouldn't want to create a false impression) by our car hire provider and enquired about a bed for the night. We got the $260 response. I said that we had been told in Provo we could get a room for $60. "No problem, I'll take you there then". I only really mention this because when we arrived at our perfectly adequate $60 lodgings and chatted with the kindly hostess, we learned that the dude trying to get us to part with $260 was her son! Family loyalty eh!? Apparently her son was trying to impress his girlfriend's parents, the owners of the $260 joint.

North Caicos is joined to Middle Caicos by a causeway. It barely seemed possible but Middle was even quieter than North. We met an English teacher and her mother on one of the many deserted beaches. She had 2 pupils in her class.

Don't quote me but I think the population of North is not much more than 1,000 and Middle 100. I wouldn't really recommend Provo: yes the main beach, Grace Bay is pretty decent, but somewhat spoiled by the ugly American chain hotels adorning it. But a visit to North and Middle if you happen to be in the area wouldn't disappoint. Finding yourself a decent gaff at a decent price would be a challenge but if you have savings you'd like to blow and like it quiet then why not? So long as you don't want a choice of eateries and don't mind mozzies.

We couldn't avoid driving past North Caicos and Middle Caicos airports. In fact, we drove down their runways. Could we count them? Don't be silly. In a contradiction of the norm the airports were abandoned once the ferry became available, to our disadvantage. Normally ferries are replaced by flights in my experience. Middle Caicos airport was completely closed but North was still available for private and emergency flights, even though the tiny terminal building was totally derelict. Bizarrely the runway lights were on full beam when we passed by at night.

My duty done - actually I repeatedly thanked Agi for making me go to North and Middle so outstanding were their beaches even if their airports remained elusive - it was time to do a bit of island hopping in the only worthwhile mode of transportation. To my delight, Salt Cay flights had reappeared on the schedule and meant that we could get all 4 of the regular serviced island airports in the basket. Accommodation remained an issue. Inter-island flights were strangely affordable in comparison to everything else in Turks. We had managed to secure a reasonable priced Airbnb in Grand Turk. South Caicos offered nothing so we planned to fly via there from Grand Turk back to Provo. If we wanted to notch all 3 airports we had little choice but to stay in Salt Cay unless we wished to be total heathens and just fly there and back - a practice I'd been guilty of in the past but truly wished to avoid wherever possible. We hit the jackpot of kindness in Salt Cay: nothing appeared on line but a diving club with accommodation. Surely divers liked a bargain bed. Maybe they did but a bargain bed in Salt Cay would set you back $250 + taxes. I explained on email that that was a little out of our price range and that we were essentially backpackers (I left out the fact that we were partial to splurging out on flying). Get this! "Dear Alan, my son has been backpacking round the world for the last year (good effort during Covid) and has experienced some incredible hospitality. On his behalf I'd like to return that hospitality. Please come and be our guests in our humble cottage". Wow, what a result.

Flying from Grand Turk to Salt Cay was our kind of flying and airport collecting. Not that the flight from Provo to Grand Turk was too shabby, but we were the only passengers on the Inter Caribbean Airways Islander flight onwards to Salt Cay. Even the pilot seemed surprised that there was only 2 donkeys and 1 fireman to greet us on arrival. His flight back was apparently empty so what was the point in any staff being there to meet us? The donkeys are left over from the time when the island, funnily enough, produced quite a lot of salt. All but a few of the humans had long gone. It was a quite bizarre place. Our hostess poodled up towards the airport in her golf buggy as we headed towards her. Unnecessary profuse apologies for being late dealt with she took us on a brief island tour - it couldn't be anything but brief even with the most thorough of tour guides - and then showed us to our delightful little gratis cottage.

All seemed quite idyllic, our chancer style of travelling paying off to the max. "There's a slight problem Alan. It doesn't look like the ferry to Grand Turk tomorrow will operate, but don't worry, we'll get you off the island if you really need to, and you're our guest as long as you need to be". There were only 2 flights a week from Salt Cay to Grand Turk so we were relying on the thrice weekly ferry to take us back to Grand Turk from whence we would catch our flight, via South Caicos, back to Provo and hot foot it out of Turks.

It would be wrong to describe Salt Cay as idyllic. For sure it had a fine beach but it all felt a bit run down and derelict. It had been hit by several hurricanes over the years and salt production was a distant memory. The "shops" reminded us, in particular Agi (she clearly had more experience), of Soviet times. It was not lost on us that the sardines were imported from Poland!! I say "shops" because the reality was that a couple of islanders had converted their living rooms into scantily clad convenience stores. Seriously there was barely anything to choose from and, of course, what there was, was prohibitively expensive. Don't get me wrong. Salt Cay had a certain charm but, for us, not one that we wanted to experience for much more than 24 hours. I preferred North and Middle even if their airports were dead. We enjoyed one portion of fish and chips for £30 in the only open restaurant and contemplated our options if the ferry didn't operate in the morning.

It didn't. Our options were limited. It transpired that Karen, our hostess, could not extend her generosity in terms of getting us off the island. Her boat could operate when the government ferry couldn't but it would set us back a tidy $400! Should the ferry operate the following morning we could still make our flight back to Provo via South. The incredibly friendly captain of the ferry, whilst not wishing to crush our optimism completely, indicated that he wasn't too hopeful of setting out any time soon.

We certainly didn't intend to spend $400 for a 20-minute boat ride so it looked like it would be the next flight from Salt Cay for us, in 3 days' time. Whilst doing some research to rebook our flights I came across a flight on the Inter Caribbean Airways from Salt Cay that day and via South Caicos to boot. This was strange as the schedule was only due to operate Monday and Friday.

We weren't too concerned that we were stuck on Salt Cay. There wasn't much point in worrying as, unless we were prepared to fork out for the divers' boat, there was nothing we could do about it. I contacted the airline by email to confirm our rebooking costs as the T&Cs were a bit ambiguous - I've just realised that T&Cs looks very much like T&C, as in Turks & Caicos but to be clear, in this instance I am referring to terms & conditions. May as well have written terms & conditions in the first place. I was shocked to get an almost immediate and helpful response. Getting back to Provo was not really an issue. It was just that in my haste to leave Turks I had already booked our escape flight on Thursday.

If the ferry didn't operate Wednesday morning there wasn't a flight from Grand Turk to Provo on Thursday or Friday that operated via South Caicos. This was the concern. I/we had to come to terms with the fact that we had seen, and would again see, South Caicos airfield from the air but would never be adding it to the collection. It's only one airfield isn't it? Tantalisingly close though. 2000 feet below us to be precise. Ah well, I would just have to add it to the list of disappointments, so close yet so far.

I'm getting slightly ahead of myself as there was still this glimmer of hope with the mysterious appearance of the additional flight on Inter Caribbean Airways' (ICA from now) website. We were hanging out on Karen's dive shop balcony. Not a bad spot but, more importantly, essential for Wi-Fi to sort ourselves out. The place was deserted apart from Francis, the dive shop engineer and odd job chappie. He was from Philippines but had been living on Salt Cay for 20 years. No flight on a Tuesday according to him. ICA confirmed this by email a little later and, another little bit later, the mystery flight mysteriously disappeared from their website. So we had a plan. Hopefully the ferry would operate on Friday and we would reach Provo for an onward flight on Monday. Swings and roundabouts: we would have 3 free nights on Salt Cay but would need to find somewhere for 3 more nights on Provo.

Whilst we were mulling all this over and thinking, as usual, that life could be so much worse and how trivial our "problems" were, we suddenly heard the unmistakable sound of a small aeroplane. We looked up to confirm what our ears had heard and, sure enough, there was an Islander from ICA coming into land. Did the mysterious flight exist after all? "Francis, look!!". "Oh that'll be a private charter" he casually replied. "Well, maybe they might want to take a couple of stowaways. What do you reckon?" "We better be quick as he won't hang around. Let's go see."

The airport was about 20 minutes' walk away, our cottage just a couple. Fortunately Francis had the golf buggy to use. We dropped Agi at the cottage to chuck our gear together in the event we were off and chugged along to the airport. As the small terminal was once again empty I walked out to the plane. The arriving passengers looked a bit bemused but unperturbed I approached the pilot and explained our predicament. Was he flying to Grand Turk? No, Provo. "Could we possibly have a lift? We do have a ticket from Grand Turk tomorrow." A quick phone call to his company, ICA, and yes we could. "Great, thanks. I'll just go and get my wife" "You'll have to be quick" he warned, pointing to a rather large and ominous looking cloud heading our way, "I need to get up and avoid that storm". 5 minutes later we were away and 30 minutes later back in Provo.

Relief was mixed with anti-climax and disappointment. One minute we were chilling by the ocean, contemplating 3 more days on Salt Cay and, quite literally 15 minutes later we were gone. Karen was nowhere to be seen so we didn't even get to say thank you and goodbye in person. Yes we were relieved that we could leave Turks as planned on Thursday but disappointed that we missed out on South Caicos, despite our pleas to the pilot to make an unscheduled stop en route to Provo. We also couldn't convince him to drop us in Grand Turk so heading straight back to Provo was anti-climatic. Although we had visited 3 outer islands I had been keen to visit Grand Turk as it was the capital and, apart from those days when cruise ships visited, apparently a sleepy place. Overall, though it was a funny situation, a good blag and the right decision to seize the unexpected opportunity.

Of course we had to check to see if the ferry operated on Wednesday. It didn't. We were vindicated. We hadn't had time to be indecisive. It did operate on Friday but we would neither have had chance to see Grand Turk nor fly via South Caicos so, if we were in any doubt, we knew we had made the right decision. We had booked an Airbnb with a lady called Molly for our planned overnight on Wednesday close to Provo airport, about an hour walk. When we came back from North Caicos I had contacted Molly, rather than impose on Winky any further, to see if her room was available that night. It wasn't but, no problem, we could have her bedroom and she would stay at a friend's house. There really were some kind folk in Turks.

Molly was originally from Jamaica. They have some strange set ups these Caribbean dudes: Winky had a daughter in Dom Rep, who only spoke Spanish and a son in Haiti, who only spoke French.

Winky only spoke English. Molly had 5 kids, 3 grown up, yet the other 2 younger ones lived in Jamaica and she'd been in Turks 10 years. Molly was new to Airbnb and we were her first overseas guests. On the Sunday night her spare room was occupied by a local. She was quite relieved to have us stay. Where had we heard this before?

Well, one of our stranger Couchsurfing experiences had been back in good old Blighty. We were spending the weekend completing the Cotswold Way but had been unsuccessful in finding anything near to the path for the Saturday overnight under £150. Couchsurfing to the rescue. I contacted a chap called Nigel to enquire if we could stay. We certainly could, although he was away at a conference so it would just be his wife but she would welcome our company. In addition, if we contacted her before 7pm she would come and pick us up from the trail, some 10 miles away. She couldn't come any later as she had her grandniece staying. Fair enough. We did contact her before 7pm. She did come and pick us up with her grandniece and very cute dog. We returned to her 5-bedroom detached house! What on earth were these guys doing on Couchsurfing? Obviously I had to ask.

Our hostess, let's call her Shirley, appeared to be a very shy, even timid, lady. Very pleasant but the little grandniece had more to say for herself. We opted for a Chinese takeaway, which Shirley declined, and a couple of bottles of red plus one for Shirley as a small token of our appreciation. Once grandniece was in bed, Shirley joined us for a glass of wine. She did become a little more talkative and it transpired that their eldest daughter had bullied them into Couchsurfing after her own experiences. Shirley and Nigel had hosted on numerous occasions but never surfed themselves. I have to say that I was somewhat shocked when Shirley said she "was quite relieved to have us stay". Really? "I really don't like to be in the house on my own with my grandniece so I was "quite relieved" when Nigel said you were coming". I wonder if Nigel would have been so eager to respond in the affirmative if I had been a single male traveller? It seemed rather odd to us that Shirley would rather invite 2 complete strangers into her home than spend the night alone with her grandniece.

It's actually rather refreshing to meet people who naturally don't think the worst of people they've never met. The next morning Shirley returned to her shy, timid demeanour (she didn't have far to go to be honest) but did admit to enjoying the evening even if she did have a hangover. She'd had one glass of wine and I thought I was a lightweight! After we'd cooked a hearty breakfast she dropped us back at the trail. I am not one to follow conversations on line which Couchsurfing prompts me to from time to time. However, one particular conversation caught my interest. A female couch surfer had apparently fled in the middle of the night when her host tried to have sex with her. After skipping through a whole host of comments damning the host I came to one who asked the unfortunate girl what she expected. The host's profile said that he only accepted female guests and that they would be expected to sleep in his bed!

Now I'm a bit slow on the uptake, as per my Oslo experience for example, but even I would've worked that one out. The opportunist host couldn't have been clearer unless he'd said "I reserve the right to have sex with you at my discretion" on his profile. I didn't go to the trouble of reading his reviews if he had any. I've never travelled as a solo female traveller, funnily enough, but I'm sure it can be a little more daunting than as a solo male. Probably best not to choose to stay with a guy who openly tells you the sleeping arrangements only include one option and that's not sleeping on the couch, even if he had one.

Maybe if I had been travelling alone I may have been a little concerned with our choice of Couchsurfing in Fort Myers a couple of years back. I admit that I do only tend to think of going down the Couchsurfing route when paid accommodation options do not wet my palate. We had a 6am flight to catch from Fort Myers - I had a devious little route planned to visit our friends in Houston that allowed us to add the secondary airports in Chicago (Midway as opposed to O'Hare), Dallas (Love Field instead of Fort Worth) and Houston (Hobby avoiding George Bush yet again) - but I couldn't find a suitably priced hotel fitting a 4am departure without an expensive taxi ride to the airport. Instead I found Andrea.

Andrea lived 10 minutes from the airport, some distance from downtown Fort Myers, but would happily meet us in town when she finished work and take us back to hers. Andrea was Shirley's opposite: an open book who chatted freely. We met her for a drink and she asked if we minded if a "man friend" joined us. Of course not. On his arrival we moved on for some food. We both noted that the dynamic between Andrea and man friend seemed a little strained and that man friend seemed considerably more interested in her than she him. Once we headed off to Andrea's she told us that she really wasn't sure about this one. Andrea was about my age and, relatively recently divorced, had been trying out several men and not in a monogamous fashion exclusively.

When we got back to Andrea's it was, again, not your typical Couchsurfing pad. Whilst not the most modern home, it was spacious, we had a choice of rooms and it had a large outdoor pool. At this point, Andrea proceeded to divulge that the reason why the atmosphere with her man friend had seemed a tad strained, was due to him learning on their previous date, that she was conducting a physical relationship with her pool maintenance boy, some 30+ years her junior. Now, I'm not prone to bigging myself up but it did cross my mind that, if Aggers had not been there to shield me, would I have been fleeing my accommodation in the middle of the night too? I had checked Andrea's profile and didn't recall any mention of male surfers only who would share her bed but she may have been a little less transparent than that much maligned male character.

Back in the real world, even though that felt a bit surreal as we learned of more of Andrea's recent conquests (do we really lead such sheltered lives!?), we were once again treated to another dollop of human kindness: Andrea simply would not let us arrange a taxi for our early departure but insisted on getting up at 4am, to take us to the airport, even though she had work that day.

Even though this digressing does stretch my limits at times, whilst on the subject of human kindness I must just regale you one other story before we head back to Turks, just to leave pretty much straightaway. On our Norway flying extravaganza we had found what looked an utterly charming Airbnb half way between Forde and Sandane and not far off the route. Furthermore the hostess was called Audrey. I have an ancient aunt called Audrey. She speaks her mind always, is very direct, blunt and regularly quite offensive. So I shouldn't have been surprised when Norway Audrey's reply to our request went along the lines of "don't be so ridiculous. It's way too far off your route. Find something nearer. Goodbye". Now we were intrigued. If her location was correct on Google it was around a 3 hour walk from the main road. It also looked a delightful walk. Agnes, who can also be quite direct, meekly, on this occasion, informed Audrey that we liked walking and that, if it wasn't too much trouble, we would love to come and stay for the night. "Well, if you really insist but I'm telling you it really is too far and won't be worth your while. Have it your way. There's nothing here. You'll have to carry your own food". I kid you not. I'm not exaggerating. Not the exact transcript but that was genuinely the frosty reception our attempt to provide Audrey with some business prompted.

We were so looking forward to meeting Audrey. When we did, after a very enjoyable stomp, the similarity with Auntie Audrey continued: how was your walk? I've left you some food. Please come and visit our museum later. Please let me know if I can do anything to make your stay more comfortable. My husband will give you a lift back to the bus stop in the morning. I did wonder if Audrey just didn't fancy the hassle of one nighters like us so I asked her. She obviously preferred longer stays but that wasn't her reason for her initial lukewarm welcome. She genuinely didn't think we were making a wise choice. We did and we had. The cottage was unbelievably charming, like a big dolls' house. We learned so much from Audrey about their life in the wilderness. It really was in the middle of nowhere and Audrey told us how they had had most of their materials, apart from the natural ones, flown in by helicopter, which could only land some 10 miles away on higher ground. Her and her husband then hauled everything to their home. They were both past retirement age at this stage. It was definitely one of those one night stands we wished had been longer and were very satisfied that Audrey failed in her best attempts to deter us.

Meanwhile, back with Molly, my youngest daughter's name. Are you seeing a pattern here? Well, if you are ever in Turks you will see a lot of Forbes as well. I fear it may be a legacy of slave trading days in this region but there's an awful lot of Forbes about, particularly in the real estate business. Molly, it turned out, didn't have anything to worry about with her other guest: his apartment was being repaired and he needed somewhere to stay for a month. He was checking her out and would indeed be going back for a month.

I had warned Molly that we were stuck in Salt Cay and asked, if necessary, if we could put our booked accommodation back a couple of days if need be. No problem. Also no problem when, not so long after, I let her know we were now back in Provo a day early. She had guests but we could have her sofa. She wanted her bedroom this time. The cheek of it! Molly was not too enamoured with her current guests: a young couple who had not left their room since they arrived only to inform her that the bed was broken. Molly knew it wasn't broken and that they had broken it. I would have probably proudly, if somewhat bashfully, owned up to it. I'm not saying this couple were more chivalrous than I. I might have just been too presumptuous but Molly planted the seed, so to speak. I found it quite odd that the girl left around 10pm not to return. Apparently she had to look after her baby. This was not the sort of business Molly was looking for, she told us.

Molly went over and above what she was obliged to provide us with: breakfast, smoothies, soup, a very nice curry, lifts to and from the airport and 2 extra nights shelter. The latter, whilst not free, as good as by Turks' standards. We were, despite the kindness we had experienced, convinced we were making the right decision to leave Turks after a week rather than five. Not because of the cost. As much as we love the beach, and we really had enjoyed some lovely beach walks, there was no charm or character to keep us there. We'd done 3 of 4 commercial airports and had stumbled across a new one to take us to our next destination.

CHAPTER TWENTY-ONE

You would probably have to be an airport collector to fully appreciate the buzz of finding airports to visit which you never knew existed. I consider my geography knowledge to be reasonable but would suggest it falls into the "jack of all trades, master of none" category. I was planning a little jaunt to Sicily a few years back for my birthday. I had previously flown with Dan Air to Catania and back from Palermo but Ryanair had again opened up more possibilities by flying to Trapani and Comiso. It would have sufficed to tick these 2 off and have a very nice time but, thanks to the folks at Skyscanner I found 2 more airports in Sicily which I'd never heard of.

Maybe I should have been familiar with Lampedusa due to its infamy with being one of the first ports of call for refugees crossing the Mediterranean from Libya, but I wasn't. Neither had I heard of Pantelleria. I didn't know that Sicily was more than its main island. As we couldn't fly to Trapani from UK we flew to Perugia on the mainland (another unexpected addition), took a 4-hour bus ride to Bologna, had some very nice dinner and then flew to Trapani. The next morning we flew to Pantelleria. What a lovely little place. I would opine that it is virtually unknown to all but the most discerning overseas tourists. A bit like some Greek islands it gets a bit busy with domestic tourism in high season but for our visit in June it was blissfully peaceful.

There are no flights between Pantelleria and Lampedusa but there was a convenient connection via Palermo which was another addition for Aggers. Lampedusa was much busier but still very charming. We flew back to Catania, one more catch up for Aggers, and after a delightful birthday stopover nearby, took a bus the next day to Comiso. 5 new airports for me, 8 for Aggers, a much better appreciation of Sicily. Happy birthday Alan!

As well as the thrill of unknown airports there's also an equal amount of euphoria when discovering that a previously visited destination has a new airport such as Paros or, as per following, a city switches its airport uses. I accompanied Aggers on a work trip to Costa Rica. The cheapest flight we could take was via Montreal. I hadn't been there since 1980 when all international flights used Mirabel. I had no reason to think that this had changed. In fact, it was only on the way back to the airport that it even occurred to me to check. Call it sixth sense? Low and behold, the Canadian government had done me a huge favour and switched all flights to Dorval. If they'd still called it Dorval and not named it after

President Trudeau I'd have realised when I booked the flight. Still, I wasn't complaining. 2 new airports planned, in Costa Rica and Nicaragua, the latter a new country too, were now supplemented with an unexpected bonus.

These unexpected bonuses occasionally make a mockery of all the planning. On a holiday to Burma/Myanmar with Aggers some 20 years after my first visit I had been desperately trying to add to the airport collection without compromising our brief visit. Although we started our journey from Yangon with a tidy little multi stopper that added 3 for Aggers and 2 for me the rest of our journey would be by train and boat. Rightly so as both modes are clearly a much better way to see and experience the country than flying. Not so fast though. Call it a sixth sense, again, if you wish or just a feeling that I was being selfish. We could fly from Nyuang U, the gateway for the magical temples of Bagan, to Mandalay from whence we would take a night train to Yangon. Nyuang U would be an addition for me but I had visited Mandalay previously. Sixth sense made me check the distance from Mandalay airport to the city. The airport was nowhere near the city. Not how I remembered it. A quick check on Wiki revealed that a new airport had been opened in 2000. It actually has (or had) the longest runway in South East Asia. The old one certainly didn't! Another unexpected addition.

Similar to football clubs moving to new grounds, bigger players in the airport world have provided opportunities to increase the numbers as well, such as Hong Kong, Bangkok, Kuala Lumpur, Athens, Munich and the aforementioned Berlin, spring to mind. Equally, as previously mentioned Ryanair's preference for redefining what constitutes a city's airport has helped swell my numbers. Oslo, Stockholm, Hamburg, Dusseldorf, Frankfurt, Warsaw, Brussels spring to mind. The latter actually featured in my first holiday with Aggers. I'm not sure too many girls would have eagerly agreed to the following itinerary at the start of a relationship: Eurostar to Brussels (admittedly in first class as an enticement - one can't be expected to remember all life's experiences but I do still remember sitting opposite Agnieszka on the early morning train out of London thinking that it was all quite pleasant), transfer to Charleroi, long wait, then flight to Tangier, overnight, late train to Fez and back to Stansted. 3 nights away in total, 3 new airports. Did we pack some experiences into those 3 days?

Before we get back to where we ended up from Turks and why this particular diversion has manifested itself I'm going to tell you in detail about our visits to Morocco as they all have a story and it's a fabulous country to visit. I had been once before I met Aggers. Dan Air flew regularly to Tangier and Agadir but I had never made it. When

GB Airways announced that they would start flying to Marrakech and that they would like our company to help promote the route I wasn't about to turn down their invitation to visit. As they hadn't started the route they kindly contacted Royal Air Maroc to provide us with tickets. The night before we travelled, Leeds had gallantly fought back from a 3-0 away defeat to Stuttgart, in their long-awaited return to the European Cup, to win the home game 4-1. Obviously this is only relevant to fellow footy fans but it does warrant a mention so bear with. I returned from Elland Road proud that we had redeemed ourselves after a pathetic performance in Germany but ultimately disappointed that we had been knocked out in the first round by the slimmest of margins, away goals.

Somewhat jaded by the long drive back from Leeds I was nonetheless bullish about a new adventure to Marrakech. I only managed 5 new airports, from memory, in following Leeds in Europe, unless I count those visited to get to a game in England as already mentioned. Marrakech would bizarrely remain connected in my brain to Leeds in Europe. Before we get there a quick word about the flight from Heathrow to Marrakech. My ex business partner, (he and his antics warrant a book to themselves), was a character. Not always a nice one but really quite amusing at times. GB Airways had kindly arranged business class travel for us with Royal Air Maroc. Royal Air Maroc kindly had old fashioned style business class seats - the big fat ones no longer seen. On this flight they only had 8 business class seats. We boarded last, or so I thought, took our seats in 2C&D. 1A/B/C/D and 2A&B were empty. Actually, it's easier to say that we were the only passengers in business class, is it not? Not so fast. Just as we thought the doors were about to close 2 passengers joined us. The guy in his shades prompted me to comment to my business partner, let's call him Boris, "look at this dude, thinks he's Mick Jagger". Quick as a flash Boris responded "that's probably because he's with Jerry Hall". He was and he was.

I'm not much into meeting famous people. Back then, 30 years ago, famous people generally earned the right to be well known. Nowadays we have A, B, C and D list celebs, apparently. The last 3 categories, in my humble opinion, generally having zero talent and little merit to be considered celebrity, let alone talented. I'm no huge Mick Jagger or Jerry Hall fan but it is difficult to deny their celebrity status. Sat miserable looking in 2A&B I saw little evidence that they would be interested in engaging in conversation with a couple of strangers. Unperturbed Boris spent the next 3 hours debating with me how he would introduce himself to Mick and Jerry. Finally he came up with his master piece, leant towards them and, more in Mr Jagger's direction, slurred

"Pleasure to meet you man". Mr Jagger, potentially less affected by his rice and water than Boris was by his juicy steak and red wine, beer and whiskies, replied "Pleasure to meet you too man".

That was it. 3 hours in the making. Still I had to give it to him. When I had spotted my all-time boyhood hero, Mr Don Revie (Greatest Leeds United manager for those of you not in the know) at Bahrain airport on a stopover back from Sydney to London I lacked the courage to just say hello and thank you to him. I vowed to redeem myself on arrival at Heathrow but it was too late. He was off like a flash. Opportunity gone forever. At least Boris had had one sentence with one of his heroes.

When we awoke in our hotel room in Marrakech the next morning we had 2 shocking pieces of information. Boris proudly called his girlfriend to tell her who he had met on the flight. Couldn't be so. It was all over the press that Mick and Jerry had gone to Paris to repair their marriage. Ha! We knew differently. This was quite amusing but paled into insignificance when I turned the TV on. We were in a posh hotel and Sky Sports were announcing to the world that Stuttgart had fielded an ineligible substitute. Leeds had a reprieve. They would play a one off replay v Stuttgart, venue TBA. A fine start to our stay in Marrakech indeed. 30 years ago Marrakech had a charm that has since been lost. Add on the fact that our return flight stopped in Casablanca and it was altogether a very successful first visit to Morocco.

An altogether different but far more enjoyable return some 20 years later followed with Agnieszka. Tangier had long had a reputation for being one of the worst destinations in the short haul mass market for hassling tourists. Apparently, in the years preceding our visit, the mayor of Tangier had done a remarkable job in turning this situation around. It mattered little to us: we were there 1 day and confident we could fight off the most persistent of locals. We liked the vibe of Tangier. We holed up in an old but incredibly atmospheric hotel. We went for a wander and the hassle went like this: "good evening, would you like something to eat? Something to drink? Something to smoke? Can I sell you a car? A house?". How could you be offended by such good-natured banter?

After an extremely pleasant day wandering, unpestered, around Tangier we took the train to Fez. What a place! Absolute must visit, despite the lack of alcohol. Our train was late and slow and didn't arrive until 1am. Of course we didn't have anywhere booked to go to bed. I offered Agnieszka the choice of the Ibis near the station or a wander into the old town. "I need a pee but I don't want to stay in an Ibis thanks". We had been dating maybe 4 or 5 months but this involved getting together once a fortnight. On reflection, I think we knew each other much better than I thought at the time.

We certainly had a similar approach to travelling. While Agnes visited the ladies I was approached by a diminutive chap who, at this considerably late hour, wished to assist us in finding somewhere to stay. I asked him if he wouldn't mind awfully not to f*ck me about on this occasion as I had a new girlfriend and didn't want to come across as a bit of a travel dick. He duly obliged.

We wandered into the maze of the old town of Fez. It was bloody fabulous and neither of us was overly concerned that we had nowhere to sleep. He banged on 2 or 3 doors to no avail. "Don't worry Mr Alan, I will find you somewhere to rest with your good lady". He duly obliged again. He threw some stones up at a window which prompted a relatively young chap to come down and open the door to his abode. He asked our man, let's call him Ali as that probably was his name, in broad English "what the devil kind of time do you call this Ali?". "You have room for Mr Alan and his good lady, Mr Mark?". He did. I offered Ali some money for his troubles. He was having none of it. Could we please visit a certain leather shop in the morning? I told him that we would visit but it was extremely unlikely that we would buy anything. Not a problem but please visit. We did but, as promised, we bought nowt.

What an interesting set up Mr Mark's place was. A very simple but stylish Riad. You can look up Riad if you are not familiar. Fez was freezing at night in February but warm during the day and, apparently, unbearably hot in summer. Riads are designed to remain cool in the summer and warm in the winter. Mark's place was not that warm but it certainly didn't lack character and charm. Nor did he. His Moroccan wife was perilously close to being unacceptably young in the eyes of all but the most free living. We spent a day getting lost in the maze that is old Fez. I say it again. What a place. Our flight on the Sunday was not until 8pm. Mark asked if we would like to accompany him and his wife on a visit to a local festival. For sure we would. The festival was taking place a couple of hours away from Fez. It really did provide an insight into local customs with not a tourist in sight. Mark's wife went to a fortune teller and came back with her eyes streaming. Had she had some bad prophecies? Not at all. It was customary for the fortune teller to squirt orange juice into her eyes. We weren't so keen on seeing goats having their throats slit in the street but we are meat eaters, and animals have to die before we eat them, so let's not get all hypocritical.

Mark then did a Campbeltown on us. He completely misjudged the time it would take him to get us to Fez airport. He was/is a tour guide so he probably knew too well how unforgiving Ryanair would be if we missed our flight. We did make it, only just. Security was closed and we had to find someone to let us through to the gate.

Once on board I felt we accomplished an all-time blag. Forget getting an upgrade on BA or whoever to business or first class. We blagged not 1 but 2 free beers each on Ryanair. Courtesy of the steward liking the company I part owned and/or he and Agnes both being Polish.

Some 4 years later we took Mark up on his offer to provide a private guided tour of Morocco. Mark didn't come cheap but he offered us a local guide at half his price. No offence to Mark but why would we pay double to be shown around Morocco by an English man when we could take the same tour with a Moroccan? It was a wonderful week starting in Agadir, merely to tick off another Dan Air destination, and ending in Marrakech via the Sahara and Atlas Mountains. My perception of Morocco when I was at Dan Air was of a cheap bucket and spade destination. What an idiot. Well, in my defence, those Dan Air passengers were going for a cheap bucket and spade holiday. Were they missing out or what? We had a fabulous week.

I was actually going to say that we have since had one other brief visit to Morocco but it actually happened 5 months before. Funny how the memory plays tricks. Aggers had a work trip to Cannes starting on Tuesday so suggested that we have a long weekend in France prior. I could not come up with a plan that included new airports in France but how about this for an alternative? Gatwick to Essaouira. Bus. Rabat to Marseille. I still shock myself occasionally with my determination to feed that airport collecting addiction. Essaouira? Where the hell is that I hear you ask. Just as I did when it popped up on Skyscanner. Clearly a lot of Brits knew where it was as when we boarded the flight, last as usual, it was full. We only paid £25 but as was the case, pre Covid, EasyJet and their pals always seemed to fill their flights.

Like I said - jack of all trades, master of none. That's me when it comes to geography. In case you're interested Essaouira is on the coast, north of Agadir. It actually has a massive, sweeping beach, an interesting old town and a hippy vibe. The latter potentially being why EasyJet could justify flying there. Rabat was mildly interesting as was the journey there. Hats off again to Aggers though. Cannes hosts a luxury travel show. I'm not sure if any of the other exhibitors from the UK, or anywhere else for that matter had travelled, with a small rucksack via Essaouira and Rabat to Cannes. I'm sure Aggers' rucksack is a tardis: somehow she had 3 different posh outfits for daytime and evening wear together with high heels.

Right then. Back to our escape from Turks. Inter Caribbean Airways offered a few international routes but one stood out for me. Santiago in Dominican Republic. I'd already been to Santiago de Compostela, Santiago de Chile and Santiago de Cuba but I had never heard of Santiago de Los Caballeros. Dominican Republic, DR from now, would not have been on our radar when we opted to travel full time but Covid has done some funny things to people. Aggers has been several times with work to Punta Cana. I had been twice before. I asked myself, and Agnes, on numerous occasions during our month there, why I went in 1987. I never came up with an answer, and still haven't.

I had flown long haul solo several times. I had ventured into Europe on my own for a few days. I hadn't set off on my own for 12 days. I know this makes me sound like a wimp but that's how it was. So what possessed me to head off to a Spanish speaking country that I recall knowing precious little about for my first long haul holiday on my own? There were so many other options. It's not like it was going to be an airport extravaganza. It's not like it was straightforward to get to: this was long before DR became an all-inclusive package holiday destination. My plan was to fly to Santo Domingo via New York and back from Puerto Plata via New York again. I can remember standing by for the flight to New York and, for the first time, not really being worried whether I got on or not. I'm just being honest. I was apprehensive about spending 12 days in my own company.

Obviously I did get on, otherwise I didn't go to DR in 1987. I made it to Santo Domingo. I remember little about it apart from my first, and last, experience of trying to change money on the black market, i.e., down a dark alley, being a dismal failure. I lost quite a few of my precious pounds for just a fraction of the pesos I hoped for. I know that I had then gone to the Samana peninsula. I remember the last part of my journey being on the back of a lorry with a bunch of locals for several hours on incredibly poor dirt tracks. I spent a few nights in a small village in a room above a bar adjacent to the most idyllic, deserted beach. It just went on for miles in both directions. I met a Canadian dude on the beach many miles from my village. He introduced me to the concept of all inclusive. This was completely unknown to me (and most of Britain I imagine). Drink and eat whatever and as much as you want? Free cigarettes? What's the catch? I didn't find one then and found out many years later that there wasn't one. At least not for the guests. Canada dude offered me a beer and a packet of fags, the latter I declined, before I made my way back to my little piece of paradise. His resort even had a short runway so that he likely saw nothing of DR bar his hotel, the beach, me and the airport.

What I do remember with absolute 100% clarity is why I returned to DR in 2013. This may have been thinly disguised as a business trip but I had a wrong to right from 26 years earlier. Apart from the fact that I didn't really speak to anybody, except for my brief encounter with aforementioned Canadian man, my first solo trip had been successful until I came to leave DR. I found the evenings especially long and lonely. The bar above which I was staying played very loud music until very late, which was out of keeping with the overall tranquillity of the village. Not speaking Spanish obviously limited my interaction with the friendly locals, unscrupulous money changers in Santo Domingo notwithstanding. Nonetheless I loved the beach and the scenery in general. I was, though, not too disappointed to be heading home. I was not then, and am still not, a loner. I like company although from that trip onwards I became at ease with travelling solo.

I made my way to Puerto Plata airport, not an insignificant journey from Samana Peninsula, for my flight back to New York. To my dismay there were around 30 standby passengers. Names were called for boarding until I was the last man standing. "Sorry we're full". Bugger me sideways. I wasn't expecting that. I'm not sure when the next flight to New York was from Puerto Plata but I doubt I would have taken a 5-hour bus ride back to Santo Domingo and an overnight if there had been one any time soon. Even back then the ball ache of returning to the capital was far outweighed by the disappointment of being at the gate, overlooking the runway but failing to add Puerto Plata to my, then, relatively short list.

So now you know why I returned to Dominican Republic in 2013. The added incentive was also being able to arrive in a new airport in DR - Punta Cana. Unlikely to have even been a pipe dream for the developers back in the 80s, at some point PUJ (I've resisted the temptation to refer to destinations by their 3 letter airport codes but I think it makes sense for DR as we have PUJ and POP - Puerto Plata) became the mega tourist destination for DR. POP feels like it had its heyday back in the last century and, to be fair, was already, and still is a city in its own right with tourism secondary. Conversely PUJ was barely a village before tourism hit in a big way.

Combining PUJ and POP by public transport was a throwback to that first visit and a refreshing change after the all-inclusive hotels which needed visiting to justify the "work" element of the trip: 2 local long distance minibuses, a ferry, an overnight in a backpacker's guest house in Samana and another long distance minibus. All that effort just to tick off POP? Of course not. It was the kind of travel that, despite the discomfort often entailed, is what I love most. That makes me think of 9-hour bus rides from El Nido to Puerto Princesa in Palawan, Philippines, Maputo to Vilanculos, Mozambique and Pokhara to Kathmandu, Nepal all in the name of adding airports and, need I say, seeing more of this wonderful world. Sorry if that sounds a bit name-droppy but I believe that's the first time.

Now I have a dilemma: do I recount 2 more near misses that spring to mind or crack on with DR? I think you know the answer. Well, while I'm in the region (of DR) there's one bizarre airport miss that occurred not so long ago, 8 years roughly. I was invited by St Kitts and Nevis Tourist Board to go and have a look. Their itinerary included a boat ride for the short hop from St Kitts to Nevis. I hadn't visited St Kitts but I had transited so this would be a zero airport addition if I followed their route. You know me well enough by now to know that I would go to some lengths not to remain barren. I set off a good few days before the official trip was due to leave and managed to fit in 2 of the US Virgin Islands, both sides of St Maarten, St Barths and Saba before joining the group.

As one of the main focuses of this book is airport collecting please allow me to go into a little more detail. I flew to St Thomas in US Virgin Islands. Now then, the flight from St Thomas to St Croix is a seaplane service. As it's a scheduled service and both "airports" have 3 letter codes and significantly larger terminals, on land obviously, than many land-based airports on my list I decided that the fact that the "runway" was in the sea wouldn't deter me from adding them to my collection. After all, if you land on the beach in Barra is it that much different? So, for me, that was 4 airports to the collection for those 2 islands as they both have land-based and sea-based airports. May just be unique? Then it was back off to St Maarten and a ferry to Saba in order to visit and tick off the famous Saba airport - reportedly the world's shortest commercial runway. Well it is certainly very short and particularly dramatically located.

It is also on the other side of the island from where the ferry docks so I enjoyed a fabulous walk up and over the island whilst feeding the addiction. The next day it was a ferry to St Barths. Another island easily visited in a day. Whilst not as dramatically located as Saba, the runway ends directly on the beach and has a pretty big hill at the other end. A very cute island but, as you may be aware, pretty much exclusively reserved for the rich and famous. Took a bit of a battering a few years back with hurricane Irma but I believe it's been pretty well repaired. The flight back from St Barths allowed me to notch Grand Case in the French side of St Maarten/St Martin. There is very little tourism there and, consequently, very few flights compared to the Dutch side. I would opine that Grand Case airport is virtually unknown compared to the famous/infamous Princess Juliana airport in the Dutch side.

Many of you will have seen the pictures of jets screaming over the beach with tourists appearing to almost be ducking for cover. Even though the jumbos rarely, if no longer, frequent this airport it's still a pretty exhilarating experience for both take offs and landings. The next day I had a flight booked with LIAT (the notoriously unreliable Caribbean airline) to Nevis where I would join the group from UK. As the saying goes, no smoke without fire, and LIAT have certainly earned their reputation. Not that on any of my previous flights with them I could claim to have suffered any inconvenience. In fact they had certainly helped to swell my numbers in the region.

Now, as this is not so many years ago, what followed is still very clear in my mind. I checked in for Nevis. I had a boarding card for Nevis. The gate showed destination Nevis. I boarded the plane and as we taxied out was welcomed aboard the LIAT flight to Antigua!! I showed the cabin attendant (see how I've modernised my terminology as it's a more modern story?) my boarding card as she passed through the cabin. She looked very puzzled and said she would check with the pilots after take-off. Was I on the wrong plane? No. After take-off she came back to me, "I'm sorry sir this plane is too big to land at Nevis. Please check with the ground staff in Antigua. I think you will have to fly to St Kitts and catch a ferry as we are not flying to Nevis today".

You can imagine how distraught I was, can't you? Not that I had gone to all these other islands just so I could arrive in Nevis. I'd had a great time and ticked off some fascinating airports but I wanted to fly to Nevis. I had a boarding card for Nevis. They announced Nevis at the gate. Why was I the only passenger who expected to go to Nevis, not Antigua? I can only assume nobody else wanted to go to Nevis in the first place. So, a flight to St Kitts and a boat it was. Nevis currently has no scheduled flights. Even if/when it does I'm not sure I'll be making a special trip there just to add Nevis. I've seen the island, and very nice it is, but can only think of Barbuda and Montserrat in the vicinity to add. You never know though.

Just before we head back to DR I have to tell you about another near miss I have since managed to rectify. If for only one reason that the initial trip was quite bizarre. Our business had a very successful year in 1993 so Boris suggested that we have a little end of year trip to celebrate. I could choose where. No need to mention that I would be choosing a new destination. We were off to Guatemala. Well, that was the plan. Back then I had no caution re connecting flights and delays. Consequently we had little or no room for any delay on our flight to Miami via Orlando to catch our connection to Guatemala City. Exceptionally strong headwinds meant that although we left Gatwick on time we arrived around an hour late in Orlando and missed our flight onwards to Miami and then to Guatemala.

Let's just say that Boris and I had slightly differing approaches to alcohol and money. I happily joined him in the drinking, I just didn't do it so regularly. His addictions were somewhat different to mine. Fair play to him though. When we finally landed in Miami it was time to invoke plan B. Our trip was too short to warrant spending a night in Miami. We needed a flight that evening. Rio de Janeiro stood out on the departure board and would seem a natural choice for some fun and games, particularly for one who played as hard as he did. What stood out for me though was La Paz. I hadn't been. He readily agreed which, as I say, fair play to him. We enquired at the desk how much for the tickets. £300 each return. Pretty reasonable I thought for a flight leaving in a few hours. "And first class?" Oh no. Here we go. He wants to blow some more cash. We went to the bar to discuss. He insisted on going back to buy the tickets. £3000 each return! Not how I would choose to spend but it was mainly his business so what could I say.

Of course we fell asleep immediately after take-off so didn't benefit whatsoever from the additional offerings included in the first class cabin. We landed in La Paz early the next morning, feeling somewhat jaded, but, by goodness, did it look bleak. The flight was carrying on to Santa Cruz and we enquired if we could continue there. Before we got the answer the delightful ground staff had convinced us that La Paz wasn't as bleak as we thought. Back then La Paz boasted the title of the highest major commercial airport in the world before the Chinese started banging them out this century. It's dropped to number 5 in that table now but I wouldn't imagine it'll lose its title as the world's highest capital city any time soon.

We didn't have a plan for when we arrived in Guatemala so, of course, we didn't for Bolivia, seeing as we didn't even know we were going there. Young Boris really wasn't your backpacking type. He liked to flash the cash at any given opportunity, so we checked into the Intercontinental hotel in downtown La Paz. 2 hours later we'd checked out! We decided that La Paz wasn't necessarily the place for us, hired a car and set off for Lake Titicaca. If we'd thought that La Paz was a bit gloomy, Copacabana on the shores of Lake Titicaca was a far cry from its namesake in Rio. It would not have been unfair of Boris to complain that he would far rather be sunning himself on Rio's finest.

To be fair, having been back to Lake Titicaca recently, the weather really did cloud my judgement. It was cold, grey and utterly miserable. Not that when the sun is out the lakeside town itself had much to recommend, but the lake and surrounding scenery, of which we saw little back in'93, is as spectacular as you may expect from the world's highest navigable body of water.

We didn't hang around the next morning, having decided to head down to much lower and therefore warmer parts of the country. This required us to pass back through La Paz so we decided to grab a spot of lunch in what looked like a relatively upmarket and safe neighbourhood. Our lunch was indeed quite dignified. Imagine my/our surprise when we returned to our hire car, some kind of hard top Suzuki jeep or similar, to see that the rear door was open and our bags gone. Shit! My 1993 diary was in my bag. It was no use to anyone but me. The poor thing was probably lying in the gutter somewhere, totally abandoned. This was December. A whole year's worth of memories. How would I remember I had a son that year, amongst other milestones!? To be honest, the contents of my bag would've been disappointing in the extreme to the new owners. Boris's on the other hand! Good job I had our passports, tickets and my credit card on my person. Inexplicably, or maybe quite explicably, he had left his wallet, containing approximately $1000 in cash and his credit cards in his bag, which was no longer his. So, basically, we had the clothes we were stood in, our passports, flight tickets and one credit card.

It was Saturday. My credit card could only be used for cash in a bank, none of which would be open until Monday. I had about £5 worth of Bolivianos to my name. Bolivia was very much still a cash society. We continued on our way down towards Santa Cruz, found an establishment where we could sleep, eat, and most importantly - to Boris, and, to be honest, me at this moment in time -

drink on my credit card. We headed back to La Paz the following day, found a hotel that said they would accept my credit card and prepared to head out to the airport the following morning to continue our adventure. Fortunately neither of us were particularly prone to body odour, just as well. I prepared by trying to demonstrate my superior levels of fitness to Boris by running up the world's highest ski slope - after consuming half of a small bottle of whisky. What a dick! I knew I was fitter than him so what was this bravado about?

Once we had descended I started to feel decidedly unwell - a classic mixture of altitude and alcohol. Boris, having more tolerance than me of the latter and not having pushed himself to the limits with the former, was ready for a night out. He found himself a new play friend while I went to our room to vomit. The next morning at check out the receptionist told us that they did not accept credit cards and proceeded to deal with her next customer. Well, we didn't have any cash, so what were we supposed to do? She didn't seem concerned, so we left.

At the airport we withdrew some cash, and, most importantly bought a ticket to Sucre. A new airport. Nothing else mattered. Sucre was, and is, a fine town. After a very pleasant lunch with our new found bundle of cash, we took a taxi to Potosi, some 3 hours away. Obviously we weren't going to fly to Sucre and back, were we? Sucre is located at around 2,800 metres. The midday sun was extremely pleasant. Potosi, on the other hand, is one of the world's highest cities at a tad over 4000 metres. It was anything but pleasant when we arrived early evening - very cold and misty. The taxi ride was notable for the fact that about half way through, I noticed that the driver was sat on the other side to his dashboard of his quite antiquated Toyota Corolla. It's another you had to be there moment, but this chap really did look quite odd, effectively sat in the passenger seat with the steering wheel for company.

If I ever write a book about that part of life I'm afraid it wouldn't all be complimentary. Many good, funny and bizarre times but not a particularly harmonious ending. Still, that book is unlikely to ever materialise so, I would, once again, salute Boris for not once saying that he could have been sunning it in Rio rather than freezing his arse off in Potosi. In addition, the litre bottle of Potosi Pilsner each that we ordered to try and drown our sorrows at ending up in this god forsaken place was really, truly undrinkable. Fear not, we were off the next day back to La Paz and I would have another airport on my list. We headed out to the airport and into the departure lounge. No sign of any plane and, before not too long after the scheduled departure time, our fellow passengers began to leave the airport. Boris's Spanish was as non-existent as mine. Fortunately a kind young lady noticed that we didn't have a clue what was going on. She explained that the flight was cancelled. That much we had gathered, but why and what was the plan was more important to us.

In keeping with that attitude of the time that everything always ran to schedule, even though it occasionally didn't, we had planned to arrive back from Miami on the morning of our first hosting of a big, by our standards, corporate Christmas party. Probably not the wisest move. So here we were, in deepest Bolivia with a flight to catch to Miami in 17 hours. There was no plan other than that maybe there would be a flight to La Paz tomorrow. Apparently the weather was too poor for the aircraft to land at Potosi. This seemed a bit flimsy as, to us, the weather seemed pretty clear. If it wasn't a lame excuse for some other problem, our operational experience told us that maybe it was genuine, and that there was an issue with suitable diversion airfields, weather wise. Whatever, the flight was cancelled and we needed to be in La Paz pronto. We learned from our kind translator that it would take at least 12 hours to reach La Paz by road. There were overnight buses but they would not leave until 6pm and, consequently, not arrive before 6am. Our flight to Miami was 7am.

Our translator, who was studying in USA and spoke perfect English, proceeded to display that kindness that has been a feature of my travels throughout the years. She took us back to her father's house for some lunch and called all the taxi companies she knew until she found one willing to take our $200 for the 350-mile road trip to La Paz. Not a bad price really for a journey of that length. The 12-hour journey actually ended up taking 14 hours. I think it would've taken even longer if we hadn't shared our bottle of whisky with the driver and his co-pilot. We weren't too fresh when we presented ourselves at the American Airlines check in desk but we had paid £3000 for the journey to Miami so I figured we could pretty much dress, and smell, as we pleased.

The disappointment of failing to register Potosi airport on my list, as well as the drive to La Paz mainly being undertaken in the dark, was somewhat offset by adding Santa Cruz to the list and, at least this time being able to appreciate some of the first-class hospitality we had paid for. We bought some fresh clothes in Miami airport, boarded our complimentary Virgin flight to London as planned and the party was a roaring success. No harm done and some karma in Boris spending the morning vomiting between our arrival and the party starting. I, meanwhile, felt pretty bullish in comparison, minus one diary and 3 airports in the bag compared to the one I had planned in Guatemala City.

Almost 400 airports later Potosi was finally added to the list. Not without a little drama and significance. On the grander scale I was able to rectify my less than favourable experience of high-altitude Bolivia. Perhaps, later in this book, or in another one, or more likely never, I will expand on my return to Bolivia. For now, I will merely recount how I returned to Potosi. Agnieszka had expressed her desire to visit Uyuni on our debut adventure after giving up work. Look it up, if you don't know it, which I didn't, and go. It's an absolutely amazing place. Depending on how you reach it so is the journey to get there. We travelled "over" from Chile and it was truly spectacular. But where were we going to go from Uyuni on our way to meet my son and his girlfriend in Peru?

Uyuni does have an airport with commercial flights but, more importantly, to me, it was a mere 3 hours by bus to Potosi. Low and behold there was a cheeky little cheap flight from Potosi to Cochabamba. Cocho where? That didn't really matter. Not only could I scratch a 25 1\2-year itch to conclusion but it just worked out that Potosi could be my 800th airport. A most scenic bus ride from Uyuni to Potosi was followed by a vision of Potosi so different to that of my previous visit that Agnieszka quite rightly wondered where was this shithole I had vividly described to her. Add to that the very tasty Potosi Pilsners we enjoyed and she couldn't be blamed for thinking that I had made it all up.

Some folk say "never go back". Frequently I am inclined to agree but in this instance I'm very glad I did. My opinion of Potosi was so grossly inflated from that miserable experience in 1993 that when we were informed in the tourist office that Potosi airport was actually closed and that we would need to take a bus to Sucre for our flight to Cochabamba I took it in my stride. Aggers seemed more concerned than me. Before I had time to truly fret about this news we had made our way to the airline office where the staff in so many words questioned the sanity of their tourist office contemporaries. Of course the airport was open. It was only closed on the days that there were no flights, in order to continue the runway lengthening works.

Due to the altitude it is indeed a long take off run, even for the smallest of jets. Our little jet was virtually empty so it almost felt like a private, executive flight. It was certainly one of the more spectacular airports for the 800 milestone. If I was religious, which I am 100% not, I would think that there is an airport god looking out for me. Not only did he allow me to right the Potosi wrong but he also commissioned the building of a new airport in Sucre during my 25 year absence. What a fella!

Just before we head back to DR I have to share with you my guilty secret of Cochabamba. We stayed with a most delightful lady, Patricia and her grown up son, Victor through Airbnb. What a lady. She was so elegant, charming, friendly, warm and welcoming. How did I return this hospitality?

Well, in mitigation, I have had a bladder issue for over 35 years. In fact, I could write yet another book about pee and pooh emergencies but I think it may have a very limited audience. After having enjoyed a delightful breakfast with Patricia and Victor we headed out to explore Cochabamba whilst they both went about their daily activities. On our return I was on a 9.9 out of 10 available to me for a pee. Aggers chose this moment to display a complete and unfathomable inability to fit a simple key in a simple lock. Whilst she dithered, I had a split second, pretty much, to make a choice: either wet myself or find somewhere this side of the unlockable door to relieve myself. To my eternal shame I chose the latter.

A couple of large and very conveniently located plant pots by the lift looked like they could do with watering. Nobody was in the vicinity so, yes, don't judge me, but pee I did. I was kind of ok with this until we ventured out again a short while later. To my horror I hadn't previously noticed the numerous screens behind the security desk, displaying CCTV footage by every lift on every floor. I simply could not shift the vision of this being reviewed and some dude being jolted from his slumber by the sight of me watering the plants. I was mortified. On reflection, perhaps I was overthinking this. The footage would likely only be reviewed in the event of a security breach. But I just could not rid the image from my brain of Patricia and/or Victor being grilled by security as to whether they knew this despicable individual relieving himself on the 2nd floor.

Aggers just found my anguish quite amusing. I felt slightly vindicated in my decision as she was still struggling with the key when I returned from my vile deed. She is still in contact with Patricia so I guess the footage has been wiped without anyone being any the wiser. I just had this nagging feeling that, at any moment, Patricia would receive a call from security, which certainly slightly dampened my enjoyment of her ongoing hospitality. Call me shallow but once we arrived at the new Sucre airport I was back on track. And so are we as we finally get back to Dominican Republic and the unexpected new airport.

CHAPTER TWENTY-TWO

Dominican Republic was everything that Turks and Caicos wasn't. Vibrant, alive, colourful, tropical, very noisy, smelly and affordable. And that was just Santiago. A large city in a big valley that I was previously unaware of, even though I must have passed through it many years previously as it is enroute from Puerto Plata (POP) to Santo Domingo (SDQ). Not really much to recommend but for me, to tick off a new airport arriving in a country I had no huge desire to visit for a third time, a start. Let's get the 2 large negatives out of the way. Not unique to DR but this country definitely has its fair share of disgustingly stinky and noisy motorbikes. I am undoubtedly, increasingly less tolerant of the smell of the nauseating fumes from these little fuckers. South East Asia absolutely has more of them but they do not give out the same level of pollution. Number 2, rubbish. Predominantly plastic. For us, it's truly heartbreaking to see the extent of manmade filth littering the most gorgeous of beaches, let alone elsewhere. Thankfully, not every beach we visited was blighted in this way. I know we're only touching the surface of this problem but it is just so sad.

Right, now I've got that out of the way, let's get positive about DR. And there's so much to be positive about. It is so refreshing to discover so many endless miles of beautiful, undeveloped beaches. We hired a car for 2 weeks from Santiago and visited all but the south east of the country. There are currently no domestic scheduled services within DR which, to airport collectors, is a little frustrating, as there's no shortage of airports and airfields. On our tour of the island we tantalised ourselves by driving to both of Samana's airports, Santo Domingo's less visited second airport, Barahona, Caba Rojo and Constanza. Let's set the record straight. DR is a fabulously diverse country with only the Punta Cana region really totally at the mercy of mass tourism. It's a great place to self-drive apart from - moan 3 - speed bumps on steroids. Seriously, I don't know how I managed to return the car some 1200 miles later without a big whole in its undercarriage.

I had actually resigned myself to one new airport and familiarity with 5 airports that would likely never feature in Alan's 1000 - seriously getting ahead of myself there so let's not tempt fate and change that to Alan's 910, even though it doesn't have the same ring to it. Ah, but not so fast. Let us not forget Aggers's positive use of FB. "Hi, does anybody know a pilot who would like to fly us to some airports in DR?" Now, as you know, dear reader, I'm not big on social media but I have already mentioned moments that have been beneficial to us. Aggers had joined a couple of local FB groups due to her urgent need to find a reliable dentist. This had been an unqualified success. Not 30 minutes later we had our Stinky in the Caribbean. It would be reasonable to say that communication wasn't entirely straightforward but after a bit of back and forth, 4 of the 6 aforementioned airports, plus one we'd never heard of were on the radar. And costs negotiated.

I'm afraid our pilot was not as exotic in name as Stinky but Jonathan, the pilot (think Neil the baby from Gavin and Stacey) was our gateway to airport heaven in DR. Now, I'm getting on a bit and, as you may have gathered, there's a few years between Aggers and I, but, bloody hell, Jonathan didn't look old enough to hold a driver's license let alone a pilot's!! On the drive from POP to Santiago he told us that, until recently, it wasn't necessary to pass a driving test, one just purchased a driving license. These days one did take a test but, as he described it, it was pretty elementary. We hoped the same didn't apply to pilots! Jonathan was 20. He bloody owned his own Piper Cherokee. Stinky had to rent one. At least at 20 Jonathan was less likely to have a heart attack than Stinky but he sure as heck didn't have the experience. To be honest, none of this was of any concern to me. We were going to add 5 new airports and it was an unexpected bonus.

What was of more concern to me was the weather. There were some big ass clouds hanging over the hills in Santiago. I thought we may be in the clear as they were to the north and we were heading south. Jonathan had added Angelina Cotui to our itinerary. Angelina who? To be fair this little gem was right up our street. An airstrip used for agricultural purposes. From there we proceeded towards Constanza. By road this was an eventful journey for us. Beware of Google. We had to turn back not once but twice before we reached Constanza. At least in the air we only turned back once. Constanza itself is nothing to write home about but its location is. Hence the problem. There were simply not enough breaks in the cloud for Jonathan to safely negotiate our passage to Constanza. There certainly was a lot of stormy weather around. Naturally we were disappointed but, to his credit, Jonathan had a plan B. We headed off to Samana to tick off both the international and domestic airports there before heading down to Santo Domingo's number 2. 4 instead of 5. Fair play to him. Whilst ideally, we would have loved to follow our initial route to Constanza and on to Barahona and Cabo Rojo the descent into Arroyo Barril (Samana's airport for private flights) and flying over Los Haitses National Park was really truly memorable. We really wanted to see the stunning Las Aguilas beach, adjacent to Cabo Rojo airport, from the air but it wasn't to be. To be fair Los Haitses was more impressive. At one point I feared that we were going to head straight to Santo Domingo, so overall, our early Christmas present to ourselves had been highly rewarding. We landed at La Isabela in Santo Domingo in torrential rain. Any nagging misgivings we still had about not being able to follow our initial route were quickly removed.

The colonial area of Santo Domingo is rather overrated in my opinion. It is a UNESCO World Heritage site but for us, 24 hours was plenty. We had found a little gem of a hostel/hotel in the centre of Puerto Plata, not 200 metres from the coast and even less from the main square. POP was much more to our liking. The Hotel Kevin was quirky and at times it seemed that dogs and cats outnumbered the guests and certainly the staff. At first, we weren't sure if they were allowed into the hotel. It swiftly became apparent that they were also residents. Only problem was it seemed that a couple of the dogs liked to use the hotel as their toilet. Not use the hotel toilet, you understand. On more than one occasion we had to alert the staff that there was pee and pooh from them. There were 4 small dogs and 2 cats. Kevin was spotlessly clean, probably due to enhanced practices because of Covid. Kevin had a rooftop that would probably have been considered out of bounds in most establishments. This worked in our favour as no other guests ventured beyond the third floor, although one of the dogs did a few times. We had a good view of the mountains and sea, sunrise and sunset.

We really did enjoy POP. It was not lost on me that we ended up spending 12 nights in a city where I had already been to the airport twice. Selfless to the last, Aggers left without adding POP to her list. The small city is blessed with some very pleasant beaches within walking distance. It also has around half a dozen or so very acceptable beach bars and restaurants. The main tourist area is a gated community a good hour or two walk from the city so downtown POP retains a very local feel. Admittedly Aggers' dentist appointments did govern the length of our stay but we were not disappointed.

Even Punta Cana, which we had to go to for our rejigged return flight to UK, was a pleasant experience for us and we left DR with very positive vibes. However, the Northern European winter was still not in our plans, apart from visiting family. We were coming up to almost 2 years of trying to travel through the Covid pandemic. Turks and DR was our first long haul trip in just over 18 months. During our brief stay in UK I had planned, and then cancelled a 2-day 10 Spoons tour, I panicked, and turned down an invitation to tick off AFC Wimbledon's new ground - the match was ultimately cancelled due to too many players testing positive for Covid. The days were too short to tackle any of the remaining National Trail miles. Not a great end to 2021 but we had added 31 airports, 125 Spoons and 4 National Trails to our collections. Not a bad return, particularly considering that the first 113 days of the year had been barren on all fronts.

I was as keen as a jar of Coleman's to get 2022 off to a grand old start on the airport front. Even keener for slightly more adventurous travel to be involved than of late, since India. We had a tentative plan in our heads to head for Colombia and this has since materialised. So I'm going into diary mode, a la India, for what is likely to be a fairly lengthy end to this book. If I don't end it soon, it's going to go on and on, isn't it, dear reader?

Colombia was on our radar when we first started full time travelling. Fortunately, no pre departure tests required for triple vaccinated folk like us. One less headache to deal with in 2020s travel. Aggers was off to a good start with our arrival in Bogotá. This baby had bitten the dust for me, not once but twice, almost 35 years ago. Back then, the good old folks at Iberia offered Dan Air staff a £28 service charge fee to travel standby anywhere on their network. Not too shabby. Mind you, it would be fair to say that Iberia's service was fairly.....shabby. Well, I just remember their crew being quite grumpy. No change there in 35 years. What has changed is that their services to South America seem to be non stop now. That first trip went Madrid - San Juan - Bogotá - Lima, with Quito thrown in on the return for good measure. Pretty attractive and convenient for an airport collector.

Lima was under a night curfew on that first trip. I would assume that my Dan Air mate, Steve, and I were blissfully unaware. We certainly couldn't check on gov.uk could we? No airport disappointments on that trip. We had only planned to fly to Cuzco and Trujillo, which we did. Our return flight from Trujillo to Lima was cancelled which did then necessitate a pretty ropey overnight bus journey to ensure we were back in Lima for our flight home. Cuzco and Machu Picchu need no introduction. It would have been grossly selfish of me to try and thwart Aggers's plans to visit in 2019. It didn't cross my mind but I admit to being more than a little anxious as to how crowded and blighted by tourism it would be.

Back in '87 Steve and I did a day trip from Cuzco to Machu Picchu by local train. I don't recall the cost and I'm sure we didn't pre plan anything. Totally different story in 2019: plenty of pre planning required and unlikely to be affordable on Dan Air wages. What I recall on the trip with Steve was that there were very few people but a lot of clouds. Aggers had done her research and, thanks to this, and the weather, I can say that my second visit to Machu Picchu was so much more rewarding than the first. Apologies Steve, but like everything in my eyes, it looks so much more spectacular with the sun and blue sky. We didn't make the 4-day hike.

We took the soft 4-hour version, where the train - the modern tourist version that is - stops in the middle of nowhere to let you off.

I'm sure the guide books explain it slightly differently but our walk brought us to Puerto del Sol, above Machu Picchu (MP). It was anything but a gate to the sun. MP was invisible, shrouded in cloud. There were around 20 or so people gathered at this viewpoint. I've no idea how long they had been there but judging by their reaction, a while. We had been there less than 5 minutes when the clouds started to part until finally they all but disappeared. The view was simply breathtaking and one I hadn't previously enjoyed. Fortunately it was late in the afternoon so all the day trippers had long gone. It would be stretching it to say that we had the place to ourselves until dusk but crowded it was not.

After overnighting in the town of Aguas Caliente which, although totally touristy, is an interesting spot too, we were back up to MP for sunrise. It was only becoming crowded around 4 hours later when it was time for us to leave and catch the train back to Cuzco. I was not only so pleased for Agnes that it had been such a fantastic experience but for myself too. On this occasion don't go back was not the winner. And we had flown to Cuzco from Arequipa, so one new airport for me as well. Should you go to Peru try and make time to visit Colca Canyon, Rainbow Mountain and that side of

Lake Titicaca as well: you won't be disappointed. We certainly weren't.

Before we go "live" to Colombia I'm going to share 2 experiences that spring to mind where going back provided that ultimate disappointment and 2 where I was none the wiser. Firstly, Boracay, Philippines: 1990, a blissful backpackers' paradise. No electricity, no roads, no cars. Boracay 2006, a South Korean and Japanese (amongst others) honeymooners "paradise". Plenty of electricity, plenty of roads and plenty of cars. Add in 1000s of excitable tourists, nightclubs, shopping malls and high(ish) rise hotels and you could rightfully ask why did I go back? Well, the first visit entailed a very circuitous route to Boracay. Why? Because the only place that the Philippines Tourist Office in London recommended, apart from Cebu, was Boracay. Therefore, in my mind that was to be avoided.

After a very long flight to Manila via Frankfurt, Karachi and Bangkok, I had chosen a connecting flight to Bacolod. Of course, I hadn't researched it or planned anything but I had 3 new airports on the list, so far. Free of charge, courtesy of Philippine Airlines. Surely every Philippine island had nice beaches? Well, it would seem not in the case of Bacolod, but what it did have was a very nice gentleman indeed. We, we being second ex-wife to be, met him on the very underwhelming beach we ventured out to the next morning. He was disappointed that we were disappointed in our first sight of his country. He insisted that we simply must go to Boracay. We wouldn't regret it. But how would we get there without flying back to Manila? This wonderful man, doctor by profession, arranged it all. We would catch the ferry that evening to Iloilo, stay at his friend's flat above the chemist shop and his friend would take us for the early morning bus to Kalibo. From there we would cram into a jeepney for the remaining few hours to reach Caticlan and take a boat for the short crossing to Boracay.

On top of all that kindness he insisted that we simply must stay in his friend's guesthouse. Not the right word for simply idyllic cottages, on stilts, directly on the beach. The island was a dream. He wasn't wrong. I was, to dismiss it in the first place. At least Kalibo airport was added before the same 24-hour routing home.

I knew Boracay had changed and no longer would it be the paradise it was. I only had one reason to return: Caticlan airport. This was how most "normal" people reached Boracay 30 years ago, unless they were full on backpackers. The same Philippines Tourist Office who suggested I go to Boracay in 1990 kindly paid for me to return in 2006! 2 years earlier they had facilitated me adding Cebu, El Nido and Puerto Princesa to my collection. They didn't question my choice of routings and I wasn't out of the closet yet. I think they just thought I was a bit odd not sticking to their itineraries. As I mentioned in the last chapter that (8-hour dirt track) bus ride from El Nido to Puerto Princesa was amongst my most memorable, despite the tourist board warning me against it. Obviously I wanted to tick off Puerto Princesa (PP) rather than fly back from El Nido. They couldn't understand why I would do that. Fortunately there was a resort, on an island just off PP which they were keen for me to visit. I was keen because the Sales Manager had the most fantastic name: LEEDS Trumpeta!

Now, if I was a Chelsea or Crystal Palace fan (god forbid) you know what I would have proposed calling a daughter. If I had a boy and was an Everton fan…… maybe there's more examples but why was this Filipino dude called Leeds? I had to meet him to find out, and treasure his business card. His father had actually studied in Leeds in the early 70s and, quite naturally, fell in love with the football club. It would have been a bit weird if he had fallen in love with the city back then. I didn't ask but I wonder if Mr Trumpeta had a nickname. Completely nothing to do with anything but sadly Leeds' resort had suffered a significant downturn in business since 2 guests had been murdered by terrorists. Sadly, I couldn't promise him that I would be sending him customers anytime soon.

When I went back 2 years later the tourist board

only had 1 itinerary on offer that entailed new airports: a combined Davao and Boracay trip. Hence, I bit the bullet in order to add Caticlan. To be honest, the island was so unrecognisable I almost felt I was somewhere new. Yes, the 4-mile beach was intact but that was it. The graffiti on a JCB reading "fuck off Shangri-La" kind of summed up my sentiments. Not against that hotel chain, as they have not only provided me with some very nice beds but also helped me add a few airports along the way, but for the over development of this once beautiful island. I'm sure some of the locals welcomed the changes to their island and their pockets but I doubt all did. Let's face it, if President Duarte felt it necessary to shut the island for 6 months to clean it up that says it all to me. Even if he's not the most stable sounding of leaders.

Cousin Michael, and wife to be, Wendy had decided to escape UK indefinitely and had holed up on Railay Beach in Krabi, Thailand for a couple of winters. I had decided to take cousin Curly, Michael's brother on a visit. So kind were Thai International that they not only provided me with a very comfy free seat for the trip but they did the same for Curly. A couple of years later cousin Michael joined me in the same way on a lightly veiled work trip to Burma, taking in the old Mandalay airport amongst others. Cousin Curly was in no position to question why we flew to Trang to reach Krabi. To be fair to me Krabi airport was not yet open to commercial flights, or if it was, Thai weren't flying there and Phuket airport was a similar distance. For once, the routing was quite easy to justify in order to add a newbie.

This was 1996. Railay beach was reached by a long boat from the tiny hamlet of Ao Nang. There was nothing there apart from the boats and a small guest house. Railay beach was very, very nice but Chicken Island, as it was then called, and maybe still is, was stunning. Crystal clear waters, beautiful sand and we had the place to ourselves, apart from our boat driver. Fast forward 9 years, yes, just 9 years. Ao Nang had turned into your worst nightmare. Unless, of course, you like to diet on MacDonalds, Burger King, KFC etc, shop 'til you drop, ladies of the night, Euro disco trash. I was astounded. I knew it had changed otherwise all the hotel chains wouldn't be there but I was quite astounded by the level. Not since Malia in Crete had I, personally, witnessed such a dramatic change. At least there was a new airport to be had in the form of Krabi. The province itself still has some redeeming features but forget Ao Nang.

I mentioned earlier that "I was none the wiser" on two occasions. To be fair it didn't look as if Syros or Naxos would have changed all that much in 30 years but I had no recollection at all, of visiting either. My diaries tell me otherwise, scant as the detail was back then. At least I knew I hadn't double counted the airports though as boat trips to both are mentioned. It never fails to fascinate me how the brain works in respect of memory, what one does and doesn't remember. I remember fragments of Paros, when I supposedly visited Naxos first. I remember going to Mykonos and Milos, but I certainly can't dredge up a memory of Syros on the same trip. I know I'm not alone in this.

Right, back to Colombia. The "live" moment has been and gone so I'll come back to that a bit later. What is "live" now is planning the flights in Colombia. Well not now exactly, as I'm writing, but what I was doing from 8 until midnight last night and from 4.15 this morning until now. This is what happens if I go into serious travel planning mode. I'm wide awake. I sleep fitfully, dreaming about flight routings amongst the usual weird and, occasionally, wonderful routine stuff, until I see no point in lying there any longer, as I realise I am no longer dreaming about flight routings. I am awake thinking about them. Terrible combination to have had a strong Colombian coffee after dinner last night too. I am wired, as the saying goes. Double wired, to be precise: strong coffee followed by attempting to feed another addiction.

Colombia just has too much choice for an airport collecting addict. I realised this as soon as I started researching. A simple Bogotá to Colombia search on Skyscanner revealed no less than 35 different direct flights to new airports in one day!

Obviously you couldn't do all 35 in one day, but you understand the possibilities this presented. That was just from Bogotá! That didn't include the airlines I subsequently found who didn't feature on Skyscanner! Prices from £9. I'm almost starting to dislike this addiction. I admit I am becoming obsessed with the 1000 target I have set myself. As I get closer to that target I want to factor in combining it with Agi's 500th. She will reach 400 very soon so there will be a little bit of selfless repetition involved for us to peak together. Colombia has everything: beaches, jungle, volcanoes, desert, very high mountains, lakes, colonial cities and towns in abundance, history, good food, friendly people and a reputation/ notoriety not unjustified. It has worked and succeeded in cleaning up the latter. Well, actually, I'm sure many folk still consider Colombia off their radar. UK Gov still warns against all but essential travel to most of the Pacific coast and the borders with Ecuador and Venezuela. That, at least, discounts quite a few of the airports as we don't really want to travel to those regions where our travel insurance will not be valid - any excuse for these insurance companies! Most of the country is considered safe for travel though.

At least in Colombia road distances seem to be very time consuming so there is a small amount of justification in flying. Unlike India there are not so many flights that do not involve starting or going via the 3 main airports and, if they do, the frequencies can be as little as 1 per week. As usual flight prices go up nearer the date of departure. Although some of the main routes can be booked for under £20 the following day. However, I struck the airport collector's jackpot when I found not one but two airlines who offer an air pass. They give you a number of coupons which work out at about £18-20 per flight. Seeing as it's only the routes with the densest frequency where the flight price drops below that, this was dreamy. Too good to be true? Well it was starting to look that way when I actually tried to buy an EasyFly (I like the fact that Stellios tried to ban them from using that name and failed) pass. I won't bore you with the details but suffice to say it was lucky Aggers has a friend in Bogotá who persevered on our behalf and the purchase of 13 flights for 1,550,000 pesos was finally completed.

There is only one restriction with utilising one's pass: one cannot book a flight within 72 hours of buying it. Other than that, even if there are only a few seats left on a flight, selling at let's say, £60-70, one can book them using the pass. Seeing as we had only managed to complete the transaction the day after we had arrived in Bogotá that meant staying there for 3 days before we could book a flight out on the pass. Luckily there were several flights the next day to Santa Marta on the Caribbean coast for £20. Even luckier one of them went via Bucaramanga on the way. We were up and running.

Not that we minded Bogotá. The old colonial city centre had a charm and the funicular up to Monserrate afforded splendid views of the city and surrounding mountains. We had a charming colonial style hotel, virtually in the city centre, with a junior suite for just £18 including a cooked breakfast. We wouldn't have planned to spend long in the capital anyway but the deterrent was the weather. It was like UK spring, or summer for that matter. Our journey to Bogotá had entailed an overnight stop in both Krakow and Madrid. There's only one thing apart from being homeless, hungry etc., etc. worse than cold weather and that's cold weather in warm weather clothing. We were done with freezing our arses off, even though Bogotá was nowhere near as chilly. It did frequently threaten rain as well, which occasionally materialised.

So, we were off to warmer climes. The landing at Bucaramanga airport is described in Lonely Planet as "quite breathtaking". Not that I needed any justification in taking the longer route to Santa Marta. We knew we would have to pick and choose the places we wanted to visit as we only had 5 weeks. Whilst there is lots to see around Bucaramanga the city has nothing to offer and the journey times to points of interest made us choose this as an area we wouldn't visit. The landing, whilst I wouldn't consider it breathtaking was certainly very interesting. I have developed a habit of looking on Wikipedia at the airports we intend to visit. This started because of the new ones I nearly missed out on. That is not relevant here. I'm just turning into an airport anorak. You could rightly argue that I made the transition 40 years ago, but this is a new level for me. I don't care. It interests me and I'm not doing anyone any harm.

Bucaramanga did previously have an airport in the valley in which the city lies. They decided to build a new one up above the city. This involved major levelling work of hills and canyons, some being up to 60 metres deep and took 7 years to build. The airport takes its name from a major battle that was fought on the site in the early 20th century. The old airport had a bad safety record. See I told you it was interesting. I actually recall now that I developed a similar trait in the latter stages of keeping the 92 football grounds current. Not using Wikipedia but a site specifically for those wanting some intricate details of the grounds they would be visiting. Interesting, again, for me.

What also interested me was that the national carrier, Avianca, didn't make any announcements in English. Fair enough? Maybe, maybe not. The landing at Santa Marta was also very interesting. Of course, there are numerous airports located by the sea but this one was very, very adjacent and provided an equally interesting approach. We shared a taxi with a young Colombian, football obsessive. I instantly warmed to him as his English team was Everton and he knew teams outside of the Premier League! We stayed in a delightful hostel on the outskirts of Santa Marta. Our host, Nicholas, was a charming chap. He greeted us with a beer on the rooftop, albeit I've never seen such a small can of beer (Budweiser). Think tonic water size as a mixer for your gin on the plane. Not that I'm being ungrateful. I really didn't know such small cans of beer existed, that's my point. No detail was spared at Nicholas's 7 room gem. He even furnished us with a glass of wine from his wine cellar on our return from dinner. More important was hearing his life story and, the next morning, him sparing the time to find out from EasyFly how we could actually use our airpass.

Santa Marta is a working port but that doesn't stop the Colombians flocking to the small beach located next to the giant Maersk container ships. It looked quite bizarre to us. It's a nicely located city, with a pleasant old centre, backed by mountains. We ventured up to Minca, a small town in the hills. Beautifully located but, it seemed, only existing for foreign tourists/travellers. Not our kind of place but we had our first walk of any note to some waterfalls nearby. Santa Marta was rocking. The end of the Colombian holidays was approaching and the place was heaving. The next day we headed out to Bahia Concha, on the edge of Tayrona National Park. We chose not to pay the £15 entrance fee to go into the National Park because Nicholas warned us it would be busy. Bahia Concha would be a compromise. Officially part of the park but strangely only an entrance fee of £1.

Neither of us had ever queued to enter a beach before. This was surreal. The 15-minute walk down to the beach from the car park was a constant stream of people of all shapes and sizes - the majority of the latter on the large end of the scale choosing to use the mopeds available to ferry them to the beach. We imagined a somewhat horrific sight would greet us at the beach. Not so. Where had all the people in front of us gone? As you may have noticed in the UK, the trend for the vast majority is to walk no further than absolutely necessary to find a spot, no matter how close to others and then to plonk themselves down. The Colombians were no different. Most of the beach was deserted as they all congregated as close as they could to one another. It was a very pleasant bay and we enjoyed a few hours in relative solitude.

We were sad to leave Nicholas and his genuine and kind demeanour but it was time to move on. Tempting as it was to hang around in the fabulous climate of the Caribbean coast there was too much to see in this country to give in to our weather preferences just yet. We had a 2-

hour bus journey to Barranquilla from where we would fly to Medellin. It was a very interesting stretch of coast to travel along. If you look at Google you'll see what I mean. We didn't go into the city as it had nothing of interest apart from hosting the world's second largest carnival after Rio, and hosting Colombia's international football matches. Neither of which were taking place in the 4 hours before our flight left.

Medellin held an added attraction to us: it has 2 airports. We arrived into the international one which, with traffic, is up to an hour and a half from the city. It seemed a much busier, hectic city than Bogotá but our hotel was located in a quiet residential area. We took a "free" walking tour to Commune 13 the following morning. I mentioned earlier about Colombia's notoriety. It's difficult to ignore it if you're of a certain age. Obviously not on a level with Auschwitz or Killing Fields for example but there was a certain level of the macabre in taking a wander to Commune 13. Whatever reservations we had about visiting the most dangerous sector of Medellin were quickly dispelled by our guide. He had grown up in the commune from the age of 2 so knew it at its worst. He explained why Medellin, and Cali, had become the homes of the major cartels, about the different factions that had caused Colombia to be at war with itself for 50 years, and how peace, of a kind, was finally reached. A very worthwhile way to learn more about Colombia and its troubles and how to live through them. The commune itself reminded us of Camden market on a big hill on a Saturday. We had a wander around, away from the tourist streets, something you would have been considered insane to have done just 5 years ago.

The powers of Facebook came in handy again. Agnes had posted a couple of pics of Colombia and the lady who she first stayed with in London commented that, if we were in Medellin, she should contact a Colombian girl who had stayed with her at the same time. Aggers couldn't remember her but made contact nonetheless. Claudia was more than keen to meet up and we spent a really enjoyable late afternoon and early evening seeing Medellin from a locals' perspective. Claudia's husband, Carlos, had also lived in London but had grown up in Medellin in the height of the drugs and guerrilla wars. He said, coming from a middle-class family, living in a well-to-do neighbourhood he was, pretty much, blissfully unaware. The highlight was the local street food in a suburb we would never have thought of going to. It was extremely tasty. Kind of like gourmet pork scratchings with lots of extras.

We had enjoyed our stay in Medellin. The weather had been fairly kind to us, but it was time to put our EasyFly pass into action.

CHAPTER TWENTY-THREE

I think I've already mentioned how much more appealing city/town centre airports are to those out in the yonder. Of course, it is not always possible to stick the airport in the city, but when it is.... For a start, it negates the possibility of the road transport from the airport to the destination costing more than the flight. A few years back Aggers and I took a little weekend trip to France with Ryanair. Dan Air had long had a scheduled service to Clermont Ferrand which I had never made it to. That was to be our return flight. We would land in Brive (even a French friend of Agnes's hadn't heard of it) and take a nice little road trip to CF. We checked the car hire prices before we left. 255 euros for one day with drop off fee! Surely not. We arrived in Brive, went to the car hire and received the same quote! We went to the taxi rank. 50 euros to town! Significantly more than we had paid for the return flights for both of us. We decided to hitch to Brive. Imagine our surprise when the first car to pass us stopped and as we gratefully hopped in, the driver was none other than the lady from the car hire company. You takes your chances and you never know.

We did have to take a bus to CF to get a reasonably priced car but still succeeded in seeing another good portion of France. Other airport collecting, long weekends in France have included Nimes to Beziers, the previously postponed Poitiers to La Rochelle, Angers to Quimper, Bergerac to Limoges and Rodez to Carcassonne. The journeys between airports providing as much enjoyment as the destinations themselves. When I finally hung up my boots at Dan Air I had 3 months to continue using my concessions for some reason. I was desperate to add some airports on the cheap while I could but time was limited with a full-time job and a baby. This resulted in some fairly rushed airport collecting which I'm not so proud of but, while mentioning France, to give you an idea one such trip included Nantes, Lorient, Lourdes, Pau, Biarritz, Bordeaux, Saint Brieuc, Rennes and Le Havre. Three other trips to Sweden, Northern Spain and Switzerland/Germany/Austria were undertaken in the same manic fashion. A lot of airports added in daily numbers only matched in Norway and with Stinky in recent times.

I/we have occasionally come unstuck in the past with lack of research on airport locations. In some instances even if we did feel resigned to using the only option of an expensive taxi this was made distinctly impossible by the lack of any taxi waiting. Things always seem to work out though.

Hitchhiking, walking and local buses usually solve the issue.

Another couple of Dan Air destinations I had failed to notch were finally ticked off in the nick of time. The continuity of the narrative here is Clermont Ferrand, in case you were wondering. I had flown to Tel Aviv with cousin Michael for a few days but the other two airports Dan Air flew to, Ovda and Eilat had eluded me. Neither of us had been particularly impressed with Israel. The people we met were decidedly unfriendly, Tel Aviv failed to impress and although the Dead Sea and Masada certainly did I was in no hurry to return. However, when we were looking at a week away, to escape winter briefly, in the January before our travel time was to become somewhat limitless a return flight with Wizzair to Ovda for £27 most certainly caught my eye. We had added the airports of the lesser-known Canary Islands of La Gomera, El Hierro and La Palma (all well worth a visit in their own right) in previous winters. We didn't feel we could justify the expense of a brief long-haul trip so close to our planned lengthy departure. A quick look to see if we could incorporate Eilat in our plan, which we could, and we were off.

Ovda airport is primarily a military airfield located around 60 kilometres from Eilat. Dan Air used it when they started to fly the Airbus A300 to carry the winter sun seekers to Eilat as Eilat airport was too small for anything above a Boeing 727/100.

Even that required a fuel stop on the way back. Sorry getting a bit technical there. I could only assume that Wizzair had received some funds from the Israeli government to operate these flights at such a low price. It didn't appear to work on the flights we were on as they were both quite empty. Ovda didn't provide much in the way of passenger comfort so I dread to think what it was like for 336 Dan Air passengers in one go. A cheap bus ride was also provided into Eilat for the Wizzair flight.

Eilat was much as I expected - a pretty soulless getaway for Northern Europeans. No need to hang around. We hired a car, which we dropped off in Jerusalem, a few days later after a journey which was really quite inspiring and spectacular in places. Jerusalem was cold and wet, but still a fairly unique and intriguing city. I felt better about Tel Aviv than on my previous visit. Whether it and its inhabitants had changed or me, is debatable. The main attraction of revisiting Tel Aviv was that, unbeknown to me, it had 2 airports! Tel Aviv Dov, walking distance from the city, had occasional flights to Eilat. Everything else went from the main Ben Gurion airport. I was excited. Not only could I finally do Eilat and Ovda but also add a 3rd. We pushed back on time but then pulled back onto stand with a technical problem. Oh no! Please!

I immediately went into panic mode. This could be an all time so close yet so far. I may have been in the departure lounge and even at the gate and failed to fulfil my obligations to myself but I'm pretty sure I had never been on the plane, taxied out, only to then be thwarted in my quest to add one more. We disembarked and the ground staff told us they would have more news in an hour. I convinced myself that this would be that we would be transferred to Ben Gurion where they had a spare aircraft to take us to Eilat. One less airport. Or even worse, that they would stick us on a coach for 4 hours to Eilat. No new airports.

Whilst waiting for an update from the airline we got chatting to a local who told us that, not only was Dov airport due to close imminently to become luxury apartments but, Eilat was going to close even sooner, once the new Ramon airport was ready. It was now or never. Well it was anyway as we didn't have any plans to retrace our steps in the future should we fail. Which we didn't. We had a happy ending. Arkia fixed their plane and we were off. Eilat airport was so central that we had around 15 minutes walk to our hotel. Eilat airport closed 2 months later, as did Ovda to commercial traffic, and Dov 5 months later. That was a first for sure: adding 3 commercial airports in one trip which would all be closed within 5 months. I don't think we will be making a return trip to go to the new Ramon airport. If the border crossings to Egypt and Jordan were simpler, then more likely.

Talking of panic mode when airport adding is

involved leads me nicely back to that "live" moment in Colombia I mentioned earlier. Our first flight with our pass had taken us to Armenia. Nothing of mention in this city but it was genuinely the closest airport, by some distance to our destinations, Salento and the Cocora Valley, both of which justified the nearby airport visit. The former being a classic colonial town in the mountains. We arrived on a Sunday afternoon and, even though the kind chap we had shared a taxi with into the city centre in Armenia had warned us that the traffic would be bad (which it ultimately was not), it being a Sunday, we were totally unprepared for the deluge of folk in the town centre, in particular the street leading to the mirador.

We decided we would take the steps to the mirador early in the morning, as the weather wasn't great anyway, and to reach it would be like taking a stroll down Wembley Way after a sell out match. Aggers had yet again come up trumps with the accommodation so we enjoyed a grand old view from the terrace for a while before venturing out once some of the weekenders had left, queuing to leave the small town.

We had the mirador to ourselves the next morning, in bright sunshine. After a sumptuous breakfast on our terrace we took a ride in one of the lovingly restored "Willy's" Jeeps to the Cocora valley. Now this is a very nice place indeed, if you like walking and nature as we do. We enjoyed a splendid hike initially surrounded by wax trees, Colombia's National tree, some reaching up to 60 metres tall apparently (I wasn't convinced) in open grassland, followed by dense cloud forest following a lovely waterfall back down, crossed several times by very rickety bridges indeed.

By the time we returned the cloud had started to set in so you could no longer see the peaks which surrounded the valley. It was a memorable walk. We spent a pleasant few hours in Salento's main (only) square sampling some, very interesting local (non-alcoholic!) drinks before catching a Willy to Filandia, a bigger version of Salento around 40 minutes away, but worth a visit too.

For some reason I had become a little jumpy about our next flight from Ibague back to Medellin. It was at 4pm the next afternoon. The information I could get on line about buses was sketchy, as was the journey time. It seemed that the journey time was anything from 3-4 hours and that there was no bus between 8.30 and 1100. The latter was definitely too late and for the former we would probably need to spend the night in featureless Armenia rather than Filandia oozing charm. Aggers got to work on line and found a bus at 1000. That was acceptable to me, even though I was still nervy that a 55-mile journey was showing 3 1/2 hours on Google, by car! What kind of road was this!?

Whilst travelling around Northern Thailand by car we had learnt a lesson the hard way. Google showed a route south to Pai, which was significantly shorter than the main route, going almost back to Chiang Mai first, then north again. At some points it only showed this route. I was concerned by the time versus distance, average around 20 miles per hour, but we agreed to risk it, for a biscuit. All was going well until the dirt track we had been following for a good hour or two took a decided turn for the worse. We had a saloon car. The crevasses crossing the dirt track had just become too deep for our mode of transport. We finally gave in and turned around, just 20 miles from Pai, but not before we had crossed two of these crevasses with Aggers directing me from outside the vehicle to avoid getting it trapped, thinking it just may get better.

In our defence we had asked the army patrol if we could pass to Pai in his direction and he indicated that it was indeed possible, or least that is what we understood. We were not only reluctant to turn back because we knew this meant missing out on Pai, as we now had no time to reach it the "real" way. We would have to renegotiate the two massive gaps in the road we had already rather foolhardily, painstakingly bumped over. We felt it was the safer choice. There were two upsides to that story. Firstly, we overnighted in one of the more bizarre lodgings we'd experienced:

quite modern and well-furnished cabins/cottages located in the middle of paddy fields, surrounded by massive Disney characters, within the gardens. The owner was clearly eccentric and we were the only guests. You had to be there, but I was mildly unnerved, and we both, were very amused by the whole experience. Secondly, Pai has an airport, so, one day, maybe we will return.

I say that we had learnt our lesson. In Dominican Republic we had clearly forgotten it in our failed attempts to reach Constanza. I had clearly forgotten it again when assessing only the journey time to Ibague, not the distance. My nervousness was not helped, once we had decided to overnight in Filandia, by the lack of any identifiable bus stop for the morning bus to Armenia. I really am, at times, becoming an old woman, with my travel worries. Fortunately not too often, and generally related to getting to the airport in time. I can think of several occasions over the years where I very, very nearly missed a flight, two of which I related earlier but only one springs to mind when we actually did miss the flight.

Aggers had very opportunely planned a work visit to Romania back in 2014 and I was able to join her. A new country and two new airports! We flew to Cluj Napoca, never heard of it, although since our visit, a little more on the map with the football team's participation in the Champion's League. We hired a car to drive to Piatra Neamt, where Aggers' first meeting would take place. There was nothing memorable about that town but leaving Cluj airport certainly was. It was over 20 years since Romania had finally got rid of their charming dictator, Mr Ceausescu, but I seriously felt we had hired a time machine not a brand-new Dacia. Don't get me wrong it was not unpleasant in the slightest. The airport was not so near the city so was surrounded by countryside. Plenty of horse and carts and very, very old, dilapidated dwellings. It really didn't feel like they had heard of the 21st century yet, or that Old Nic was no longer.

After the meeting we proceeded to Sigisoara. I think I've mentioned Lonely Planet's description: so beautiful it should be arrested. It really was a stunner with great bars and restaurants as well as its history. This was mid-November yet we enjoyed Sunday brunch in warm sunshine on a wonderfully located terrace, with superb sounds to boot. We went for breakfast but stayed so long it became lunch too. Next stop Bucharest. Not without its appeal, but there's better capital cities in Eastern Europe for sure. We were then to drive to Sibiu, another fine town according to LP for our flight home. En route we wanted to go via the Transfagarasan Highway, rated as one of the world's great drives by Top Gear, according to LP. One small problem: it was supposedly closed October to May.

Well, we'll see about that. We hadn't seen much

snow and it still felt mild for the time of year. We figured that even if we got 90% of the way, and then had to turn around, that we still had time to backtrack and take the main highway to Sibiu. Off we went, ignoring the regular road closed signs. As we approached the peak of this mountain pass there was plenty of snow but the road was clear and the views delightful. What's the problem? Well, we soon found out. The road was most definitely closed. Under one of those overhangs (they must have a proper name but it is not known to me) to protect from falling snow and/or rocks the road was simply boarded up. Never seen that before. Ah well, win some, lose a few along the way.

We had plenty of time but less than an hour from Sibiu we were done for. There had been a major accident ahead. We sat motionless for a couple of hours until it was certain that, even if the road cleared, we would miss our flight. Nothing for it but a 3-hour drive back to Bucharest and first flight out the next morning - one of us had work and, after all, it was a work trip for one of us. Our frustration was only mild and, non-existent when we learned that there had been two deaths in the accident.

We didn't need an excuse to return to Romania. We'd loved our brief visit but of course we did go back to Sibiu a year later. It's a great country to fly into one, and out of another, whilst seeing some country as well. We combined Sibiu with Targu Mures and have since been back to Craiova and Timisoara. We also combined Chisinau, Moldova with Iasi. A bizarre journey made even stranger by a day trip to the "country" of Transdniestria, a classic example of the stupidity and politics of world leaders. It's a country recognised by nobody, except maybe the Russians, but they probably think it's part of Russia. Moldova thinks it's theirs but that didn't stop us having to go through full immigration procedures to go there and back. Apparently its citizens have either Ukraine or Moldova passports should they wish to travel. We still have two more trips to finish off the last four remaining commercial airports, that I am aware of, and we will be pleased to return.

OK, so back to the (non) "live" panic moment in Colombia. After a pleasant enough evening in Filandia I was perturbed to be woken by torrential rain. As you may have remembered, I was already a bit jumpy about the day's journey. We had no wet gear and, although our host had assured us that the bus to Armenia started its journey just down the road from us we had seen no sign of any bus activity the previous evening. It was currently not the weather to be wandering around aimlessly in, looking for a potentially imaginary bus stop. First panic over: it stopped raining a couple of hours later. Second panic over: there indeed was a bus waiting down the road. Third panic over: we caught an earlier bus to Ibague at 9.15. I knew I was being a silly old worrier for nothing.

Not so fast. No sooner were we out of town than the traffic ground to a halt. Not only did all the truck drivers have their engines off but they were out of their cabins wandering around chatting. The flight left in 6 hours!!! Actually I didn't think we were screwed. I knew we could sit here for a couple of hours and still likely make our flight. Fourth panic over: the traffic started to move about 20 minutes later and we enjoyed a stunning ride through breath-taking scenery at an understandably leisurely pace. As we approached Ibague it was time for panic five. This was serious now. We had made it to Ibague with loads of time to spare but the city was shrouded in thick, very low cloud. Not conducive to flying in mountainous terrain.

I blame it on Potosi. When that flight was cancelled, supposedly because of weather, it didn't enter my head that the cloud base was too low. This is not the first weather related, airport collecting panic but this one seemed justified. We'd seen nothing to keep us in Ibague so decided to catch a cab out to the airport, figuring we could grab a coffee or something during our 3-hour scheduled wait. The airport was deserted, save for an extraordinary large presence of army. Probably no more than 15 soldiers but there was nobody there and zero facilities. I hate the airports that almost resemble shopping malls but some kind of refreshment offerings are not always unwelcome.

This was no Papa Westray. It was a reasonable sized terminal building but it had nothing. As we had left Ibague the weather looked even worse. I was resigned, Aggers unmoved. She rightly does not join me in my moments of airport collecting worry. Even she though thought that our chances were slim when we started to hear loud claps of thunder not too far away. The time passed swiftly, the weather improved slightly and we all lived happily ever after again. Relax. We were back in Medellin downtown airport in no time. Only problem was that it was really chucking it down. EasyFly did not give us the option to run for cover. Instead they waited nearly half an hour for some umbrellas and then proceeded to offload us in groups of 6 as that was their total umbrella stock. Quite sweet and caring really.

The next morning, after another pleasant evening in Medellin, we were off back down south to Neiva. The purpose of this airport visit justified by the nearby "desert". How anybody could call this a desert was beyond us. Tatacoa desert has almost 30% more rainfall than London! Nonetheless it was a fascinating landscape as were our overnight lodgings. We hitched a ride in the back of a pick-up truck from the nearby town of Villavieja. The tuk tuk drivers in the town square wanted 30,000 pesos and we had been advised to pay 20,000.

We settled on 25,000 but then the dude who had agreed with us seemed to get the hump that we had tried to get cheaper with one of his buddies so refused to take us! We stomped off in a huff. Seriously, these guys would rather sit there and do sweet f.a. than take a fare they had agreed on!? If they were that wealthy they hid it well. Our first unfriendly experience in Colombia.

The "desert" consisted of some weird rock formations, one area being very reddish in colour and a few miles away changing to grey. The ground underfoot was incredibly gooey and soggy. They'd had some of the rain we'd had in Filandia. A fellow traveller told us that the red desert had been closed off the previous day. Our luck was holding out, weatherwise. Our overnight was a very basic affair in the middle of the desert but run by the most friendly of folk and provided a delicious dinner and breakfast. We awoke to a frog by our bed. I wouldn't mention this other than when we went to leave for breakfast I thought the fella, about the size of your average female fist had gone for his. Fortunately when I went to put my shoe on I did so quite gently. It felt a bit squidgy inside. No wonder, froggy clearly liked the smell of my feet and was hiding in my shoe!

After visiting the grey desert that morning we headed off to our next destination, San Augustin, home of Colombia's most important archaeological sites, apparently! It was a full day travelling from 9 until 6 but great scenery as usual. We were, once again, spoiled with our accommodation. Our tactic of selecting accommodation on booking.com then booking at a lower price on arrival did not work in Colombia. We had experienced in Filandia that, if they did not like the price you quoted from booking, having quoted us a significantly higher price, they simply closed booking.com inventory there and then. I mention this because, on arrival the chap in our first choice did the same thing. Not only did he lose two nights business but he did us a huge favour. Bambu hostel was so much nicer than his establishment. The terrace afforded the most delightful views of the surrounding countryside and our room was very, very pleasant.

It was quite grey and miserable when we arrived in San Augustin and the forecast was rubbish. The reality was lovely. The small colonial town is beautifully located and quite peaceful. Partly due to a lack of options and partly because we wanted to walk and enjoy the surroundings, after a pleasant breakfast in the town square we headed off to the main archaeological park. To be honest I was somewhat underwhelmed. I was expecting ruins of the statues in their original places but what we had was more like an outdoor museum, with the statues placed alongside a path and covered. It kind of took away the authenticity of the place for me. Still the surrounding flora and views were lovely and, at the end of the day, sometimes it's all about expectations, as Aggers would say.

We took a hike over to La Chaquira – another archaeological site, but with carvings in the rocks, rather than statues. Well, a carving to be precise! Fortunately, our main motivation to visit this site was for the views of the Rio Magdalena, in the canyon far below us. The views certainly did not disappoint but it was warm, the terrain hilly and a long way for one carving, to heathens like us.

When we awoke on our first morning in San Augustin it was the first time I wondered if I should have allowed more time. If we were to do some serious hiking then yes we should have, but by the afternoon, I felt we had enough time to see the main archaeological site and it seemed that the others were not necessarily worth devoting our precious time to.

The following morning involved a 5-hour minivan ride to Popayan. Agnes had sounded the alarm bells a few days earlier as she had read that the road from San Augustin was often closed because of landslides. It's an 85-mile journey so that equates to a speed of around 17 miles per hour. Not particularly ambitious. We realised that our route needed to cross over one section of the Andes. A fact for you: the Andes in Colombia consists of three separate mountain ranges in parts. Temporarily it seemed that my homework was a failure and that I really needed to pay more attention to transport between the airports I had chosen.

Fortunately Aggers had temporarily assumed the role of ground transportation co-ordinator as well as accommodation provider, via her friend in Cali, so we knew before we arrived in San Augustin that I hadn't screwed up after all. It was a spectacular ride at the start and the finish. The visibility was such up the top of the drive that we were left to imagine what could be seen of the mountains. The immediate terrain was full of cactuses and other flora with no humans to be seen. The road was fine for the first hour, terrible for the middle three hours and fine again for the last hour down to Popayan. Rather than moan about the state of the dirt road, we marvelled at the fact that there was a road of any description to be had.

I allowed myself a few moments of panic and pessimism regarding our flight from Popayan the following morning as we descended through thick cloud to the city. Why would I do anything else?! The airport is fabulously located in the city, right next to the bus terminal, so about a half a mile walk from the old colonial centre. Popayan is rated as second to Cartagena for its colonial architecture. It is certainly a fine city in a lovely location. Views can be enjoyed from three of the nearby hills close to the centre. It's a bit of a shame about the graffiti soiling a lot of the whitewashed buildings. Street art abounds in Colombia in the form of some fantastic murals but sadly, self-centred, meaningless (to all but the vandals who write it) graffiti is all too common.

Jumping down from my high horse our only other negative view on Popayan was the complete lack of eating establishments in the centre. When we asked our hostel receptionist for some recommendations she suggested that the best options were located around the bus station. Really? Not from what we saw on arrival. When pressed she recommended one restaurant nearby. We "enjoyed" cow's tongue and pork cordon bleu. The next morning they enjoyed Aggers and for the next 3 days my stomach also took a distinct disliking to one or the other, both, or the accompanying salad. I couldn't possibly allow Aggers to have this one exclusively could I? Although it seemed so for a good few hours before I caught up in some style.

Regrettably, Agnes's stomach was too unstable for us to walk to the airport, as close as it was, so we jumped in a cab. I had read that work had started on a new terminal due for completion in 2020. I figured Covid had probably put paid to that and it had in some style. We were accommodated in a temporary outdoor shelter prior to going through security. The new structure dwarfed what remained of the old terminal but looked some years off being ready for use.

Obviously my previous day's doom and gloom was unfounded again and we enjoyed another scenic flight back to Medellin from where we caught a bus out to Piedra del Penol, near Guatape, around 2 hours from Medellin. This is a delightful area of man-made lakes created in the 1970s to supply electricity to Medellin, but the main attraction is probably the Piedra - a huge granite rock with 659 steps required to reach the top. Unfortunately we weren't going anywhere near it that afternoon. Aggers was understandably weak from lack of food and her bathroom activities that morning and I was in no state to be further than around 5-10 seconds from the bathroom. Fortunately our view from our lodgings and our room of the rock and the lakes was superb. We hoped that the weather would hold for the morning, my bathroom needs would subside and proceeded to binge on series 4 of Ozark. It's a cracker!

We headed off up the steps as soon as they opened the next morning at 8. Neither of us in ideal nick for the walk up to the steps, let alone the steps themselves. I was spurred on by the need to reach the bathroom I hoped and prayed would materialise at the top. The views from the top were fabulous but I was quite relieved to be back near our bathroom. Having starved myself for over 48 hours my visits were becoming less frequent and I appeared to have some level of control. We headed off to the international airport for our next stop,

San Andres Island.

CHAPTER TWENTY-FOUR

As I said just now, it's all about expectations. I didn't expect much from San Andres. It's quite easy to gauge how busy a place may be by taking into account the number of flights it receives compared to its relative size. I had been keen to visit Northern Cyprus for some time. It's another of those places which smacks of political intrigue. Back in Autumn 2019, Aggers had expressed her wish to have a couple of weeks not doing much, other than creating a platform for her blog. Obviously we wanted somewhere warm with not too many distractions.

Wizz Air came up trumps as usual with a cheap little number to Larnaca. There are still no direct flights to Ercan, the only commercial airport in Northern Cyprus. You have to fly via Turkey and it's not cheap. What is cheap and plentiful is the number of flights from Ercan to multiple different destinations in Turkey, many of which I had not heard of. It was easy to take our pick of where to fly to in Turkey: a Dan Air destination which, to the best of my knowledge, they had only flown to from Berlin, for the Turkish workers, Adana. Before we headed there we had to find a place for Aggers to concentrate.

We took a bus from Larnaca to Nicosia, apparently the only remaining divided capital in the world. Until fairly recently it wasn't possible for tourists to cross from Cyprus to Northern Cyprus but now it was quite straightforward, if weird, to pass from Cypriot/Greek Nicosia to Turkish/Northern Cypriot Nicosia. Let's not get too caught up in the politically correct terminology. Suffice to say, the contrast between them is stark and we know which one we preferred by some distance.

For those of you who have not been to the Cypriot border there is the most bizarre no man's land running from north west to south east, varying in width. In Nicosia it quite literally cuts through buildings in places. It is a simply classic example of how unbelievably stupid man can be. Intriguing nonetheless. Greek Nicosia is full of shops, smart neighbourhoods with not a soul in sight. Not totally unpleasant but the Turkish side, in contrast, is full of life. Kids playing on the streets, people's doors to their homes permanently open and more old buildings to admire than the other side. We needed to find somewhere to relax beachside though.

As we drove north to Kyrenia, a charming port city in its centre, we got the first taste of why there were so many flights every day to Ercan. Miles upon miles of the most unsightly holiday home/timeshare development you could possibly imagine. It was bloody horrible. We drove west from Kyrenia along the coast, nothing of any use to us whatsoever. We drove along the north east coast. The same. My expectations had been quite low, but nowhere near as low as the reality. If there were any nice beaches we never found them until, that is, we reached Golden Beach in the very far north east of the island.

It never ceases to amaze us how people travel and what they expect from their holidays. In our opinion most of the Turkish Cypriot coastline has been brutally destroyed by over development. Yet this is where nearly everyone goes for their holiday off those numerous flights from all parts of Turkey. OK so we are not casino collectors. We don't like shopping, but, praise the lord that other people do, or have been told they will. Golden Beach, currently designated a national park by the Turkish government is a most beautiful 3-mile beach with, quite literally, no development on it and consequently, very few people. There are two very basic accommodations, both consist of around 8 little wooden shacks, one set back from the beach at sea level. The other, Big Beach was located on the hillside above the far north end of the beach and was to be our home for the next 2 weeks.

It was perfect for us. Although 40 euros per night, admittedly including a very substantial breakfast, seemed a bit steep for what amounted to nothing more than a big shed with a bed and toilet, the location was just perfect. Hakan our host from Trabzon, a city we would later visit on our Turkish airport odyssey, had the right balance of socialising with us and leaving us in peace. His two Zimbabwean helpers kept themselves to themselves when not serving. Only the numerous kittens occasionally outstayed their welcome at meal times. However, after they had disappeared for a few days we were happy to have them back and their ever bolder attempts to steal our nosh.

There was a monastery, a mile or so north of Hakan's, which supposedly attracted coach loads of day tripping tourists. We never saw any. We virtually had the place and the beach to ourselves most days. There were a few other guests from time to time but it was exactly what we had been looking for. Apart from one pretty fierce storm we enjoyed virtually unbroken sunshine. If most of Northern Cyprus failed to reach even our very low expectations, Golden Beach far exceeded those we had from reading what LP had to say about it.

Aggers got the platform for her blog up and running. She spent a considerable amount of time on it, in between our double to triple daily beach walks, but I'm sorry to report that she has yet to add to her first article which she penned at Hakan's. My book may be rubbish, but at least I've (nearly) written it. It was still a pipe dream back then so I could spend as long as I wanted to plan our flying around Turkey before we headed off to

South East Asia.

Our departure from Hakan's to Ercan airport was not without incident. Hakan assured us that there was an early morning bus from the nearby (20 minutes by car) village of Dipkarpaz. He took us there with one of his Zimbabwean girls, who didn't say very much, but I think she was off to Famagusta to try and legalise her stay. Hakan dropped us in the deserted village. It was only 6.30 after all. He insisted that there would be a bus at 6.45. There was. Only problem was it was a school bus and quite rightly, we were not welcome. I went for a little wander to see if I could find anyone to ask about the likelihood of a bus for grown-ups appearing anytime soon. Fortunately I bumped into Hakan who, for some unknown reason, was still lurking around the village.

In my brief absence Agnieszka had flagged down an improbable but possible taxi. The only problem with this was that, while she was trying to explain to the driver where she wanted to go, three cheeky school kids hopped in the back. Luckily I returned with Hakan in tow while Agi was, in her own non-confrontational manner, trying to point out to the boys that she had flagged the car down for herself, not for them. Hakan was not quite so discreet. He almost literally pulled the boys out of the back of the ageing Mercedes, shoved us in it, barked some orders to the driver and we were off. As we were about to speed away I shouted to Hakan "cheers,

but where is he taking us and what do we pay?".
"Don't worry, just give him a few euros."

Now, we've all seen the odd dude trying to look cool with his seat laid back as far as possible but this smiler took it to another level. He was virtually horizontal as he tried to break the all-time speed record to we knew not where. Seriously, James Hunt (or Lewis Hamilton if you don't remember F1's coolest) would've been proud of his cornering, particularly the laidback - literally, manner in which he performed his manoeuvres. The fun continued for only around 20 minutes until we passed a minibus and our young driver screeched to a halt and motioned, with a beaming smile, which became even broader when I gave him some money, that we should hail the minibus.

I don't know where the minibus had come from but it certainly hadn't started its journey in Dipkarpaz. I can highly recommend Golden Beach, the old harbour of Kyrenia, Nicosia and Famugusta. It took a while but our expectations of Northern Cyprus had been exceeded. We chose to fly to Gaziantep on the mainland of Turkey as it was around 2-3 hours by bus to Adana. It was a fascinating city and such a contrast to Cyprus. Airbnb got their directions to our accommodation hopelessly wrong so we ended up on an extended tour of the city, still in our Western Europe holiday gear. Agi's attire did not meet with the locals' approval. This was Muslim Turkey far removed from the Mediterranean resorts.

I first went to Turkey in 1986. Prior to that visit I can honestly say that it was the only time I had ever become complacent about travel. I was, momentarily, starting to believe those Dan Air colleagues and other friends who opined that I'd seen everything the world had to offer. What a load of bollocks! 35 years later and there is still so much to discover. Back in '86 cousin Michael had packed in his job and was spending a few months in Turkey with his friend, Simeon Jupp.

Whilst I wasn't over the moon that my marriage to Jackie had ended, one huge positive was that I could really take advantage of the ludicrous amount of holidays I had at Dan Air. My original book notes (see epilogue) state that I spent 108 days overseas in 1986 whilst in full time employment and only 160 days at work (compared to most folks' 220-230 minimum). I've no idea why this is the only year that I mentioned these totals, to myself. Maybe because it was my first year without Jackie's 4 weeks holiday restriction? There have been many barren years where my new airport total was in single figures, reaching an all-time low of 3 in 2000. Disgraceful, or maybe an effort to become teetotal and free of my addictions. I very much doubt that!

Back to 1986. It was a bumper year. I had finally

reached the hallowed 92 club, taking in 5 new airports for the last ground, Blackpool, which I believe I may have mentioned. I had already visited India, USA and Mexico, learnt, belatedly to ski, getting in 2 new airports in the process, taken 5 trips to Greek islands, with 2 to follow, and Calvi in Corsica – one of my favourite airports up until then, providing a particularly memorable flight deck landing. Michael was going to be in Kusadasi, a resort town favoured by Germans, when I planned to arrive.

It's so interesting to reminisce how we managed to make arrangements pre mobile phones and email etc. Quite how I managed to contact Michael to advise him of my intended arrival I do not recall. I imagine I would have told him I intended to join them and maybe a rough date, before they left UK. I vaguely remember a phone-call to him at Dan Air's expense one night shift. I remember asking him if they would be kind enough to stay put for a couple of days so I could hook up with them.

Back then Air Europe provided a fortnightly flight to Dalaman from Gatwick. Bodrum airport didn't even exist. Turkey was in its very infancy of welcoming British holiday makers. Dan Air was still only interested in Turkey as a repatriation route for Turkish workers in Berlin. I managed to cover the 250 kilometres by bus that same evening and successfully met up with cousin Michael and Simeon. Highlights, that quickly made me realise how wrong those who had tried to convince me that I had seen the world were, included Pamukkale and Cappadocia. Yet to be discovered by hordes of Chinese, the latter in particular, was unlike anything I had previously witnessed.

I thoroughly enjoyed that first visit to Turkey, which also included my first taste of Istanbul. My return journey involved a Turkish workers' flight from Izmir to Berlin, a fisherman's charter from there to Shannon, a bus to Dublin and a flight to Heathrow. Michael and I returned for a long weekend to Olu Deniz, a couple of years later, just before mass tourism got the better of it, ticking off the new Izmir (me, not him) airport on our return. The previous year I had flown to Istanbul, onwards to Ankara and was on a bus to Antalya, all before my night shift at Dan Air had officially finished. This was how much fun could be had "working" for Dan Air. In fact, I was planning to fly to Istanbul in the morning once my shift had finished. My friend and supervisor for that night shift; John Dixon, had other ideas. He'd seen I had come in with a small bag and asked me where I was going. He then proceeded to tell me there was a flight in an hour, one hour into my shift, to Istanbul with Orion Airways and why didn't I catch that. He even phoned Orion to ask them to accept my Dan Air ticket!

Turkey was a fabulous place to travel around in the late 80s. It still was in 2019, if you avoided

ALAN FORBES

the Mediterranean coast. Domestic flying was at a level I could only have dreamt of 30+ years previously. My only experience of Turkey that was so terribly negative was the murder of the 2 Leeds fans prior to our UEFA Cup semi-final in 2000. I didn't know the 2 guys but the lack of remorse from the Turkish in general, and in particular the Galatasaray fans, beggared belief. Me and my mate Rob did manage to escape our hotel through the kitchen so we could spend the day in Istanbul, rather than in our hotel room. It was impossible though to enjoy the city knowing what had happened. UEFA's decision, and Leeds' acceptance, to play the game was a disgrace. Being escorted to the ground by armoured UN trucks told you all you needed to know about how pointless a football match had become that evening.

Nearly 20 years on it was time to return to Istanbul, not least because they had built a new airport to help Turkish Airlines (I much preferred THY Turk Hava Yollari as they were known back in the day) in their quest to compete with Emirates, Etihad and Qatar with worldwide domination. Before we reached Istanbul though, our journey took us to Bodrum airport from Adana. Pegasus was doing wonders providing cheap domestic flights and Anadolujet, THY's low-cost company, was matching them. We had no intention or desire to stay or visit Bodrum so took two buses straight to Denizli, our next airport. Having, as usual, not researched much I had no idea how close we were in Denizli to Pamukkale. So close -20 minutes by bus - that we were able to enjoy the afternoon there.

Pamukkale was so much larger than I remembered it and fortunately, relatively uncrowded. It was a pleasure to revisit somewhere that I'd told Agnes about, most likely on several occasions. It was another "don't go back" positive. Our next flight from Denizli, one of those airports with one flight per day, via Istanbul SAW took us to the north coast of Turkey to Ordu-Giresun airport from whence we took a bus via Giresun to Trabzon - a fine city, as Hakan had promised us. The next day we took a flight to Bursa/Yenisehir with a couple of hours on the bus back to Istanbul SAW again. The next morning we took an early flight to Erzincan, followed by a delightful 4 hour train ride to Erzurum. I can assure you I had heard of none of these places either, prior to searching Skyscanner.

Erzurum was a memorable experience. Our train from Erzincan was the twice weekly Ankara to Van, Vangolu Express, a 26 hour, 750 mile journey of which we covered around 150 miles. Both our departure and arrival stations were eerily deserted, as was the train itself. As you may, or may not recall, we love a train journey. This was airport collecting at its best and most justified. When we arrived in Erzurum we had no plan, of course. An old dude with not very many teeth approached us. His English was surprisingly good. It was a Sunday and it was his day off, he informed us. He would like nothing better than to show us around his city. He assured us that he did not want any money. It would be his pleasure to share the time with us. We dropped our bags at our chosen hotel and spent the remainder of the day with Nuri, learning about his life and his city.

The city was memorable to us for only one thing. In 1873 Queen Victoria gifted a huge church bell to the city which was made in Croydon!! My home town was famous in this Turkish city. We visited the clock tower with Nuri and, sure enough, the bell was inscribed with "Made in Croydon". I was very excited. This was on a par with discovering a Forbes airport in Australia. What fascinated us was how, 150 years ago, they had transported this huge contraption to Erzurum, let alone why. We never found out about either. What puzzled us was that Erzurum is about 750 miles from Istanbul, or Constantinople, as it was then. The Black Sea coast is significantly closer but separated by a not insignificant mountain range. Either way it would've been one heck of a journey without motorised transport.

Nuri worked on the Vangolu Express, refreshing the train's water supply. We never really established what he did on the days there was no train or the hours either side of replenishing its water. He had 6 daughters. He worked as a guide in the summer. It was late October and already dropping to freezing at night. He had visited Exeter, neighbouring Iran (neighbouring to Turkey, not Exeter!) amongst other places. He insisted to join us for dinner but refused to eat anything as he said his wife would already be annoyed that he was late home, let alone if he then refused her dinner. He very much wanted to meet us the next morning at the station to ensure that we caught the right bus out to the airport. Nuri must've led a tougher life than I. He was actually 2 years younger than me. Aggers agreed with me that he looked at least 10-15 years older. Age is but a number and 6 daughters are enough to age any man, I imagine.

Finally it was time to tick off Istanbul NEW. I was interested to see a brand-new airport even though these biggies are not my favourite. Sure enough it was big and out of the city. It took over an hour and a half to reach the city by bus. I was pleased to see Istanbul again, even though it held sad memories from my last visit. It's a fascinating city. The receptionist at our delightful little accommodation was from Turkmenistan. Never met anyone from there before!

Just before I head back to San Andres and how it fared with our expectations, I'd like to recount two other "don't go back" experiences if I may. Our journey from Istanbul had taken us via a 3-day layover in Abu Dhabi, visiting yet another of Agnes's worldwide friends, a week in Chiang Mai with my old mucker Budgie then onwards to Cambodia. I had managed to add 2 airports to the Thailand collection en route to Cambodia and clearly we were not going there without a return visit (for me) to the Angkor Wat complex. It is, beyond any doubt, one of the world's must-see sites. Aggers had done her research on how to avoid the busiest times at the major sites and it worked. We spent 3 fabulous days exploring, one by tuk tuk, another on bicycles, and the third on a scooter.

Siem Reap was changing rapidly when I visited some 15 years previously, but it had gone into overdrive since. We had to visit "Pub Street". It was more awful than we simply could ever have imagined. It's an all too frequently reoccurring theme the world over: something so wonderfully created by previous generations or nature alone, completely fucked up (sorry but ruined isn't strong enough) by our modern generation either on site itself, or nearby. Siem Reap fitted the latter description. Thankfully Angkor Wat itself was left pretty much as it was found - the huge ticketing complex being thoughtfully situated some distance away.

Overall it was a total pleasure to go back to Angkor Wat and we had found an oasis of a homestay in Siem Reap far away from Pub Street: think Pattaya without the beach and all that it entailed. Next revisit was to be another wonder, this time natural, in North Vietnam, Halong Bay. Vietnam was yet another country that allowed the airport collector in me to indulge far greater than my previous visit 25 years ago. This addiction and Lonely Planet enabled us to enjoy a simply fabulous visit to Halong Bay via an alternative route. We had crossed from Cambodia to Vietnam by bus, after Agi's rather ambitious attempt to hitchhike hadn't quite worked as she hoped. We did manage two lifts but we were still some way from the border when a bus appeared. An outrageous attempt to fleece us from the bus conductor successfully negotiated and we reached Pleiku for our onward journey to Qui Nhon - a pleasant seaside city not frequented by foreigners it seemed.

From Qui Nhon we took our first flight with the wonderfully named Bamboo Airways to Hai Phong. Rather confusingly most airports in Vietnam seemed to serve more than one city and have up to 3 different names. Qui Nhon/Phu Cat airport took us to Hai Phong/Cat Bi for example. The journey to Cat Ba island, the Lonely Planet recommendation to avoid the crowds of Halong Bay, was somewhat confusing on paper, and no less so in reality initially. We made it via bus, ferry, bus to the main; only, town of Cat Ba. If this was the quiet alternative to Halong Bay town itself I dread to think how ruined that had become. Cat

Ba was busy, not unbearably so, but certainly no hidden gem.

We booked a day tour of Halong Bay for the following morning. It was a fabulous trip, totally devoid of crowds. Southern Halong Bay, reached from Cat Ba, receiving just a fraction of the visitors that the northern area receives. Our boat was around a quarter full, if that. One of the guides remarked how, for us Europeans, he knew this was perfect. In contrast he told us that the Vietnamese and Chinese would consider their day a total failure if the boat was anything less than 100% packed out. I would opine that most Indians would feel the same. It was an eye-opening observation.

We decided to treat ourselves to an overnight on a floating homestay. I say treat because our accommodation in Cat Ba was £2 including breakfast!! I don't recall the cost of the floating homestay but it was yet another fabulous experience, not totally dissimilar to our overnight in Uros Islands on Lake Titicaca. The latter though being made of natural weeds and homing families as well as offering Airbnb for the likes of us.

Next stop on our airport inspired trip was a five-hour journey by bus, ferry and bus, south to Ninh Binh. Of course we had to have a reason to visit this area other than just the obvious one. Not far from Ninh Binh is a fascinating area called Trang An, a network of rivers, caves and temples, hugely popular with Vietnamese (and likely Chinese) but not with many of our sort, it seemed. We took a train the next evening one hour further south to Thanh Hoa for our next flight the following morning. Thanh Hoa was memorable for 2 reasons: a genuine 5-star hotel stay with a massive buffet breakfast included for £10. Ridiculous. As was the journey to the airport the next morning. I had one of those fortunately pretty rare experiences when my need for a pooh goes from 1 to 9.9 in about ten minutes. Not ideal when this happens about 5 minutes into a one-hour packed minibus ride. I was in serious trouble. There was no way I could last up to an hour on 9.9. One of the local ladies seemed to recognise the anguished look on my face and, maybe (obviously I have no idea what she said to the driver but guessed that it may have been along the lines of "mate, if you don't let this bloke off the bus you may have an incident to clear up) assisted in my attempts to persuade the driver to stop for me at, what I perceived to be some kind of eating establishment.

It is to my eternal shame that it actually transpired that this was somebody's home but, at the time I cared not as I ran past their astonished glances saying "toilet, toilet emergency". What makes my shame so long lasting is that, no sooner had I breathed an enormous sigh of relief at removing my emergency status, I realised that this toilet had no running water. What could I do other than shrug and smile and hop back on the bus, which fortunately had waited. I won't digress onto other toilet emergencies, of which there are a few as I'm thankfully not addicted to them and they're not very interesting for other people. This, though, is the number 1 for me.

Thanh Hoa/Tho Xuan airport took us further south to Nha Trang/Cam Ranh airport. You get my drift. We had chosen not to stay in Nha Trang as we knew it to be favoured by TUI charters amongst others, a sure sign that mass tourism had arrived. The little we saw of it before we took a train to Tuy Hoa confirmed what we expected. The next morning we flew to the island of Phu Quoc via Saigon/Ho Chi Minh. Lonely Planet had pretty much managed our expectations for this island - back on the expectations theme - together, again, with the fact that TUI flew there. I have nothing personal against TUI, you understand. It's just that I think it would be fair to say that they don't fly anywhere off the beaten track.

No matter how many times we reread LP's description of the overdevelopment and destruction of Phu Quoc it still didn't really prepare us for the reality. It was, beyond any doubt, the worst example of destruction by mass tourism, of what must have once been a stunning island that we had ever experienced. It's difficult to over-stress just how screwed up it was, and they were still building and destroying what remained of any unaffected beaches. The place was a mess. It even had its very own Vietnamese style of Disneyworld. It was huge and totally out of place. Those Vietnamese and Chinese who felt robbed of their holiday experience if they weren't surrounded by crowds would not have been disappointed.

Having said all that we did manage to find a couple of pockets yet to be blitzed, although the best of them, with a nice beach, was due for development very soon. It's fair to say that our decision to go there was motivated by airport adding as we could take a ferry off the island to the mainland with a flight from Can Tho back to Bangkok for our journey back to Poland for Christmas.

That little jaunt finished off 2019 with 21 new airports for me which, ironically is the planned total for this Colombia trip. San Andres airport could not have been more in town unless the planes landed on the main road. It was about 10 minutes' walk to our accommodation. It had a nice airy terminal building and the runway stretched roughly east to west on the northern tip of the island. It provided a similar, but nowhere near as dramatic, experience as St Maarten, as the planes land and take off both ends over the beach/ocean. That was the highlight of San Andres for us, particularly as it was a milestone number for Agi, number 400! Bloody good effort as her number 100 was only just over 6 years previous. That's roughly one a week, with 2 of those years Covid restricted.

No doubt we have been spoiled by the number of times we've enjoyed the turquoise ocean around the world. San Andres is encircled by a beautiful coloured ocean but the beaches are few and far between and littered with rubbish, tourists or both. The town is overdeveloped and the rest of the island does not have much going for it other than the ocean. It was pleasant to hear the Caribbean lilt on some of the natives as the rather bizarre history involves Spanish and English colonial periods. The island and neighbouring Providencia, which sounded far more alluring, but was sadly closed to tourists since a 2019 hurricane, are way closer to Nicaragua than Colombia. Consequently Nicaragua thinks they should belong to them.

It was cheaper to fly there from Medellin than the cost of the obligatory tourist card for foreigners and mainland tourists alike. LATAM gives no warning of this when you book. Since LP's last Colombia print run in 2018 this had increased from £8 to £24. With 20-30 jet flights per day that's an awful lot of £24s. Of course there was zero sign of the islanders benefitting from this "tax" on tourists whatsoever. The place was tatty and in much need of some investment. I was glad that I had only booked us 2 nights and one full day there. I had no regrets as we hot footed it south to Cali.

Cali felt edgy compared to Medellin but it was good to spend a day there, in particular to visit the extremely odd cat park. It does have a pleasant old colonial area, where we stayed, but this was mainly given over to tourist restaurants, bars and shops and lacked a locals' vibe. Again I didn't feel that our departure the next morning was premature. It was time to try out a new airline, Satena, who unfortunately didn't offer an airpass. They did offer an infrequent service to Ipiales, a border town with Ecuador, which was where we were heading.

Ipiales had a very different feel to it, many more indigenous folk and a nip in the air. From Ipiales LP describes the 2-hour drive north to Pasto as breathtaking which it certainly was. Sadly we learnt from one of our fellow minibus passengers, or at least Agnes did, that earlier that day a coach had crashed on this stretch of road killing 5 passengers. We saw the remains of the coach one hour into the drive. It was a horrible sight. Worryingly it didn't cause our driver to proceed with a reasonable level of caution. Although my excuse to tick off Ipiales and Pasto was primarily the section of the Pan American highway where between the two, time permitting, there was a rather odd sounding opportunity near to Ipiales.

I felt we were taking the soft option of a taxi a little too frequently for my liking. They were so cheap that farting around with buses made little sense. Ipiales airport is north west of the small city and our attraction was south east. Imagine our surprise when the bus we caught from the main road near the terminal not only whisked us off to the city but proceeded directly to Santuario de Las Lajes - a rather bizarre church built in a stunning location in a deep gorge. Apparently an image of the Virgin Mary made a brief appearance there in the mid-18th century. That doesn't make a great impression on an agnostic such as myself but the location certainly did. My New York friend Colin, of some 32 years standing- we met in deepest Africa on a 3-week camping trip to see gorillas in Zaire, as it was then - is very religious though. We had received the extremely sad news that he had been diagnosed with a brain tumour just after Christmas. We lit a candle for him and said a prayer in the church - both firsts for me. It meant a lot to him when we sent him a short video and it was heartwarming to feel that we had helped him in some small way in his battle.

That 3-week camping trip to Zaire, with Explore, was part of a 3-month sabbatical I took from work. Dan Air encouraged unpaid leave in the winter. I kind of wish I had taken advantage on more than one occasion. My knowledge of Africa to that point had been restricted to South Africa, Cameroon, Zimbabwe, Zambia and Tanzania. The Cameroon trip was particularly memorable as my school friend Ian was working there for a year or so at the time. I had a free ticket with UTA, a now defunct French airline serving their former and current colonial outposts. I'm sure Ian was delighted to have a visitor. He kindly treated me to a safari which included 4 more airports in addition to Douala. Delightfully named Maroua, Garoua and Ngaoundere as well as the capital city, Yaoundé are proud additions to my collection.

Ethiopian Airlines were another airline kind to Dan Air staff. £28 took me from Heathrow to Addis Ababa via Frankfurt and Rome, onwards to Nairobi and Kigali. After the safari which started in Rwanda and took in Uganda as well as Zaire, my journey continued with them on a bizarre route from Nairobi via Brazzaville and Accra to Abidjan. Obviously I like an unusual flight routing and that trans Africa fitted the bill. It seemed bizarre that a country that had suffered so badly with famine and civil war maintained an airline with, by African standards, a significant network.

All that for £28! I could have taken a softer option and returned to London, at no extra cost and flown onwards to Brazil from there. However, I was keen to visit another country in Ivory Coast and Varig, the since defunct Brazilian flag carrier, had a once weekly flight from Abidjan to Rio. I had no way of finding out the flight load on this route but was inclined to risk it. I didn't much care for what I saw of Ivory Coast - the locals were too frenchy for my liking, very pushy and even hassled you in airport security for money. As it was the Varig DC10 (loved that aircraft) was virtually empty for the 5 1/2-hour flight from Africa to South America.

I kept a diary for that 3-month trip which, if I can find someone to type it up for me, may very well feature at the end of this book. I shared a tent with Colin for 3 weeks which no doubt had a bearing on why we've remained friends for so long.

I appear to have digressed yet again - I haven't mentioned that for a while - so back to Colombia and religion. They don't seem a particularly religious lot here. All the cities have a fine church or two but not so many for the size of the populations. LP advised us that the Santuario would be heaving at the weekend but that we would almost have it to ourselves during the week, which we almost did. It seemed quite bizarre, but very handy, that there was a gondola to take you to/from the gorge. We were happy to take it as we had our bags with us, even if they are only Ryanair/Wizzair free carry-on size.

It was time for another panic when we got to Pasto. A beautifully located city, according to LP. We believed them but it was hammering it down and the clouds were so low we had no idea. Wikipedia told me that flights were regularly cancelled due to weather. LP only told me to panic about Manizales airport and its weather record. I had a few days to build up to that one. The rain subsided overnight and we caught a brief glimpse of the mightily impressive volcano overlooking Pasto. There was no need to hang around the city. Its location was the best thing about it, although it had a couple of nice churches and ok plazas. We took a bus out to the airport which was beautifully located between the mountains on a plateau. Unlike India, nearly all the airports so far in Colombia had been in interesting locations.

Pasto was the best so far. Panic at the airport was fairly short lived, thankfully, as a couple of jets came in before ours and the weather, 80% chance of thunderstorms as well as the cloud base causing my anxiety, held steady. We overnighted at Aggers' friend's apartment in Bogotá before an early morning; 6.20, flight to Pereira. Neither LP or Wikipedia made mention of weather issues here so I was back to my more chilled self. We pushed back on time, only to taxi to another stand and park up. Agi translated from the pilot's announcement that the weather was below limits in Pereira and we would have to wait. It seemed weird that they didn't decide that to be the case before they wasted all that fuel to start up, taxi and shut down again.

I was pretty relaxed as we had no tight connection to think of and there were a bunch of daily flights from Bogotá to Pereira. We only had to wait around 40 minutes and we were off again. There was a whole lot of low cloud around when we landed at Pereira and as we walked away from the airport, we heard the sound of an overshoot and turned to see that the end of the runway where we had just landed was covered in thick fog. Lucky us. Agi had booked us a stay on a coffee plantation, half way between Pereira and Manizales. It was absolutely idyllic. The weather cleared and we were surrounded by fabulous hilly/mountainous terrain. Should you ever visit Colombia do be sure to visit one of these plantations that offer a tour and accommodation. We will definitely never look at coffee in the same light. The manual labour involved is staggering. We certainly had no idea that the coffee beans we buy at home are coated in sugar. The coffee tasting session was completely different to what we were used to.

It was serene and so chilled at the plantation that I even gave myself a few hours off from worrying about the flight from Manizales. My concern stemmed from LP's advice not to book a connecting flight due to frequent cancellations. Obviously I ignored this advice and booked a connecting flight! Which only operated twice per week! LP didn't really say much about Manizales but what a magnificently located city. Surrounded by mountains and built over hills, some of the streets were like San Francisco on steroids.

Aggers found a rooftop bar on line. Finding it in reality was another matter. The entrance, with no signage, was located in an office block. The 360-degree views from the 15th floor were brilliant.

The beers on offer weren't bad either. We couldn't see all the mountains because of the clouds but we had a pretty good picture. We saw a plane making its way to land which gave me some optimism for the morning. Amazingly we woke to some sunshine. Not much, but some. We took a bus out to the airport. It was a stunner. I don't think I've ever seen an airport on such a slope. No jets could land there due to the terrain rather than the runway length, I think.

It was actually sunny and warm as we waited for our plane. Two landed from Bogotá but then the weather started to close in! Now I could really go into panic overdrive. Flightradar24, which Aggers introduced me to a while ago, had accurately shown the other two flights on their way in but there was no sign of ours. I was getting, quite illogically, to the levels of tension normally only reserved for watching Leeds. Illogical because surely they wouldn't call us to the gate if they knew the plane hadn't left Medellin. I really need to have a word with myself. Naturally we all lived happily ever after and were soon enjoying a late morning beer on the terrace at Medellin downtown airport, with bags of time for our connection to Corozal.

We only had a couple of tickets left on our EasyFly pass and were gutted to learn that they had discontinued the promotion. We were very keen to visit Mompos; Mompox in Spanish times, rated as second to Cartagena for its colonial buildings. I'm sure they said the same about Popayan! It is quite a remote town, 6 hours by road from Cartagena and much further from anywhere else with an airport, apart from its own airport and Corozal. Both Mompos airport and Corozal only have 2 flights per week but they pretty much fitted our schedule. No weather or terrain issues in this part of Colombia. Flat as a pancake but an awful lot of lakes and rivers.

Google told us that it would take 2-3 hours by car from Corozal to Mompos and LP made no mention of any boats needed to get from Cartagena, which joined the same road near to Corozal. All Aggers' research though showed that we needed to get a boat from Magangue, half way between Corozal and Mompos, for part of the journey. I had no choice but to give us the best part of 3 days to make the short journey if required as that was when the next flight from Mompos was.

The reality was quite straightforward. We walked from Corozal airport to the main road and caught a bus to Magangue quite swiftly. We had booked a hotel for an overnight in Magangue as there was very little choice. We could have potentially continued our journey to Mompos that evening but for some unknown reason the comfortable bus that stopped for us, transferred us quite swiftly to a particularly uncomfortable minibus. I may as well have been sitting on the floor my seat was so low. The windows were 80% blacked out so I could basically see jack. Aggers didn't fare much better but at least she was higher up. The driver, having failed in his attempt to convince us to continue to Mompos with him, dropped us outside our hotel on the outskirts of Magangue. It was nondescript, which is the kindest way to describe the town.

It is an unfortunate fact that if somewhere has not geared itself to tourism or simply has nothing to offer that, well, it has nothing to offer the traveller. However, what Magangue did offer was a very stark contrast to Mompos. Situated on the same Magdalena river it could have developed itself into something of interest. It seems the Spanish didn't fancy that location so it had no history as such. There were a few extremely basic bars on the riverside but pretty much no infrastructure to speak of. The city/town felt rundown and it was debatable whether we were wandering in the safest neighbourhoods.

As we made our way back to our hotel the outskirts seemed to offer a little more in the way of eating establishments but we had already gone down the cheese and wine option for the first time on this trip. Our hotel had suggested we could take a shared taxi to Mompos, surprisingly for the same price as the minibus driver was offering us the previous evening. Fortunately a shared taxi in Colombia seems to stick to the numbers that the car was designed for: a driver and four passengers.

A few years back I was fortunate enough to blag a work trip to Sierra Leone. I had wanted to visit this country for a while. I'm not sure why. Maybe because of the colonial history? Perhaps because British Caledonian used to have a regular flight to Freetown during the country's long lasting civil war?

I found an English guy promoting a hotel on the beach near to Freetown at World Travel Market. His offer to host me for a few days was all the encouragement I needed. British Airways were now flying to Freetown so I was off. It wasn't going to be an airport extravaganza trip but I was excited to visit a country that had been pretty much off limits for so long unless you're a war zone collector. Talking of which, I read a few months ago about an English dick whose sole intention was to visit the most dangerous places he could think of. I say dick because he was flown out of Afghanistan when seats were at a premium and his could've been utilised by a much more desperate Afghani than he, who had voluntarily decided to go there when the country was in its most precarious state for some time. Who am I to judge but that's my opinion.

By the way I also heard the back end of a story on the radio a couple of months ago where an American/Chinese guy had visited nearly 8,000 Chinese restaurants. I wanted to know more. I googled it and found that he's been visiting for

40 years. That's still one almost every other day!! Apparently he has a spreadsheet detailing what he ate. I guess, like me, his list was manual before the advent of spreadsheets. He has a way to go mind: there are more than 45,000 Chinese restaurants in USA, which is more than the total of MacDonald's, Wendy's, KFC and Burger King combined.

The hotel in Sierra Leone was very nice, deserted and so was the beach it was situated on but, if I just stayed there it would be a travesty. As luck would have it a lady approached me on the beach with her husband and asked where I was from. When I told her Croydon she was excited, "ha, we live in Norbury" (that's just a couple of miles up the road from Croydon, for those who don't know their sarf London suburbs). I forget her name but, her delightful husband Godfrey's father had been the first president of the country after independence from UK in the early 60s. I was in exalted company. They were intrigued that I would choose to visit their home country and, to my extreme pleasure and excitement invited me to stay at their home in Freetown.

If you are wondering how this story is linked to a shared taxi in Colombia here it is. The hotel I was staying in was around an hour and a half from the city centre. Godfrey suggested I should book a private taxi to come and visit him but I baulked at the price and the lack of authenticity that would entail. I had already been reduced to a private transfer from the airport to the hotel but it was kind of fair enough seeing as it was 10 o'clock in the evening and I didn't have the faintest idea how else I would get there.

Godfrey reluctantly suggested I would need to take a shared taxi from the small village next to the hotel to a bigger town and then another shared taxi onwards from there. The first taxi was not too abnormal - 4 passengers in the back and me in the front. The next one, however, was interesting. Somehow 5 people squeezed in the back and I shared the front passenger seat with one other. Still we didn't leave. There was room for one more apparently. I've got to admit to being a bit shocked when the driver shuffled towards me so he could fit a passenger in on his left-hand side. We're talking Toyota Corolla here, not some old Cadillac with a bench seat in the front.

Off we went. The locals were not phased that some foreigner was joining them in their discomfort. As always, out of the cities in Africa, the locals are friendly at best or disinterested at worse. Godfrey was horrified when I told him where I had been "sightseeing" in Freetown claiming that it was totally unsafe. I had nothing on me to be robbed of apart from my toothbrush and it was enlightening to see how local life carried on in one of the hardest hit cities in modern times.

I met up with Godfrey and his wife a couple of times back in Blighty. Their home in Freetown was quite basic and they were in the elite. His wife told me that when she came to boarding school in England in the early 60s some of the girls had asked, innocently, to see her tail! Racism is 100% wrong but hearing what she had to put up with does make you wonder whether we've gone too far the other way these days. They took me to the point where the slaves had been shipped to the Caribbean and US. It was quite eerie to say the least. Godfrey had built a small "resort" on a nearby island and took me there. The island was quite charming in a way but the accommodation he had built was too basic, even by my standards. Godfrey had lived many years in Houston and although they had not been married long, they bickered like an old couple. I'm sorry I lost touch with them.

I'm sorry, I digressed yet again, not really. Our taxi did not pick up any more passengers than it was designed for so we enjoyed a comfortable ride to Mompos. What an utterly delightful place it was too. The Spanish certainly treated the natives particularly badly in their colonies, by all accounts. I'm not saying that the Brits were any better. I believe we did help with infrastructure in some of our old haunts as well as being pretty horrible to the locals, but, my goodness, those Spaniards knew how to build villages, towns and cities that, if they haven't been somewhat destroyed, are just so pleasing on the eye. The contrast with Magangue could not have been starker. If Mompos was a person and it had been any more laid back, it would've been horizontal.

As I've most likely said before, the balance between having enough infrastructure for a traveller to enjoy as opposed to a tourist is a very fine one. Mompos had fallen into disrepair because the Spanish had diverted their trade onto a different tributary of the splendid Magdalena river, for reasons we know not. It's only fairly recently that some of its splendid buildings have been restored. Those that haven't are equally charming. The jewel in the crown is the riverside promenade, about a mile long, which is where most restaurants and hostels, but not all, are found. For us, the balance between local life and tourism was just about right. As we had been warned it was damned hot, not that we minded. We were extremely pleased that there wasn't a flight until Thursday so, apart from numerous strolls along the promenade and the other streets we could sit and watch the world go by, or at least the river, while enjoying beers, iced coffees and pretty tasty food. An absolute must if you make it to Colombia, dear reader.

It was time for us to take a stroll out to the airport, head back to Medellin for the penultimate time and head back to the Caribbean coast.

CHAPTER TWENTY-FIVE

We knew Cartagena would be a shock to our systems after Mompos. Peaceful and tranquil it would not be. We felt compelled to visit but figured on a fairly short stay. LP amongst others warn of constant hassle from folks trying to earn a living from tourists any which way they can. Well, they had nowt on the Egyptians and, to be fair, this negative aspect was very mild in reality. Crikey it was busy though. There is no doubting that it is another fabulous creation by the Spanish and far more worthy of its UNESCO status than Santo Domingo. Definitely worth a visit.

We had 5 days until our next flight but it was never our intention to spend most of that time in Cartagena. We had a good wander around that first evening but the crowds of, including a lot of Colombian, tourists were too much for us. We decided we could probably have the city to ourselves early the next morning, just after sunrise. Sure enough, only the locals were out and about and it was an altogether more pleasant experience. We were done with the big city though so, after a late breakfast, we headed out to the bus station.

Surprisingly not mentioned by LP, Aggers had found a blog about Rincon del Mar whilst researching how to reach the San Bernardo Islands. The blog was only 3 years old and, with Covid affecting 2 of those, we didn't think it could have changed too much. It sounded idyllic. It was. The government is in the process of turning the dirt track from San Onofre, where the bus drops you from Cartagena, into a paved road. It's around 25% completed. I imagine it will change Rincon del Mar beyond recognition in time. We learnt that 4 years ago there were only 2 hostels. Now there are 17 but they are very small and most of them quite rubbish. We know because we had a look inside most of them.

Currently locals far outnumber travellers/tourists, massively, 100+/1. There are certainly better beaches in the world but this one stretches unbroken for 2 miles either side of the village. It was, thankfully, almost devoid of any human generated garbage and no other humans in sight once you left the village. For us, the balance was perfect. A few places on the beach to eat and drink. A basic room with a fabulous common area balcony directly on the beach. It was paradise, apart from Leeds losing to bloody "Frank Lampard's Everton" prompting beers on the beach before breakfast.

We had a couple of nights there before treating ourselves to a private boat trip to San Bernardo

Islands finishing on the bizarre Santa Cruz del Islote for our overnight. From where I'm writing the next morning. I'm up to date. The end is in sight, of the book and Colombia. The end of the book feels natural: I don't have a natural digression coming into my head. The end of Colombia feels anything but natural: there's still so many airports and so much of this country to discover.

Our friendly captain firstly took us to a couple of islands, as yet, unaffected by tourism. Apparently the locals live there Monday-Friday to fish and return to Rincon for the weekend, about an hour by boat. They were no Maldivian beauties as mangrove was the main coastline with next to no beach but authentic for sure. We then headed off to the 2 main tourist islands of Murcura and Tintipan, the former filling up rapidly with so many day trippers that, after a quick breakfast, we were off sharpish. The day trippers come from as far afield as Cartagena, a few from Rincon but mainly from Tolu, our next destination.

Although we could have stayed on Murcura, Tintipan or one of the small hotels offshore of these islands we chose Santa Cruz. Not because it was cheaper, although, naturally for the 50% Scot in me this appealed too, but because it's weird. It lays claim to being the most densely populated island in the world. It is the size of 1 1/2 football pitches and population estimates vary from 900-1200. Imagine that many people living on the pitch, not invading it, at Elland Road plus half again. The island is built on coral. It came about because many, many years ago the fishermen realised that when they stopped at the coral overnight they were not plagued by mosquitoes, as they were on the islands with mangrove. Gradually it grew to what it is now; described aptly, by LP as a tropical aquatic shanty town.

Unsurprisingly in this day and age there is one hostel featured on Airbnb. It has 4 pretty decent rooms, running water for showers 1700-1830 and power from 1700-0500. You can see sunrise and sunset. The beer fridge seems well stocked, the cocktails are cheap and tasty and if the breakfast is as good as the dinner what more could we want?

The breakfast was indeed tasty but I'm afraid I have to change the opinion of the cocktails. We had enjoyed a coco loco the previous day but the pina coladas looked and tasted decidedly different to any other pina colada we had set eyes on and/or consumed. When we enquired to our host what exactly he put in them we were quite shocked to learn that both drinks contained artificial flavouring in addition to the normal ingredients. Clearly the coconut flavouring was less invasive than the pineapple. Why you would add artificial flavouring when you have an abundance of the natural contents is beyond me. To be fair Andreas, our host, did offer Aggers a complimentary coco loco. He didn't need to ask her twice. I spied at least 20 bottles of these artificial flavourings in the kitchen.

We had a couple of wanders around Santa Cruz. It's not the first time we've seen people living in such close proximity surrounded by water but it certainly had a rather unique feeling. The locals were either friendly or indifferent. There are no police on the island, in contrast to the mainland where we've always seen a police presence. It's difficult to establish what is a public or private space. It's difficult to imagine that 1000+ people all get on with each other. Maybe they do or maybe they just ignore each other if they don't. It's a credit to the islanders that there is precious little rubbish in the surrounding, stunningly turquoise sea. Apparently Mondays aren't great though as the losing chickens/cocks can be seen floating in the sea after the weekend fights. I would've thought they would eat them.

I found the men's public urinal quite amusing: a standard one-man porcelain with surrounding wall but the short exit pipe lead directly into the sea. I didn't try it out but you would basically pee into the urinal, only to watch it coming out into the sea. We both found it intriguing too that our dwelling had an area behind the rooms where you could have fitted at least 5 large cars. Obviously there are no cars on the island. Considering that space really is at a premium this seems an astonishing waste. They could have easily built another 4-5 homes in that area.

After sitting around admiring the beautiful sea and watching the locals go about their day, we took a relatively uncomfortable one-hour boat trip back to the mainland in the afternoon. The sea didn't appear overly choppy but, by heck, it was a lumpy, bumpy crossing to Tolu, from where we would fly back to Medellin for the last time.

We had booked into Hotel Kevin's, no relation to Puerto Plata Kevin as far as we were aware but a similar friendly vibe with an unused rooftop. Tolu is a fairly pleasant, reasonably sized, seaside town. For the first time in Colombia we witnessed an impressive amount of bicycle usage, both taxi and individual varieties. We took an evening stroll along the coast to the airport as it's so close to town. It looked as in use as North Caicos. Actually make that Middle Caicos. At least North Caicos had runway lights. Tolu doesn't.

The next morning we took a stroll to the airport, stopping on the beach to consume a four pack of 3 Cordilleras that we had bought in the pretty decent looking supermarket. Beer in Colombia is basically rubbish, with 2 exceptions. Poker, Aguila, Nativa and Club Colombia are the mainstay local beers, normally only available in 33cl cans or bottles. They're on a par with Carling Black Label. 3 Cordilleras come in 6 varieties and are full of taste. Only problem is they are not widely available. The stouts and IPA, in particular, do the trick. Even rarer are BBC (Bogotá Brewing Company) offerings. They are also an improvement on the others but we will be looking forward to a decent pint in Spoons.

After an uneventful departure, apart from the fact that security at the airport, strangely of the manual variety, confiscated a shaver that Aggers had, which had passed through the scanner before every other flight (they didn't find her other shaver), we were back in Medellin for the last time. We found an even closer hostel to the airport with an excellent rooftop providing great views of parts of the city and the surrounding mountains. We met with Agnes' friends who were happy to take us again to the best takeaway joint I've ever experienced. In general Colombian food is not particularly inspiring but the options these guys offer are just exceptional. The store next door stocks 3 Cordilleras. Back of the net!

We were pretty fond of Medellin. After Rincon and Santa Cruz Island the choice of coffee shops, bars and restaurants was quite overwhelming. The fact that we could walk to our hostels from the downtown airport was a real bonus. Our only negative experience on all our visits to Medellin was on our visit to Community 13. Towards the top they have a series of escalators. Quite strange but what was so totally bizarre, rather than negative actually, was this dude (with 2 very nice dogs) motioning to us not to walk up the escalators. It never ceases to amaze us that 90-100% of the population stand still for an age on downward escalators. Even on moving conveyors at airports. Fair enough if you don't want to walk up I suppose. Anyway, we figured this guy, who did not appear to be an official of any kind, became very angry with us because we really couldn't understand why we could not walk if we chose to. We started to walk on the next escalator. This was too much for him. He shouted at us and became really quite aggressive. We decided that it probably was best to do as he wished but, seriously? There's no such thing as health and safety in Colombia yet you cannot walk up an escalator!

We took our last EasyFly flight, paying full whack as we were out of passes, to Valledupar the following morning. Our hope was to visit the remote far north east coast of Colombia. Of course, any normal person would've flown to Riohacha. Obviously not us. We took a taxi to the bus terminal to save time as we really wanted to get to Cabo de la Vela the same day if at all possible. LP and several blogs said if we didn't get to Uribia before 3pm we would have to stay the night in Uribia. As soon as we got out of the taxi in Valledupar we were descended upon by colectivo drivers, whose enthusiasm was beyond belief to take us somewhere, anywhere! We headed into the bus station, so they followed. There was no bus to

Uribia, only Riohacha, which made no sense for us. Time to negotiate in earnest.

We knew we needed to get to Quatro Vias; funnily enough a crossroads. From there we could get to Uribia. We started off at 80,000 pesos each and were down to 50,000 to the crossroads. The driver locked our bags in his boot, so that we wouldn't change our minds, while he went to find one more passenger. The other passenger he had already bagged was looking like he was fed up. I must point out that the 50,000 for each of us, was on a shared basis and he needed four passengers to make it worth his while. We waited and then started to get a little restless. Fortunately the driver had left his keys in the ignition so I retrieved our bags and went off to try and expedite our departure. I got us down to 85,000 each with another driver, just the 2 of us. I should point out that all this to and fro took place on a very busy road over a huge roundabout. I should also point out that the crossroads was about 110 miles away and Uribia another 30.

I thought the original driver was going to have a heart attack when I told him we were off. He was desperate so he agreed to take us all the way to Uribia, just the 2 of us for 140,000 -£26 for 140 miles. I know there is no comparison but I cannot help but compare with UK costs. After a couple of false starts we were off. He was quite a pleasant chap, apart from lobbing his plastic out of the window. We weren't surprised, just sad. As the journey went on, through very pleasant scenery and small towns the driver moaned to Aggers that he wasn't making any money. Not our problem. He almost bullied us into going with him. I didn't anticipate it, as a deal is a deal, and we had paid his office upfront and received a ticket for the journey, but Aggers did. At the crossroads he told us he couldn't take us any further and showed us another shared taxi that would take us. He told us we would have to pay 20,000 each to continue. No way Pedro! You pay him if you don't want to go any further. Which he did reluctantly. Cheeky git!

The performance was repeated at Uribia. Amongst the melee though we heard an English speaker. Not only could we get to Cabo de la Vela (Cabo from now on) but he could arrange a tour the next day, onward transport to Punta Gallinas (Punta) the day after, another tour and transport back to Uribia on day 4. All for a very nice sum. We had to wait until he had 3 more passengers but, luckily, that was done in an hour. The outskirts of Uribia contained the worst plastic rubbish we have seen anywhere on our travels. The landscape is dry, flat and with thorny bushes everywhere, combined with a strong wind; ideal conditions for discarded plastic bags to get shredded and caught up. It was both heart-breaking and soul destroying. There really is no hope for this planet.

We never made it into Uribia town but if it was

as dirty and messy as the outskirts it would be a truly god-forsaken place. We headed off on the dirt road to take us to Cabo. Once we turned off the main drag it was amazing how the driver managed to negotiate his way in the dark through the numerous tracks. Cabo gets rave reviews from LP and bloggers. Arriving at night we weren't certain what the appeal was. The accommodation was extremely basic: no running water, electricity 7pm - midnight but directly on the beach and a friendly and efficient Venezuelan manageress. She made us some dinner, which wasn't too bad and we had a stroll down the main drag and back along the beach. There really wasn't much about and it was extremely basic. We decided to wait until daylight to decide whether it had been worth the hassle to get there.

And it most certainly was. Not long after sunrise the turquoise colour of the sea was astounding, as far as the horizon. We met a German girl on the beach who said we could get banana pancakes and yoghurt, fruit and granola at the kitesurfing club. She knew because she would be making it. This was music to our ears as breakfasts so far had been mainly uninspiring, apart from a couple, and always scrambled eggs, toast and an arepa - an unappetising local bread. It was delightful and in a fabulous setting by the beach. The sea was pond calm, the local kids chatty and not begging.

This is Wayuu country, the indigenous people who

have occupied the land here for centuries. They do speak Spanish but also have their own local language. It really was serene. We headed off for our tour in the afternoon, which consisted of a few different beaches and viewpoints. The difference in the sea state compared to Cabo, the town/ village, was extreme. The sea was very, very rough so lacked the colour of Cabo but it was pretty impressive, as was the scenery. It is bizarre that more is not made of the desert here. At times we felt like we were back in the Sahara on the drive to Punta. The almost perfect day was finished off with a large and very tasty pizza on the beach, with our new friend Luis, from France. The lack of anything but the usual rank average beers was the only thing that was less than perfect.

We set off with 2 Colombian couples and Luis at 5.30 the next morning. That was 8 of us in total in a pretty ancient Toyota Landcruiser; pretty uncomfortable for the 3 Colombians in the back. They were at least a foot shorter than us 3 Europeans so we weren't about to offer to swap seats. All was going quite well. The scenery was superb and we felt like we were in true wilderness. Even in daylight it was amazing the driver knew which of the numerous tracks to take. Then, thwack, from the engine. Our driver putting his head in his hands was not a great sign. Whether it was good fortune or the company we were using insisted on travelling in convoy we know not, but we were very grateful that we were not alone, miles from life.

It was soon confirmed that our clutch had gone. Now I'm no mechanic that's for sure but I figured this wasn't great. I imagined we would either have to wait for a replacement vehicle from Cabo, if it existed, or for our companions to be dropped at Punta and then their driver could come back and rescue us. Neither was too appealing as it would involve sitting in the desert for 3 hours. It was hot! What I actually didn't realise is that you can drive a car without a clutch. So after pushing the vehicle out of the sand, no mean feat, about half an hour or so later, we were off.

We had made it to Punta Gallinas, the northern most point of South America. I had no plans to add this to Ushuaia, the southernmost city on mainland South America, but it wasn't a bad little number. After the obligatory photos we headed off to Playa Taroa, our overnight stop, consisting of one hostel and some pretty impressive sand dunes. I guess that if you had never seen sand dunes before, as the friendlier of the two Colombian couples told Agnes they hadn't, you would probably be quite amazed. They were high enough for us to make our first attempt at sandboarding, which was predictably a failure after about 10 metres. However, attempts two and three ended up with us successfully making it into the sea.

We were surprised at the number of other

Landcruisers that had made it to Taroa as we had not seen another one on our way or at Punta. We're not talking a convoy but maybe 8-10, so we didn't have the place to ourselves until near sunset. We chose to sleep in hammocks outside, but under cover. Another first. I'd never heard of it before but it is very popular in parts of the Colombian Coast. It would have been just fine apart from some local little fuckers (sorry, no other word for them) who decided to play their music at full volume from midnight onwards. They had the whole frickin' desert to do it in so why they had to congregate in our vicinity...?! Had the music been at full volume it may have been tolerable but they seemed to only have a setting of 1 or 100 and flicked through their songs so it was all ridiculously disjointed and impossible to sleep through. I did lose my rag with them and swore quite well. Of course, they didn't understand but decided to pay me a visit in my hammock and try to look threatening. I've never had a fight in my life. Probably just as well, as a fighter would have beat the crap out of them. They were drunk and so persisted to antagonise. Why none of the Spanish speakers, including our drivers didn't intervene was a bit of a mystery. They all admitted, the next morning, to being woken up and unable to sleep, or were woken by my yelling.

Finally they wandered off into the desert but no sooner had they than the dreaded snoring started.

Talking of snoring and Landcruisers reminds me of a trip to Botswana with cousin Michael and his wife, Wendy. Wendy had a cousin in Gaborone, named Quill. They planned to visit him and tour around Botswana and invited me along, or I invited myself along. They were still living in Cape Town at this point so we met in Johannesburg and took a minibus onto Gaborone. Quite why I didn't take a connecting flight to Gaborone and meet them there is beyond me. It remained a trip devoid of any new airports. Shame on me. I was quite proud of my stamina though. I had flown into Heathrow the previous morning from Calgary via Toronto, 10 hours at home and then the night flight to Johannesburg.

I enjoy flying as you probably realise and normally, no sooner do I get off one flight and I'm looking forward to the next. Other brief visits to UK include returning overnight from Cape Town via Windhoek and flying onwards to Muscat the same evening. Also landing from Dhaka in the afternoon and flying onwards to Union Island via Barbados the next morning. I bit off more than I could handle on one occasion where I landed from Bangkok into Heathrow at 0700 and flew from Gatwick to Barbados at 1000. I got my comeuppance as by 10pm that evening my stomach had decided it didn't fancy that little jaunt. The next 2 days of hospitality were wasted on me as I really couldn't eat or drink anything.

On another occasion I flew into Gatwick from Perpignan at 8pm and left for Ibiza 2 hours later. Clearly the anxieties that I have mentioned with missing flights on this trip did not enter my head back in the day. Meanwhile back to Quill, his Landcruiser and his snoring. We headed right up to the north of Botswana, to Maun, another airport that remains off the list. We slept on camp beds out in the open while Quill slept on the roof of his Landcruiser. Whilst on safari I asked Quill if he wouldn't mind if I took the Landcruiser rooftop option. He duly obliged. Michael and Wendy were in a tent as only an old diehard like Quill would contemplate sleeping on a camp bed with all that game about.

I was enjoying my evening under a tree on the rooftop when I was awoken by some rustling above me. It was a clear night so I could see what the rustling was caused by. Literally within a foot or two of my face was a very large trunk. Clearly it was not alone and belonged to a very large elephant. I was a little bit petrified to say the least. What if this giant fella got bored with the leaves and branches and decided to explore the rooftop. I could be in a spot of bother. Not that I thought I would be eaten but if Jumbo did decide to pick me up with his trunk, he probably would have caused me some serious damage before realising he didn't fancy eating me.

As I'm writing this I clearly didn't come to any

mortal harm. After what seemed a considerable time but was probably only a minute or two the elephant decided to wander off again. I've no idea how long he had been there before I woke up. I tried to warn Quill that he could be in danger as he was sleeping just a few metres from the Landcruiser but, it's possible that his snoring was what caused the elephant to move on. He really could push them out. I whispered loudly to Michael who had either been woken by the goings on or by me. I didn't fancy staying up on the roof in case Jumbo returned so joined them in the tent for the remainder of the evening with Quill none the wiser.

The snoring in Playa Taroa was just impossibly loud. It never ceases to amaze me that the snorer sleeps through their noise, as they are the closest to it. Aggers and I waited to see if it would abate but finally gave in and snuck into the room that had been offered to us the previous afternoon. We managed to grab a couple of hours sleep before our proposed departure at 0600. Everybody was quite jovial about the night time shenanigans and more light-hearted banter ensued when the nice Colombian girl (the other couple didn't speak to anyone else the whole trip) realised she had left her phone at the ranch after a few 100 metres. Now, the problem with not having a clutch is getting the car into gear in the first place. You really don't want to be stopping, once you've started. After a half hour or so of tinkering we were on our way.

Whilst I admired the tenacity of our driver to keep the show on the road, let's just say that anticipation was not his forte. The Wayuu grown-ups put a rope or chain across the tracks on their land and charge around 2000 pesos (40p) to lower it. They are plentiful. The Wayuu kids also put a rope across the track in the hope of getting the drivers to stop and give them some biscuits, drinks, money, whatever. Prior to clutch disintegration on the way to Punta we stopped and paid all the tolls. Luckily there weren't any afterwards. Logic would have been, on the way back, to allow the other driver to go ahead so that he could warn the Wayuu that we had no clutch and, if we stopped, it would be a right old palaver to get going again. That is what transpired at first. However, the other vehicle took a wrong track and we got stuck in the not so firm sand. We had to push both vehicles back onto firmer ground, and ours, once more to get it started. We then wandered off across the desert for a few hundred metres while the Landcruisers backtracked to find the correct track.

This was slowly becoming quite radical but, as time was on our side, amusing at the same time. As we were now approaching the Wayuu rope sections it would've made sense for us to follow the other driver in spite of his earlier mishap. Oh no. Not our driver. He appeared to be senior and he would lead the way from now on. The kids ropes/strings were no problem. He shouted out of the window for them to lower them and they duly obeyed. Even if they hadn't their ropes were so thin we could have just driven through them. The adults were a different proposition. Our driver left it to the last seconds to yell out of his window "no clutch, no clutch". The male attendants lowered their ropes just in time. The ladies were more reluctant. They had wares to sell to tourists. They also had chains instead of ropes.

After one very close shave, our driver finally got his comeuppance for his lack of foresight. This old dear wasn't lowering her chain for anyone, without them seeing her baskets she had for sale. What's more she was on a slight uphill. We were in a spot of bother. I think the young Colombians in the other vehicle were becoming a little tired of coming to our rescue and having to push us each time our driver screwed up. Can you believe who, in pretty much the middle of nowhere, came to our rescue? Yes, you've got it. The army. What the hell were they doing out here, all tooled up? Can you also believe that our driver was too scared to ask them for help? Not Aggers. How could they turn her down. Six very muscular lads and us 6, less than muscular, tourists succeeded in getting our driver out of his latest pickle.

We made it back to Uribia, pretty much at the agreed schedule. It was a fantastic trip. The only negative? Yep, you guessed it. Even if there were just a few Wayuu dwellings there was plastic everywhere. Apart from that, which, fortunately, with there being so few people around it didn't occur too often, it was a real highlight of our trip. We took a taxi with Luis to Riohacha without any of the dramas of the taxi to Uribia, although our driver stopped 3 times because of an unnerving noise coming from under his bonnet. He was certainly more concerned than us.

We didn't expect much from Riohacha and just as well. The weather was splendid but the seafront, which has potential, was lacking in eating and drinking opportunities. The wind had not abated so sitting on the large beach was not an option. Only the usual rank beers were available. Tolú, although smaller, had much more to offer. Our stay there was not unpleasant though and we made the most of what we thought would be the last warmth we would enjoy.

In times gone by I would probably have booked us a flight to Bogotá to arrive as close as possible to our departure to Madrid. Not so these days. Mr Cautious Airport, football ground, National Trails and Wetherspoon collector is altogether a different animal from the one who booked a flight to Los Angeles with a once-a-week onward connection to Papeete within 3 hours of his arrival - amongst other tight schedules of days gone by. So it was that we were on the Viva Air Colombia

8.05 departure from Riohacha with 32 hours and 35 minutes until our flight to Madrid.

We didn't want to spend that time in Bogotá so we hired a car and set off, via Tunja, not very highly rated by LP but supposedly worth a visit, to the very highly rated Villa de la Leyva (Villa). The traffic to get out of Bogotá was horrendous. The roads were crap, the drivers, many equally so and let's not forget another of our pet hates - diesel belching vehicles. After an hour and a half we had managed to get 12 miles. We were beginning to regret our decision not to suck it up and stay in Bogotá. Gradually the traffic eased and the scenery became more appealing. It poured with rain when we got to Tunja, about 80 miles north east of Bogotá, but, honestly, we didn't feel that we missed much. The weather brightened as we set off to Villa - a very pleasant drive of just an hour.

What a place! It almost felt like we had saved the best until last. A perfectly preserved colonial village with the largest plaza in Colombia. All cobbled streets, red roofed buildings and surrounded by undulating hills - picture postcard stuff. It was an absolute delight. Admittedly it was touristy but with that came an abundance of eating and drinking opportunities. We found ourselves the most delightful of boutique hotels at a ridiculously cheap price for what it offered and the friendliest staff you could wish for.

It was Sunday afternoon and the Colombian

tourists were still out in force. As dusk approached though the vast majority headed off. We enjoyed the best beers of the whole trip at a tiny brewery followed by, after the Medellin takeaways, the best dinner in Happy Monkey - lasagne with plantain instead of pasta sheets, yummy! The weather even behaved. Showers and thunderstorms were forecast but did not materialise. The following morning warm sunshine and a divine breakfast at the hotel finished off what had been an unexpected but idyllic end to our Colombian odyssey. No "well the best thing about Madras was the sunset" ending to this 21-airport blinder.

We had no dramas on our return trip back to Bogotá and I finish off, as I did with India, on our return flight home. The next collecting missions hopefully to commence on home soil before we fly off again.

I did say I was not writing a travel book as there are already plenty of them. Maybe I've become a tad self-indulgent writing about Colombia, but it is such a fabulous country and I can only write so much about addictions, collecting and how I've got to the numbers I have before even I get bored of the sound of my own voice. If you've got this far.... good on you. Cheers for now.

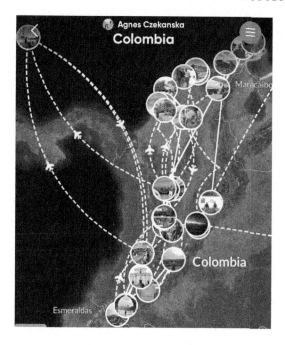

EPILOGUE

May 11th 2009. Just a normal Monday afternoon, quite pleasant actually. I set off to take Molly, my youngest daughter, 8 at the time, to cricket practice. Not 500 metres down the road from home, on the straight up to the village and what the hell!!? A car is speeding towards me on my side of the road. It was all over in a split second. Do I swerve into the ditch or onto their side of the road to avoid the inevitable head on? Before I could make that decision, the car returned to their side of the road. Jesus that was close. BANG! It was back on my side of the road and I had no time to make any decision.

My neck hurt like hell but, of course, my immediate concern was Molly. She was, unsurprisingly, quite upset. My first lucky break: the car behind was driven by an off-duty police traffic officer. She told me to stand still. Molly was fine, just shaken. It took 45 minutes or so for the ambulance to arrive. Second lucky break: one of the firemen in attendance was my good friend Nigel. When the paramedic asked me if I was OK to walk to the ambulance, which I thought I was, he motioned to me, in no uncertain terms, that I was not to walk anywhere. They had had me propped up against a board from the moment they had arrived, taking turns to hold me upright and motionless.

Without being over dramatic, their actions saved my life. I learnt, many hours later that I had suffered a broken neck, the C34 (or 32?) vertebrae, coming within 1 16th of an inch of snapping my spinal cord. The result of which being at best, paralysis from the neck down, at worst and more likely, the end of my particular innings. I was to have a metal frame fitted to my body which I would wear for 3 months. This involved 2 holes being drilled into my forehead and 2 more into the side of my head to hold the frame in place.

Why had I never seen anyone in one of these in all my 48 years? Well, most folks weren't as lucky as me with that injury. I certainly wouldn't be attending the second leg of the play off semi-final on Thursday up in Leeds v our old friends from South Bermondsey (we lost on aggregate). It was very unlikely I would be adding Bratislava and Brno to the airport collection as planned in a couple of weeks.

In fact I did very little in the following 3 months. What a perfect time to start writing the book. I set about collecting my information from nearly 30 years of diaries. That was an interesting exercise and took some time. I wrote the first few sentences, not dissimilar to the above first paragraph, but that was it. I had writer's block.

Must be some kind of record so early into the proceedings. What were my excuses? Well, I was quite uncomfortable for a start? I didn't know which direction to head in with the writing? Pretty feeble really. I guess my heart wasn't in it.

A little under 11 years later and the writer's block finally lifted. To be fair there had been no further attempts on my behalf. Had I continued after those first few sentences in 2009 there would have been no Wetherspoon visits or national trail stompings to drone on about. There's no doubt that the airport collecting was as addictive to me in 2009 as it is now. I had just returned not 2 weeks earlier from a nice little trip to Lamezia, returning from Bari (2 ex Dan Air destinations unvisited during their time) via "Frankfurt" Hahn and Zweibrucken. However, my book back then would have only consisted of travel and footy primarily.

Well, I've written it. It's a mess but it's done. 25 chapters. I'm a little bit obsessed with numbers. I was delighted to learn on a trip to Derby with my son, Callum, probably 10 years ago now that he already had the same affliction: the radio volume has to be set on even numbers! He is now "collecting" golf courses. He's not addicted but he's got a list! I've stopped at 25 because it's a good number; for me, anyway. I've stopped because it's almost 2 years to the day that I started. I've stopped because I can handle stopping the book on 931 airports, 681 Spoons, 87 of the current 92 footy grounds and 13 1/2 of the 15 National Trails.

Did I make it to 1000 airports/airfields? Did I get back to 92/92 (passing 150 in total on the way) English football league grounds? Did we finish all the National Trails? And did we raise a glass to Tim Martin as we ticked off the last of his magnificent pubs? Mind your own business!

Am I/are we cured? Done? If so, what next? Who knows, but it's been a bloody lot of fun so far. Bye - for now.

AFTERWORD

If you would like to see pictures and learn more about some of our adventures my darling wife, Agnieszka, has lovingly created www.aatravels.info

BOOKS BY THIS AUTHOR

Let Me Finish

Coming soon … the follow up.

Did I make it to 1000 (Agi to 500) airports/airfields?

Did I get back to 92/92 (passing 150 in total on the way) English football league grounds?

Did we finish all the National Trails?

And did we raise a glass to Tim Martin as we ticked off the last of his magnificent pubs?

Printed in Great Britain
by Amazon